There Is Life
After Death

There Is Life
After Death

*Compelling Reports From
Those Who Have Glimpsed
the After-Life*

By Roy Abraham Varghese

New Page Books
A Division of The Career Press, Inc.
Franklin Lakes, NJ

THERE IS LIFE AFTER DEATH
EDITED AND TYPESET BY GINA TALUCCI
Cover design by Dutton & Sherman Design
Printed in the U.S.A. by Courier

To order this title, please call toll-free 1-800-CAREER-1 (NJ and Canada: 201-848-0310) to order using VISA or MasterCard, or for further information on books from Career Press.

The Career Press, Inc., 3 Tice Road, PO Box 687,
Franklin Lakes, NJ 07417
www.careerpress.com
www.newpagebooks.com

Library of Congress Cataloging-in-Publication Data

CIP data available upon request.

Dedication

For Daniel K. Hennessy—you made it happen!

Acknowledgments

In writing this book, I have been fortunate in securing the assistance of a number of the leading thinkers in this line of research. These include Dr. Raymond Moody, the pioneer of near-death experiences; Dr. C.T.K. Chari, a parapsychologist and philosopher of science who has carried out major studies of the reincarnation hypothesis; Sir John Eccles, the Nobel Prize-winning neuroscientist; Professor H.D. Lewis, a prolific philosopher of mind; Sir Alfred Ayer, the celebrated atheist philosopher who underwent an NDE himself; Dr. Pim Van Lommel, author of the path-breaking study on NDEs in *The Lancet* based on his research; Dr. Michael Sabom, another pioneering NDE researcher and author of systematic scientific analyses of NDEs; Dr. Peter Fenwick and Dr. Sam Parnia, the leading NDE researchers in the UK; and Dr. Janice Holden, past president of the International Association for Near Death Studies. Many thanks also for the NDE subjects who have kindly shared their experiences in this book, principally Dr. Howard Storm and Dr. Gloria Polo. I want to thank my good friend Alan Napleton for encouraging me to write this book. On another level, I want to thank my wife Anila and our children, Rachel, Mary, and Michael, for their support throughout the writing of this book. Finally, I specially remember my cousin Deepu Joseph who passed away at the age of 39 during the writing of this book; his faith was an inspiration to all who knew him. I am immensely indebted to them all. Nevertheless, the views expressed here are strictly my own as are any defects of argument and expression.

I am also grateful to the various permissions to reprint; in particular Yale University Press, the University of Notre Dame Press, Hay House, Paraclete Press, the *Review of Metaphysics*, and William R. Cash.

Contents

Foreword

The NDE Phenomenon
By Dr. Raymond Moody

If you look at the thousands of cases of near-death experiences (NDEs), there is wide variation within certain limits. I find there are about 15 or so common elements that tend to be repeated. An individual experience may have two or three or four of these elements, or seven or eight or nine and, in a few rare cases, all the way up to 15 of these common features. In effect, there is a continuum or a spectrum type effect, so that not everyone has all of the standard or common elements. My impression from hearing many experiences and also in talking to many physicians who interviewed NDE patients is that it seems to correlate in a rough and ready way with the length of the cardiac arrest. Or, in effect, how close they were to death. If people were really in extremis such that it is hard to imagine how they survived—if, say, the cardiac arrest was very lengthy—it seems to me much more likely that they would have this full-blown effect of 10 or 12 or 15 of these common elements. But in cases where there was only a momentary cardiac arrest, or where the person was very sick, but didn't get really all the way into the cardiac arrest and so on, then those patients would tend to report that maybe three or four or five or six of these elements were experienced. So there is this kind of spread.

Two Basic Categories

In terms of the things I have heard from patients, I would divide the elements of the NDE into two different general categories: the framing and the actual content.

Ineffability

What I call the "framing elements" affect the whole rest of the story. The main framing element is ineffability. That is to say, a large percentage of these people, however articulate they may be, however many languages they may speak, however much education they may have, will tell you, "I just can't describe it to you" or, "there are no words" or, "this is beyond our ability to put into language." And this is the quality of profound spiritual experience that William James called "ineffability" or "indescribability."

Outside Our Space-Time

Another kind of thing these people say about their experiences is that it did not take place in the space-time framework that you and I understand. It was not space as you and I understand it. For example, they might say that, when they get far into the NDE state, just by formulating the idea that they want to go to a place they seem to be instantaneously there. They will say that time as you and I understand it was just not present. A dear friend of mine had her Near-Death Experience in 1971. She said to me, "Raymond, you can say that my experience took one second or you can say that it took 10,000 years. It wouldn't make one bit of difference which way you said it." For example, when people see their life in review, everything is there instantly at once. So in other words, we're talking here about an ineffable experience, which is not in space and time as we experience it. And these are the kinds of things that I refer to as framing elements.

Out of Body Experience

In terms of the content of the NDE, here are some of the things that people tell me. First of all, at the moment when their heart stops beating or when they reach a point at which they are extremely ill and near death, they undergo a radical transformation of perspective. They tell us they seem to rise up and they look down and they see their physical body lying on the operating room table or on the table in the emergency room or sometimes at the scene of an accident.

They say they are above their bodies looking down and they see their own physical bodies. Now another complicating thing here is that, by and large, people say in one way or another that although they are out of their physical bodies, they still seem to be in something that they would call a body. They even describe it as something that seems to have extension, like a form. Nonetheless, this is very difficult for them to describe. Once in a while you have people who feel they are just a point of consciousness, but the more common way people put this is that they still feel that they're in some kind of body. And at this point, they begin to notice some very unusual properties of the situation they're in.

Communications

Number one, they seem to be able to hear and understand perfectly what others in the situation are saying or communicating with one another. For example they hear the doctor or a nurse say, "He's dead" or, "We've lost them" or words to that effect. An interesting thing is that, because of our language, they have to say they heard it, but it wasn't really that they hear this as an audible sensation. It's more that they become aware of what the doctors or nurses are communicating in a heart-to-heart or mind-to-mind way. For example, a nurse who told me about her experience when I was in medical school, used the following words. She said: "I became aware of what the doctor was about to say a moment before I saw him open his mouth to say it." And yet when they try to communicate in turn, when they try to say something to the doctor or nurse, they realize that no one can hear them. They may try to touch someone to get their attention. But when they do, when they touch the doctor, they find they can make no contact; they seem to go through. Incidentally, one of my own patients, whom I was resuscitating, said when she came back that she was trying hard to tell me not to resuscitate her because she was fine where she was. She said in her mind she reached out to try to get hold of my hand to keep me from inserting the IV. When she did she just went right through. But when she went through my arm, she felt something that she could not describe except with an analogy: it was like when you hold two magnets together, you feel the force. She said that it was something like an electric sensation; she felt there was an electrical field of some sort there, but there was no sensation of touch.

Once in a while when people realize that no one can see them and no one can hear them, they can see their bodies lying there useless on the table—they try to go to some other location in the hospital to talk with someone else or to see a relative. They may go and try to communicate with their relatives gathered there in the waiting room of the hospital, again to no avail. No one can see them. No one can hear them.

Awareness of Being Dead

My impression from thousands of cases is that a very common next phase is when they realize that they are isolated and they make the association that this is death. They say something like, "I realized that I was dying" or, "This was death."

The Tunnel

Often, it is this realization that triggers the next phase of the experience, which is the transcendent phase. And this is when people face the ineffability problem. They say that, although they are forced to use words, there are no words to convey an adequate sense of this state. They tell you that they become aware of a passageway of some sort. They may describe it as a tube or a tunnel. They proceed down this tunnel and they come out on the other side into an incredibly brilliant and loving and joyous light.

The Light

People say that this light is far brighter than anything we have experienced while we were alive. Nonetheless, it's not something that makes your eyes hurt. As a matter of fact, it's very comforting. As they go into this light, they feel almost taken up into love, comfort, peace, and joy. But again, this is a kind of love and warmth that goes beyond what they have experienced while they were alive.

Friends and Family

Very often in this light realm, they encounter relatives or friends who have already passed away; again there is an ineffability difficulty. This is not like seeing a regular physical person, but there still seems to be a form there. You recognize the people that you knew, not because of what we might refer to as a physical appearance, but because you meet the person there. There is a sense of the presence of that person—the memories and the personality—although it's not a physical form. They say that people in this frame of existence are timeless; they don't appear to be any particular age, but they do have a number of notable exceptions that I will talk about.

The Prime of Life

I remember very vividly in the 1980s of being in Paris. This wonderful French woman, in her 50s at the time, said that when she saw her relatives, they were in the prime of life. And that's a phrase I hear from people all the time: when you meet your relatives in this situation, they are in the prime of life. Incidentally, every once in a while I go back to patients with specific questions, specifically: What do you mean by "the prime of life"?

And what they will often say is that if you have to put a time on them, it appears that they are about the age of 30 or somewhere around there. This is something I hear from people all over the world. But even this is said within the framework of "they don't really appear to have any age at all."

I've had a number of cases throughout the years where people met up with a relative that they had been at loggerheads with. There was tension and hate in that relationship, but in the NDE state, that is all healed. When they come back, the difficulty in that relationship is erased.

Life Review

With the proviso here that not everyone has all of the features, at some point, many people say that in this field of light the light takes on its own personal identity. The light becomes so powerful that everything else is blotted out. They feel themselves surrounded by a panorama—full-color, three-dimensional, and instantaneous—which consists, in many cases, of every single action that they have ever taken in their lives. Some say, as they describe it in detail, that in this context, they don't see the events of their lives from the perspective they had when they did the actions. Rather, they find themselves empathically identified with those with whom they had interacted. Hence, in this context, if you see yourself doing an unkind or unloving action to someone else then, when that action has its consequence, you feel the pain that you brought about in that other person's life. Or, if you see yourself doing a kind-hearted action to someone else, you feel the good results that were brought about in that person's life.

Throughout the years, I have often asked patients, "You say that when you see the good things you did for others, you get good feelings, and if you did bad things to others, you feel the hurt that you brought about. What I've noticed about life is that there are many people who, no matter how much good you do for them, they turn it back on you. What about that?" The answer I invariably get is that it's what's in your heart that comes back to you.

Another aspect of the life review was described to me by a very wonderful man I met in 1988, Goran Grip. Goran was a professor of anesthesiology at Upsala and he had his near-death experience when he was a very young boy. Goran described his life review to me this way: If you try to imagine this life-review, if you try to condense it into a flat table-top right before you, every action you do is represented by a point on that table-top. And just by an effort of attention, you have a choice of looking at any action in that framework in one of two different ways. You can tilt the table and look at the action-point in one direction, and you can see all of the events in your life that led up to that action trailing off behind it. But just by switching your attention and looking at the action-point on the level of a horizontal plane, all of the consequences that action had not just for you, but for other people with whom you had interacted, taking off in another direction.

Another man who was a 38-year-old electrical engineer in London when his experience took place gave a similar analogy. He said that if you try to imagine the panorama of your life as a pond, then each action of your life is like flipping a little pebble into the pond, and you can see the ripples moving on from that pebble. But when those ripples are impinge on some other person you can see the secondary ripples moving off from that person. And yet all of this is seen instantaneously.

After one man recounted his experience to me, I said, "You told me that in this review of your life you saw every single thing you had ever done. Now I want to ask you: Do you mean that literally, literally every single thing?" And he answered me, "Yes including my own birth by Caesarean section." So it's that detailed, and it's instantaneous, because time, as you and I appreciate it, just does not exist in this framework.

How Have I Learned to Love?

Often these reviews will be in the company of a being of total love. They say that although there are no words to describe their encounter, in order to recount it they have to put it into words. They say it's as though he asked them a question in the presence of all of the events of their lives, which are surrounding them. The questions asked were something like: "How have you learned to love?" "Have you learned to love?" "What can you show me about loving?" The focus is on love. They say words are unnecessary because there you are in the presence of a being of total love. So your natural desire is that you wish that you were capable of that love, too. So then you look at the panorama of your life from that perspective: How have I learned to love?

Cities of Light

Now there are other parts of the NDE phenomenon that are much rarer. These tend to occur only in cases where the cardiac arrest lasted so long that it seems almost inconceivable that the person could have lived. Those people say they see what they can only describe (again words fail) as cities of light. The general idea I get from people all over is that this is a structured state of existence, which they can only describe as a city of light—a composite, not physical substance, as you and I appreciate it. The label they can best put on it is light energy. People say that they see colors that we don't have in our frame of reference.

The Return

Another part of the NDE that you often hear is some sort of account of how they got back. Now some people say, "I have no idea how I got back. At one moment, I was in this beautiful light. The next moment I found myself back in the operating room with no sense of transition." Another group tells you that someone there, either this light or perhaps some relative or friend of theirs who has passed away, says at some point, "You've got to go back. There are things left to do, you have things you've got to finish." Incidentally, hardly ever are they given any idea of what it is they have to finish. They don't know. I've known some of these people over a long period of years and with the passage of time they come to say, "Now I understand why I came back." They're not told why they have to come back, but this may become apparent to them as time goes on.

A third group says they were given a choice: They are told they can either go back to the lives they were leading, or continue with the experience they were having then. Almost invariably the reason they give is the same: they have young children left to raise. The variants on this are some people who say it's for some other relative or friend. One woman told me that she chose to go back because her husband was a bad alcoholic and she wanted to go on helping him. Three people have told me that they had prepared all their lives to be in a helping profession, nursing, social work, or medicine. And when given that choice, they were young people and they chose to come back, but it was always directed toward helping others. People say for themselves they don't want to come back. They would rather stay in this light.

Transformation

When they do get back, they say that the NDE has had very profound effects on them. The most common effect is this: whatever they had been chasing before—knowledge, power, fame, money, and so on—they say that they really do have a conviction now that the purpose of all this is to learn how to love. So what they want to do is to develop, to learn how to love. Incidentally, the NDE doesn't make that task any easier. They say you come back and you're still a human being.

Another thing they say is that it totally wipes out the fear of death. Not that they want to die any time soon, or that they would want to die in a painful or unpleasant way. But their experience to them conveys utter conviction that what we call death is just stepping into another framework of existence. Do they really persist with this? Having talked with so many thousands of people and having actually been present at the deaths of those who previously had NDEs, when they died, I would say yes. I first knew them because they had a near-death experience, then I maintained a friendship with them, then I helped them through their final illness, and I was there with some of them when they died. Their equanimity, even years after their experiences are complete. They just face death with a sort of complete assurance.

Prologue

L et's suppose for a moment that there exists a world beyond our space-time continuum, a realm that falls outside our timelines and space coordinates. Let's assume also that when we die, the intrinsically transphysical element of our being, the element that enables us to think in concepts and retain our identity through every cellular change, call it the soul, enters this new world, call it World 2. No communication is possible between the two worlds because the first, World 1, is a field of psychophysical organisms and quantum particles, while the second is a state of conscious, conceptual "centers" that communicate directly without mediating systems. Because World 2 does not have physical dimensions or quantitatively measurable properties, it is pointless to seek it with the instruments and methodologies of World 1. Let's suppose also that World 2 is the state of being for which we were created, but that entry there depends on our receiving our identity and being in World 1 through the unique union of physical and transphysical that I call "I." We say "created" because worlds and programs of ultimate destiny do not pop into existence out of thin air.

Now we ask: is there a World 2 and, if so, how can we find out about it? Are there any clues? Everyday experience tells us that we are conscious physical beings, but that our consciousness, while relayed through physical media, has no physical properties; that our ability to understand and to think in concepts and symbols cannot be thought of as a physical process; that the I, the center of our consciousness and unifier of our experiences, makes us see things from a first-person perspective unlike anything else in the physical world. This much we know about ourselves—it hints that there is something strange about human beings from a purely physical standpoint. But World 2? Well, if there is indeed such a realm, where could we find pointers to it? Perhaps in the experiences of people who stepped through the doorway of death and then returned—no matter how mystifying their missives from "the other side." And the Creator—wouldn't you expect some word from the Creator in so important a matter? And how could we tell if such "word" had been sent or received? Perhaps it can be found somewhere in the collective memory of the human race since World 2 is not something one is "shown" as much as told about. Or in the claims of direct divine revelation. Or in encounters with eternity while here on earth, if that were possible.

Chapter 1

A New Paradigm

This is a book about a question we all have to think about at some point. Is death the end? Or, to put it another way, do we survive bodily death? Some shrug their shoulders, muttering "we can't possibly know." Others—pointing to something they call "modern science"—scornfully say "no." And a few, flying their philosophical colors, pretentiously profess not to even understand the question ("survival," they sniff, simply makes no sense if death is taken to mean that "you" cease to exist). Curiously, the overwhelming majority of human beings across the course of history have given an entirely different answer to this question. They have taken it for granted that death is not the end, that the human person in some fashion lives to tell the tale, that there is a life after death. This striking and seemingly instinctive belief has been embodied in the religious traditions and philosophical reflections of most cultures. In some instances, it has claimed confirmation in a series of experiences and encounters.

Paradoxically, the modern era, notorious for its doctrinaire skepticism, has given a new and concrete shape to the affirmation of a life after death. The technological advances of today have been known to revive the clinically dead. Those who have been thus "revived" have often given graphic accounts of the moments when they were, so to speak, dead to rights. The meeting of old and new, of science (if you will) and religion, of belief and experience, of affirmation and encounter—as it relates to the possibility of a life after death—has created a new paradigm of the after-life and it is this that we will consider here.

There is Life After Death—Compelling Reports From Those Who Have Glimpsed the After-Life is a

- ➱ cross-cultural
- ➱ trans-historical
- ➱ inter-religious
- ➱ multi-disciplinary

study of the question of whether or not the human person continues in being after biological death.

Most previous studies have focused on:

- ➱ esoteric anecdotes.
- ➱ religious teaching.
- ➱ metaphysical speculation.
- ➱ scientific critique.
- ➱ pious devotion.
- ➱ "returnee" testimony.
- ➱ communications from "beyond."

But there has been no overarching paradigm or grand scheme that has tied together these and other relevant streams of data. The goal of this book is to see if there is a picture emerging from all the shapes and colors that have been splashed across the canvas of the hereafter. If such a picture does emerge, is it true to reality?

I will try to show here that there is a comprehensive and compelling case for a life after death. And I speak not simply of life-after-death in a lifeless sort of way, but of an after-life that has its own topography and temporality. To be sure, by its very nature, the after-life cannot be "proved" scientifically, because it is not susceptible to quantitative measurement. We cannot touch the intangible or see the invisible. We are not dealing here with science or philosophy per se. Rather, we have to consider streams of data of different kinds that form a pattern visible to any who care to connect the dots. Those who take the time and energy to connect them see a picture, while those who prefer to compartmentalize or caricature only see dots.

Can We Speak of Life After the Cessation of Life?

It may be asked how we can talk about life after death when death is by definition the cessation of life. How can we talk coherently of life *after* the cessation of life? The answer is: it all depends on what we mean by "life" and "death." In this book, we shall see that there is good reason to believe that, by its very nature, the human soul (the principle of life of the human person) transcends matter and does not depend on matter for its continued existence. If the soul ceases to animate its body, then that body is "dead." But, because of the nature of its being, the soul, the principle of life of the body, continues in existence after the two are separated. This separation of soul and body we call death. To speak of "life after death" is to say that a person's life (the soul) continues in being after the "death" of that person's body.

Do We Need Another Book on Life After Death?

But why another book on life after death when we have already had so many works on so-called near-death experiences (NDEs) starting with Raymond Moody's classic *Life After Life*?

First, it should be said that this is not simply a book on NDEs, but on a panoply of phenomena relevant to the question of an after-life. It is a treatment that integrates and synthesizes a vast variety of ingredients and components, events and experiences, one of which happens to be the NDE phenomenon.

Secondly, this question itself is astounding. Shouldn't anyone alive have some level of interest in whether or not they "continue" after death? And, if indeed they do survive, this is surely relevant to the kind of life they lead here and now, even the very purpose of their lives. We are here for a short voyage from womb to tomb. If the tomb is not the last stop on our voyage then life is not simply a series of accidents—it is part of a larger story, perhaps a never-ending story. The meaning of life depends on whether or not it is part of something enduring and ultimately significant. Some atheists have said that we can create our own purposes in life even if there is no purpose *of* life. True enough, but our concern is whether there is any ultimate significance, purpose, or meaning to our life here and now. If there is no life beyond death, the answer quite simply is no. Said the atheist Jean Paul Sartre, "Death is never that which gives life its meaning; it is on the contrary that which on principle removes all meaning from life."[1]

After-Life Ruminations of Two Atheist Scientists

It should be noted that two famous atheist scientists (both now deceased) at least drew attention to the importance of the question of an after-life. In one of his last writings, the astronomer Carl Sagan wrote, "I would love to believe that when I die I will live again, that some thinking, feeling, remembering part of me will continue," but then went on to add that "I know of nothing to suggest that it is more than wishful thinking."[2] Shortly after Sagan's death, his friend the paleontologist Stephen Jay Gould (who passed away in 2002) wrote an essay in his memory starting with this dedication: "Carl also shared my personal suspicion about the nonexistence of souls—but I cannot think of a better reason for hoping we are wrong than the prospect of spending eternity roaming the cosmos in friendship and conversation with this wonderful soul."[3]

What Happened to the Billions Who Have Died and the Hundreds Who Are Dying?

Finally, at another level, the query of whether we need another book on this topic is perplexing. Tens of billions of humans have died since the dawn of humanity. Have these billions faded away into nothingness or are they still around (with appropriate qualifications about what we mean by "they" and "around")? These are the two basic possibilities. Wouldn't anyone with a bare minimum of curiosity wish to explore the question at least as often as we speculate about whether or not there is intelligent life in other parts of the Universe—especially when we consider the fact that most humans have seen good reason to believe that death is not the end? And the quest for the dimension beyond death deserves at least as much time and energy as the quest for the (purportedly) unseen dimensions of the Universe that is high on the agenda of theoretical physics—given, again, that many living people have felt that they have been in "touch" with this dimension. Approximately 100 billion people have died since the beginning of history according to demographer Carl Haub at the Population Reference Bureau.[4] Approximately, 234 people will die while you're reading this page. And, sooner or later, you who are reading this will also die. And you still ask why a book on this topic is important!

Death, Interrupted

What could be more fascinating than an exploration of the possible existence that follows death, the "other" world that could indeed await us all? But this is not the kind of world that can be explored with a big enough budget *a la* NASA or displayed on a TV set. We who live in modern times have been so mesmerized by its creature comforts and sensory fantasies that we have lost the capability of coming to grips with *non-virtual* reality. We have no interest in any singularity that cannot be digitized or downloaded. We are like children who refuse to grow up. We think we can shut out death by sanitizing it with cosmetologists, crematoriums, and corpse-free memorial services. But it's time to grow up, to get serious. Death is real no matter how well you stifle its stench or hide its horror. Like it or not, the question of whether or not we survive it is always on the table.

New Deal

Let's start off by admitting that on a natural plane no one really *knows* anything about life after death. Some scientists claim to have shown that there is no after-life because it is not verifiable by scientific methodologies. Philosophers claim that the "survival" of the human person is not possible simply because there is no such thing as a "person." The naïvete of such skeptics is matched only by their dogmatism.

In actual fact, we *know* that they—the scientists and the philosophers—don't know because they have never died. Their experience is limited by the very same boundaries as ours. They have no special insight into whether earthly existence is a prelude to another state of being. They have no esoteric equipment or intellectual black box that enables them to make informed judgments on the question. Many, if not most of them, have never even considered the available evidence in its entirety. They are as helpless as anyone else with regard to the "other side" (if indeed there is an "other side"). The eminent cancer specialist and popular science writer Lewis Thomas admitted, "We do not understand the process of dying, nor can we say anything clear, for sure, about what happens to human thought after death." [5]

Despite the inevitable limitations of the human condition, we are not condemned to languish in the mental prisons that the skeptics create for themselves. Those who are curious and serious have access to a treasury of evidence that points to a realm beyond the temporal and the tangible. We can expand our horizons anytime we please. The dots abound and if we choose we can connect them. The picture that emerges from the dots is not a proof or a theorem. But it is a picture of logical and plausible inferences drawn from the raw data of human experience. Is it a true-to-life picture? Does it correspond to reality? This is a personal question in the sense that you must answer it on your own. Does it integrate all the data to which you are privy? Does it mesh with your daily experience and deepest intuitions? The pursuit of answers to these questions is necessarily a journey you have to make on our own. The buck stops with you!

Four Sets of Data

There are four interlocking sets of data that are relevant to our inquiry:

1. What has been encountered by individuals today and through the centuries (taking into consideration only claims of encounters that have some measure of authentication).

2. What has been universally accepted from ancient times.

3. What we can reasonably surmise to be "revealed" by a divine Source, if such there be.

4. What we know of our being from everyday (pre-death!) experience.

These four points of reference form a new framework of inquiry that takes us beyond the stalemates and cul-de-sacs of the past and furnishes us with a brand new template of the after-life. Take NDEs. Do near-death experiences begin and end with brain biochemistry or point to a continued life beyond death? After three decades of study, the debate has reached an indefinite standoff. Both sides present equally plausible accounts of their positions. The same could be said of scientists and philosophers debating the body-mind question. As for claims of after-life-related encounters, these have been dismissed as anecdotal and too isolated to be relevant. And religious beliefs on the hereafter have been banished from public discourse because they are allegedly based simply on blind faith.

Parts in Light of the Whole

What is forgotten by most of the duelists in such debates is that the part makes sense only in the context of the whole. The nature and function of an eye or a wing can be determined only if we know something about the animal or bird as a whole. Hydrogen and oxygen by themselves tell us nothing about water. The same can be said about the role of the four points of reference highlighted here. The affirmation that there is a life after death cannot be based on one isolated datum or inexplicable event. It is a synthesis of numerous data-points, a connecting of the dots that

- ⬥ begins with the reported other-world journeys of NDE survivors.
- ⬥ moves to the intuitions of humankind across the ages.
- ⬥ includes encounters with those considered deceased as also purported glimpses of the hereafter (we will call these After-Life Visitations or ALVs).
- ⬥ maps the nature of the human person as experienced in this life.

It is a paradigm that makes sense of a whole host of data. On the one hand, we have historical intuitions and revelations of an after-life, the idea of the intercession of the holy ones, reported visions of the hereafter and a plethora of NDEs. On the other, we have our own non-physical acts, such as the use of language, and our sense that our identity is dependent as much on our body as on its soul. If the debate over NDEs seems to have reached an NDE state itself, we can make progress only by pulling together relevant data from other dimensions. NDEs per se cannot serve as the basis of belief in an after-life. But they supplement and sustain the underlying dynamic of such a belief. In short, the paradigm proposed here is not based on random anecdotes or conjectures. Rather it is an engine driven by what is obvious in our experience along with the cross-cultural transhistorical testimony of humankind.

Real-world Consequences

There is another dimension to some of the after-life phenomena discussed here. They have this-world consequences and effects. They cannot simply be dismissed as happenings "in your head," which is how some view NDEs. Let's consider non-NDE instances. If you believe in the intercession of the saints, you affirm that their celestial actions bring about events here and now. If, outside of an NDE, you are given a vision of the hereafter or encounter a person long deceased, your choices and actions in the present world may thereafter take a new trajectory. Such phenomena indicate also that there is some interaction between the here-and-now and the hereafter. Of course, NDEs too have real-world consequences in terms of the transformation of the experiencer.

A Divine Blueprint

We have spoken of divine revelation as one potential data source. This inclusion will be a red flag for many. In fact, most professional discussions of the after-life, even of NDEs, say nothing about God. But this quarantine policy makes no sense. An attempt to study life after death without reference to the question of God is like Newton explaining the fall of the apple without reference to the laws of gravity, or a scientist researching photosynthesis while denying the existence of the sun.

If there is a mechanism whereby human persons survive death and enter another state of existence, then the obvious question is how the mechanism was brought into being, how the laws and systems required for such an infrastructure came to be. Historically, most people who have affirmed an after-life saw it in relation to a divine blueprint of some sort. Their entire idea of the eternal destiny of human persons, in fact, was in terms of separation from or union with the divine. Personally, I hold that our experience of consciousness, thought, and the self is unmistakable evidence of an infinite-eternal Mind. This is not the place to pursue that discussion, but I have presented my case in *The Wonder of the World—A Journey from Modern Science to the Mind of God* and in my contribution to *There is a God—How the World's Most Notorious Atheist Changed His Mind*.

But what is relevant for our purposes is the fact that life after death cannot be studied in a vacuum. We cannot ignore the workings of the brain or the soul. Neither can we ignore the Source of both. Once we realize this, we can make progress. If there is indeed a God and that God has created us for an eternal destiny, then all the other phenomena make sense:

- Primordial humanity would receive some sort of primordial revelation as to the nature of human destiny.
- Near-death experiences for those resuscitated with modern technologies would tally with the primordial revelation.
- After-life visitations through the centuries and across societies would not seem out of order.
- Our experience of ourselves would indicate a transphysical dimension. By "transphysical" we refer to a reality that is not physical and yet interacts with the physical. Pre-death experience complements the data of near-death experiences and after-life visitations.

As to the question of whether there is a God, we simply need to face the obvious fact that selves cannot spring from quantum fields or thoughts from rocks.

The overall point is that only a unified perspective of the kind laid out here can help us to assess and assimilate the data available from the four-point framework of inquiry. This is the only way to break the logjam. It is the sword that cuts the Gordian Knot of the philosophers and the scientists. In any case, our scientific and philosophical categories are our own constructs. They are provisional and destined to be dated before we know it. No one quotes Hegel any more as an authority. Nor do we rely on medieval manuals of science. We can only trust our immediate experience and any indications of divine revelation that we find credible—everything else is provisional, forgotten a hundred or a mere 10 years from now.

"Natural," Not Supernatural

Having paid due homage to the Divine, I should clarify that the kind of experience considered here is by and large of the "natural" kind. Although we do consider what might be called supernatural experiences, the predominant source of inputs for our database is the natural realm. Thus, the NDEs constitute a natural body of knowledge built on the experiences of those who claim to have left their body due to natural causes. By stripping aside cultural and subjective elements, we arrive at a certain core narrative. These kinds of experience or our experience of the self do not show the nature of the after-life: they indicate only that there is an after-life.

The classic arguments for God's existence can show us only THAT there is a God, but not the inner nature of God. Likewise, the kind of data we consider here only indicate THAT there is an after-life, but not much more—except perhaps that this after-life can be either positive or negative. For more "details," the only available route is a revelation of our ultimate destiny from an unimpeachable source. This indeed is the province of religion in general and revealed religion in particular. We must decide for ourselves which vision of ultimate destiny is credible, plausible, and deserving of belief. In the interests of full disclosure, I should say that I am a Christian. But because this is not a work of comparative religion, we will restrict ourselves simply to the question of whether there is a life after death.

But religion is not something we ignore entirely in our inquiry. Most of the traditional accounts of life after death appear in a religious context. Yet our

concern here is only the common core insight in all these religious conceptions—that we do continue to subsist after death. Although we cannot offer a
definitive guidebook to the after-life, we can certainly offer a picture that con-
nects the dots. The choice is not necessarily between answering all questions or
none. Here, we show a new way not simply of answering the old questions, but
also of rephrasing them.

A Copernican Revolution

We can better understand the path taken here by comparing it to other
routes. Students of after-life-related claims and allegedly preternatural phenomena have taken two different approaches.

First, there are the "scientific"-minded who say:

- none of these phenomena meet the criteria of quantitative mea-
  surability, experimental repeatability, and universal observability.
- hence they are anecdotal accounts.
- hence they are scientifically worthless and not deserving of rational acceptance.

Second, there are the "mystical"-minded who say:

- the scientists are dogmatists who have no understanding of matters that lie outside their narrow specialties.
- there are a lot of phenomena that cannot be explained by science.
- all claims of paranormal and mystical phenomena should be
  accepted without further ado.

One says "nothing is acceptable," while the other says "everything is
acceptable."

But neither approach is satisfactory:

- It is obvious that principles applicable in studying, describing, and
  explaining the behavior of the physical world are valid only for the
  physical world. If there is a transphysical world, evidence for its
  existence will not be of the same kind as that for the physical.
- But this does not mean that there are no principles that can be
  applied in studying claims made about the transphysical. We cannot accept any and every claim in this area at face value. We
  have to be both critical and open to all the evidence.
- The two basic issues are these: does the substance of a given
  claim concerning the transphysical correspond to something that

really exists? Does the actuality of such a phenomena cohere well with what we know to be the case from everyday and universal experience?

Anecdotal vs. Scientific

The choice we face is not between the anecdotal and the scientific. It is between the rational and the irrational, the real and the imaginary. So what is a rationally acceptable approach to evaluating the evidence for the reality of the after-life? Simply this. We have to assemble all the claims concerning the after-life that have *spontaneously* emerged in the course of history. I emphasize "spontaneous" because claims involving mediums, ouija boards, channeling, hypnotic regression to past lives, and the like are "artificial" and hence, in my view, inadmissible. They are induced from "this world" and can well be accused of being "manufactured" or manipulated. Our concern is what comes to us unbidden from "the other side."

Granted, the kinds of claims and data that are available in this domain cannot be investigated or tested with any scientific methodology or instrument. They cannot even be described or experienced in terms of the scientific. What we have are:

- ↝ "Eye-witness" accounts of journeys beyond the space-time world and of encounters with individuals from another realm.
- ↝ Reports of revelations from external sources not of this world that corroborate the accounts of the eyewitnesses.
- ↝ Phenomena that cannot be explained in terms of the physical (celestial intercession for instance), but cohere with the accounts and revelations.
- ↝ Transformations of character, personality, values, and attitudes that follow these experiences and encounters.

Our everyday experience of thought and the self indicate a "life" that transcends the physical. In itself, this points to the possibility of a life after death without proving it. But when it is coupled with the after-life data highlighted above, we are drawn in a new direction.

In brief, after considering the evidence in its entirety, dynamism and concreteness, we soon see a pattern begin to form. The phenomena are extraordinarily diverse and yet strikingly specific. Cumulatively, they give us a coherent and comprehensive picture of the world beyond death. Yes, there is a life and a world beyond death, and there is a lot we can learn about it if we wish. The sooner we grasp this fact, the better for us.

We have lost so much time and squandered so many opportunities for exploring the extraordinary wealth of data that has become available throughout the centuries and particularly in modern times. We have been blinkered by superstitions and dogmatic preconceptions.

The time is ripe for a Copernican Revolution in after-life studies.

Copernicus and Ptolemy's Epicycles

By the 16th century, growing cosmological evidence had indicated that, contrary to Ptolemy's ancient theory, it was the sun and not the earth that was at the center of the solar system. But Ptolemy's followers created new extensions to his theory that sought to explain away each new piece of evidence while holding fast to the original theory. The observed movement of the planets had to be reconciled with the claim that the earth was the fixed center of the universe. This gave birth to the Ptolemaic idea of epicycles, of planets moving in small circles. Copernicus, followed by Kepler, Galileo, and Newton, managed to establish an entirely new vision of a heliocentric Universe, because they were willing to let the data frame the theory rather than the other way around. And this is precisely what is required today in studying life after death.

Certainly the data to be studied is not observable with scientific devices. Nor is it mathematically measurable. But it is the kind of data we would expect if we are dealing with a reality that transcends the physically perceptible. And it is not just one datum in isolation that creates the theory or model. The Copernician theory needed Galileo's observations and Newton's laws to establish itself. Likewise, in the present case we need:

- ↦ A model/"theory" of the after-life (as provided in the primordial religions).
- ↦ A basis/"law" for its existence (namely God).
- ↦ A diverse range of "experiential" data/"observations" to support its actuality (our experience of the non-physical in everyday life, near-death experiences, revelations from reliable sources, visions of and from the other world, the intercession of the saints).

Once we have embraced the Copernician Revolution, all the data avidly assembled by the human race across all of history makes sense. We no longer have to invent epicycles. The Copernicians of cosmology showed that Planet

Earth is a part of the Universe, but not its center. The Copernicians of anthropology show that the physical world is a part of reality, but not its center.

Connecting the Dots

We said earlier that a picture emerges from the dots. So what are the dots we are connecting? I have given my own names to these dots guided by their function:

- ✧ The "smoking gun" dot is made up of the near-death experiences that have been reported across centuries, but in greater clarity and quantity in the present day.
- ✧ The "pie-in-the-sky" dot relates to the data furnished from the religious traditions and experiences of ancient humanity.
- ✧ The "extra-terrestrial" dot is constituted by reports of visitations from the after-life or visions thereof.
- ✧ The "touchy-feely" dot comprises the kind of data available from science as it relates to consciousness, thought, and the self.
- ✧ The "it's all in your head" dot references the philosophical reflections that have given greater clarity to the idea of a soul that can survive the death of the body.

The need for connecting the dots should be obvious. Let's take a particular claim about life after death, for instance, the claim of a near-death experience. We can reliably evaluate this claim only in the context of all other data relating to the after-life. We can understand each dot only by relating it to the picture formed from connecting all the dots.

At the risk of giving away the ending before I even start, let me share the picture that *I* have drawn from the dots:

- ✧ The human person is an irreducible union of matter and spirit.
- ✧ Upon death, the person continues to exist, albeit in an unnatural state.
- ✧ Depending on the choices made in this life, one spends eternity with God or in self-imposed separation from God.
- ✧ At some point, the soul of the person animates a body again, but one which is free of earthly imperfections and also capable of

restoring you to the fullness of the person you were on earth (this last idea is a central tenet of Zoroastrianism, Judaism, Christianity, and Islam, and can only be justified on the basis of acceptance of a specific claim of divine revelation).

The previous picture is the one, in different hues and colors, that was painted by the primordial peoples of the earth as also ancient India, China, and Persia and, finally, Judaism and Christianity. Even the most ancient peoples believed in a Heaven, a Hell, and a domain in between. The Vedic Hindus did not know anything of reincarnation and taught that after death you enter a permanent state of joy or sorrow. The ancient Persians, Egyptians, Mesopotamians, Greeks, the primordial tribes, the Chinese, the Japanese, and the Jews all believed in an after-life where one's deeds in this life affected one's destiny in the next. In classical Christianity we find a highly structured description of the after-life. We have the Holy Ones now united with God (Heaven), those who are being purified in preparation for divine union (Purgatory), and the damned who are separated from God (Hell). There is also a resurrection of the body at the end of history.

The Christian Dispensation

One radical development in the Christian dispensation was the proclamation that the sacrificial death of Jesus made it possible for those who chose God to go to Heaven. This idea was radical in one sense and yet strangely continuous with the intuitions in some religious traditions of a sacrificial Savior (Hinduism, Judaism, and Zoroastrianism in particular). Although some Christians have said that only professed Christians can go to Heaven, Christian writers as far back as St. Paul and St. Augustine had said that Heaven is open to all who trust in God and do his Will (see also the teaching of Jesus in Matthew 25). Paul said that God wills the salvation of all. At the same time Christian teaching was clear that the reality of human freedom made it possible to reject God. It held that those who do so will be eternally separated from him.

Another element of the Christian dispensation of particular relevance to our inquiry is the claim that Jesus of Nazareth was not only crucified but also rose from the dead. The proclamation of his resurrection is central to Christianity and, for Christians, serves as an enduring foundation for the reality of life after death. Hence, we will examine the claim more closely in our study.

In the ancient world, and in Christianity through the centuries, there was a constant awareness of the "connection" between the living and the dead. Central to the fabric of the human reality as they understood it was:

- ✦ the intercession of the saints for those on earth.
- ✦ the travails of the souls in Purgatory.
- ✦ the appearances of these saints and "Poor Souls" to those on earth.
- ✦ journeys made by the living to the "other world."

The world of "departed" souls was just as real as the physical world. Heaven and earth, the blessed dead and the living—it was all an inter-connected web, a web far more enduring and extensive than the web of life. We are surrounded by a "great cloud of witnesses," said the Epistle to the Hebrews.

Invasion of the Supernatural

Now this picture of a continuum between the here-and-now and the here-after was torn to shreds by the modern era. But the strenuous efforts to stamp out all sense of the transcendent, all ties with the Other, could not long be successful. You can fool all of the people only some of the time. Reports of supernatural invasions persisted on the periphery of the modern consciousness (a few are reviewed later in this book). Moreover, the physicalist and behaviorist philosophies of academia kept unraveling because they could not deal with our very real experience of consciousness and understanding.

Then came the 1970s and the startling reports of clinically dead subjects who reported life on the other side of death. By the 1980s, according to a Gallup poll, more than 8 million in the United States alone reported NDEs (one such subject happened to be a world-famous atheist from the UK); today, according to researcher Nancy Bush, the number of NDE subjects has been estimated to reach 22 million. There were positive NDEs and negative NDEs (also called "distress" NDEs)—shades of Heaven and Hell! To top it all, a survey of US scientists conducted in 1998 showed that 40 percent believed in "personal immortality."[6] Not surprisingly, a national survey released by the Pew Forum on Religion and Public Life in June 2008 showed that 74 percent of Americans believed in life after death with 74 percent believing in Heaven and 59 percent in Hell. Erlendur Haraldsson, a veteran researcher in this area, notes that "Recent survey data indicate a widespread belief in life after death in most countries of Western Europe and North America.... Some persons not only believe in life after death, but they also report encounters with the dead."[7]

Skunk at the Party

The skeptics, of course, we will always have with us. No matter how strong the evidence for a claim, there's always someone who aspires to be the skunk at the party. When it comes to life after death, there are five kinds of skeptics, although the same skeptic can profess more than one variation of skepticism. The five kinds are:

1. Physicalists who reduce everything to matter no matter how strong the evidence for the non-physical (Neal Grossman appropriately calls them the fundamaterialists).

2. Relativists who hold that belief in a life after death springs from external influences that have no basis in factual reality (such influences include psychological and sociological factors and linguistic illusions).

3. Naturalists (atheists, deists, and pantheists) who deny the possibility of any supernatural revelation and therefore reject any claim of such a revelation concerning life after death.

4. Supernaturalists who reject the possibility of learning of a life after death from natural sources.

5. New Age reincarnationists who do not accept the continuing identity and existence of the human person as absolute and ultimate.

Although there's good reason to be skeptical about convincing the skeptics, we do have a body of data that should be universally acceptable as a starting point. How we treat this body will define where we stand with regard to a life after death. Here then is what we know:

- ↪ Our present-day conscious life requires a functioning brain and damage to this brain does affect the exercise of our mental powers.

- ↪ We are conscious, we think in concepts, we use language (a capacity that requires the user to be in a potential infinity of states of understanding), we have a continued identity as an "I." None of these phenomena can be described in physical terms or tagged with physical properties.

- ↪ A small percentage of humans who died "clinically," but were then resuscitated (usually with the help of modern technologies) have reported what they describe as "after-life" experiences that share certain common characteristics. Curiously, two hard-core skeptics (Sir Alfred Ayer, Howard Storm) were themselves the subjects of such experiences.

✧ Numerous societies have reported stories of visits of the dead (for example, ghosts and suffering souls) while others have seen a continuing connection with the deceased, who are now active in the after-life (the saints for instance).

We do not include here induced experiences such as alleged memories of past lives that appear after hypnosis or alleged contact with the dead claimed by mediums and spiritualists. Only those phenomena that emerge spontaneously can be considered free of obvious taint.

Now this body of data is uncontroversial because it simply concerns what "appears" to be the case. It is the movement from description to explanation that is controversial and disputable. What is responsible for each one of these phenomena? What explains them? What conclusions do they entail about human nature and destiny? The different kinds of skeptics have different spins on the same data.

Physicalism

The garden-variety skeptic is the physicalist reductionist who refuses to admit the existence of anything non-physical. Any kind of apparent non-physical reality is reduced to matter, pure and simple. Our sense of being conscious is, at best, an illusion. The idea of a self is a grammatical error. The cruder physicalists are the no-nonsense scientists who matter-of-factly state that the neuron is the ultimate matrix of all mental activity.

Slightly more sophisticated are the philosophers who analyze our usage of words such as *conscious*, *intention*, and *self* to show that all notions of the non-physical can be "cured" by appropriate linguistic therapy. Certainly the physicalists can claim some prima facie plausibility by pointing to the mental deterioration that accompanies dementia or brain disorders. Nevertheless, they face an uphill task when facing such phenomena as language and the ability to think in concepts. And try as they might, they face a losing battle in their constant attempts to persuade us to deny the undeniable. Not only am I conscious of being conscious, but there is an "I" who is thus conscious.

Relativism

The physicalist claims that we know that we are physical through and through. The relativist says we cannot know this for the simple reason that we really cannot know anything (although we do know that we cannot know!). The relativist says all reports of near-death experiences are simply portrayals of the subjects' "inner world." Their accounts of the hereafter are "culturally formed" and should not be taken literally.

As for the narratives of the afterlife in religious texts and traditions, these are a product both of particular cultures and our own desires. The link between desire (wish) and belief (fulfillment) was highlighted most famously by Sigmund Freud. The sociological relativists like Marx said that Heaven was a creation of the rich to keep the poor happy with their lot.

The fundamental assumption of the relativists is that we have no access to the way things are with respect to the hereafter. But this assumption is simply a belief with no evidence. If there is indeed a life after death and if information about this life can be transmitted through direct experience or revelation, then the assumption is simply mistaken. And that is precisely what we wish to find out in our inquiry. By connecting the dots that seem to transcend culture and subjective preference, we can rescue ourselves from the quicksand of the relativists. We can thereby determine whether or not there is an after-life. As to the role of desire, this is a knife that cuts both ways. Let's say that you don't want to believe that your choices in this life could have consequences in the next. In that case, the denial of an after-life is a wish-fulfillment for you.

There is no question that our experience of the present world colors and forms our images of the next. In his *Life After Death—A History of the Afterlife in the Religions of the West*, Alan Segal shows that each society mirrors its values and structures in its portrayal of the afterlife. Nevertheless, we are not entirely at the mercy of our sociological and psychological environments. This is because there are three "third-party" sources for our belief in the afterlife. The first relates to a seemingly innate intuition found in the heart of humanity. The second concerns claims of divine revelation. The third involves the next world actually interacting with the present world. It is possible to dismiss each one of these three sources as somehow deriving from social conditioning. But if you take each on its own, and if you find one or more of them to be factually grounded, then the after-life is no longer just a social construct.

Naturalism

Like the relativists, the naturalists who deny any supernatural revelation on life after death rest their denial on a prior claim that there is no possibility of supernatural revelation. But this prior claim needs to be proven. Whether or not there can be such revelation depends on whether or not there is such a supernatural realm and whether we can find out about it. In short, the question is not simply whether there is a God, but whether that God has revealed anything to humanity. Although not all religions claim direct divine revelation, many do claim that there is much that we can know about the supernatural realm and, in particular, about our destiny beyond death. At the very least, we should consider what is claimed in the primordial religions instead of dogmatically dismissing the very possibility of supernatural revelation.

Supernaturalism

Paradoxically, some supernaturalists present an equal and opposite problem. They hold to a particular claim of divine revelation about the hereafter. This leads them to deny the possibility of knowing anything about the hereafter from any other source. Thus, the insights provided by our own direct experience and by the encounters of credible subjects are ipso facto taken off the table. But there is no logical or theological requirement that a definitive divine revelation on the after-life rules out the possibility of any other revelation or experience concerning it. Unlike physicalists, relativists, and naturalists, the supernaturalists should be open to all the available evidence.

This all leads to the question of what constitutes evidence. And here we have to address the New Age reincarnationists. Although they profess open-mindedness and tolerance, the reincarnationists dogmatically deny the possibility of the human person being able to continue as the same person after physical death. In their view, at the point of death, what was you in this life morphs into another person, a process that continues in successive lives until you "dissolve" into the Universal Spirit. But how do they know this?

At the end of the day, the evidence boils down to a few cases of people who seem to have amazing recollections of one or more past lives. So our immediate experience of individual identity and personhood and the plethora of evidence in favor of our continued existence *as ourselves* after death is dismissed in favor of a few alleged memories. The framework, of course, raises a Pandora's Box of questions:

- How did the reincarnation mechanism get started and how does it keep going (with vast quantities of new bodies being added) if, as we know, there were very few humans around just a few thousand years ago?
- Who or what monitors and administers the "fit" between the soul that dies and the soul that is reborn?
- How does the idea of old souls being inserted into a new body fit in with the current idea of the flow of information in modern genetics (one of the most prominent reincarnationists has said that the orthodoxy in biology must be challenged)?
- Are there other explanations for the memories of past lives? A number of other plausible explanations have been proposed—telepathic interactions with discarnate souls, and so on.
- How can a soul "dissolve" into a universal mind?

Some of the reincarnationists defend themselves by locating themselves in the traditions of Hinduism and Buddhism. But Vedic Hinduism knew nothing of reincarnation—and presented the traditional view of the hereafter defended here. Buddhism is a later break-away from Hinduism and its version of rebirth is dramatically different from the modern Hindu view of reincarnation.

Please note that this evaluation of reincarnation is not intended as an attack. Even those who consider reincarnation to be a religious belief do not think of it as an attractive belief. It is regarded by them as the manifestation of a "fallen" state. Moreover, no one wishes to see either themselves or their loved ones go through innumerable rebirths since they are separated forever from those they love. If it turns out that human persons retain their identity in an after-life, no one should be happier than the religious reincarnationist. In fact, Hinduism as practiced in Vedic times did not include belief in reincarnation.

The Data Point to One Paradigm

We have said that the various skeptical views offer different perspectives on the same data. So the question before us is whether we can make any progress at all or if we simply have to agree to disagree. Our objective in this book is to show that the data supports a particular paradigm, one that affirms the continued existence of each human person after physical death. In making the case for this, we will inevitably have to address the skeptical alternatives and show where and why they fail.

A Synthesis

Our case is not built on one or two fragments of fact, but on an entire panorama of truths, facts, and reasonable inferences. We begin with the dramatic after-life reports of the many through the ages who physically died and were then resuscitated. Second, we consider the universal testimony to a life beyond death that is the common heritage of humanity. Third, we review purported visions of the after-life and encounters with the "dead" who are "alive" in God. Finally, we tie these encounters and events to truths that are self-evident. For instance, we cannot deny that we are conscious—or else we would have to say we are conscious that we are not conscious. We cannot say there is no "I" for that is to say that "I" know there is no "I." Moreover, the touchstone of a sound philosophy is whether or not it can be lived. Is it possible to live our daily lives on the assumption that our thoughts are purely the actions of neurons or that there we do not make deliberate choices for which we are responsible? Thus, our experience of the transphysical dimension of the human person in everyday life is consistent with the idea that this dimension can survive death.

Burden of Proof

We will certainly give the skeptics a hearing, but we do so with the stipulation that the burden of proof is on them. If someone tells you that the world around you is an illusion (and there are philosophers who have said this) then the onus is on them to prove their ludicrous point. Now, the world beyond is not evident to the senses in the same way as the world around us. Nonetheless, we have been furnished with the kind of evidence in support of its existence that is appropriate to its kind of reality. Hence, the human race has found compelling grounds for believing that there is such a world. If the skeptics wish to deny this belief without considering the evidence in its favor, then it is up to them to show that their denial is well-grounded.

The skeptic might retort that the "majority" argument does not work. After all, most of the human race once believed that the earth was flat and that the sun moved around the earth—but they were wrong. Here, we have to distinguish between beliefs that are based on quantitative study—which is what science is all about—and beliefs that are derived from sources that are, by their very nature, outside the physical. Science can pronounce authoritatively on any reality that can be quantitatively measured. Hence, our beliefs about planets and stars, bacteria and brain cells must be based on the results of scientific research and experiment. But science can tell us nothing about the non-quantifiable and the non-physical. Here we rely on the testimony of credible witnesses, immediate experience, and self-evident truths. And when it comes to beliefs about life after death, the 21st century AD has no special advantage over the 21st century BC.

God of the Gaps

Often, physicalists reject belief in non-physical realities by dismissing these as gods of the gaps that will become untenable with the advance of science. But the very term gaps assumes that everything is "physical" and should be studied by science—and this begs the question of whether everything is physical. Certainly any "gaps" in the physical order should be (and can only be) studied by science. Nevertheless there are certain domains that clearly go beyond the physical. In such instances we are not dealing with a question of "gaps," but of different orders of being. To address the challenge, we need to adopt methodologies appropriate to each such order. The metaphor of gaps is simply mistaken in this context.

So the challenge faced by the skeptics is simply this: they are out of touch with reality as experienced by most of humanity. Of course they can claim that the greater portion of humanity is simply deluded or ignorant. But here we are not talking about a scientific theory that requires rigorous methodologies and sophisticated validation technologies. We are talking about a different state of being. Whether it exists can only be known from experience and encounter. So our own experience and the testimonies of those who have encountered this way of being is what is relevant. Knowledge of the laws of the physical world is of no help when you're dealing with a world beyond the physical. And a refusal to remain true to experience will blind even the most intelligent to a reality that can only be known through experience.

Anecdotal Again

Another favorite gambit of the skeptic is to dismiss all after-life data as anecdotal and therefore worthless from a scientific standpoint. We admit, of course, that the available data is not "scientific" in the sense that it issues forth from controlled experiments that can be replicated by anyone, anywhere. In this respect, it's anecdotal. But there's anecdotal and there's anecdotal. Does the world exist? No controlled experiments can prove that the world is not an illusion because they all have to assume the existence of the world. So also there are plenty of things that are not quantifiable or measurable that we take for granted on the basis of judgment calls using "anecdotal" evidence—the trustworthiness of a friend, for instance. When it comes to matters that cannot be quantified, we rely on the credibility of our background framework and the plausibility and coherence of the available evidence. As noted before, in such instances, we do not have to make a choice between the anecdotal and the scientific, but between the rational and the irrational. On the after-life, the solid foundation supporting it is the synergy of everyday experience, universal affirmation, and other-world narrative.

No Scientific Proof for the Meta-Scientific

By the nature of the case we cannot have a "scientific" proof for something that is meta-scientific. Nevertheless, the most rationally plausible explanation for a wide range of phenomena is a life after death. We have just enough evidence from experience and encounter to say yes—not too much (it is not coercive) nor too little (it is not speculative). In this respect, affirmation of another world is as rational as affirmation of the present world (which cannot be proven to exist to the satisfaction of philosophers). In both cases, rational affirmation of the world concerned is a mark of sanity.

A Petition Campaign Against Hell

Some skeptics find notions of the after-life objectionable because of the beliefs they embody, given that these sometimes include the ideas of Heaven, Hell, and Purgatory. To those who reject a doctrine of Hell or Purgatory, any narrative involving them is, ipso facto, unacceptable. In response we can say that these notions are echoed in some fashion or are otherwise "present" in all the primordial world religions. And whether Hell is "politically correct" or not in the present day, it has made an appearance not simply in the world religions, but in many contemporary NDEs. In any case, what we are pursuing in this book is an investigation into what we can know about the after-life. We are not launching a program or petition campaign for changing the structure of the after-life to satisfy our sensibilities!

Structure of the Book

The approach of this book is to begin *in medias res,* that is, start the narrative in the middle of the action, as was common in the great epic poems of history (*The Illiad, The Mahabharata, Kalevala*). This means starting with a blitzkrieg of extra-terrestrial "hard facts" that have thrust themselves into the life of humankind.

In Medias Res

The hard facts include:

- "Journeys" of the near-dead to another realm.
- The after-life chronicles of the primordial religions of humanity.
- Visions of the next world witnessed by children.
- Encounters with those who have long been deceased.
- The intercessory activity of "celestial citizens" in the affairs of this world.

These phenomena were neither expected nor sought. They simply happened. They were literally flung in our faces. At the very least, they demand an explanation.

Critics at Two Ends of the Spectrum

As is to be expected, there are those who dismiss these accounts as the product of hallucination, myth, fraud, or a disorder of the brain. On the other end of the spectrum, we have religious critics who explain them as demonic deceptions. These experiences, say the latter, are real, but they are products of Satan masquerading as an angel of light. On both ends of the spectrum, the critics approach the phenomena with their own preconceptions and preconditions. They do not consider the body of data on its own terms.

In the case of the skeptics, there is a superstitious faith in matter as the only reality, no matter what the evidence to the contrary.

The religious critics, on the other hand, have a blind faith in the belief that all transphysical phenomena are necessarily diabolic. This belief has no basis in Christian scripture, which advises believers to test the spirits to see if they are good (which means some are good and some not). Moreover, the world of the Gospels is one that takes for granted an interaction between departed souls and the present world. In one of the resurrection narratives, Jesus tells his disciples, "Look at my hands and my feet, that it is I myself. Touch me and see, because a ghost does not have flesh and bones as you can see I have." (Luke 24:39). He takes it for granted that the souls of the dead not only exist, but are capable of manifesting themselves to the living. The first followers of Jesus, right from the first century, took it as a fundamental truth that those who die in Christ not only continue to exist, but in some cases, intervene in the affairs of the present world. This is the truth denied today by the religious critics.

Grounding the Other Side in Everyday Experience

After considering the hard facts that have come to us from the "other side," we turn to our own everyday experience. Here we find "facts" that testify to our transphysical reality. These data are important because they "ground" after-life-related phenomena in the here-and-now. Let's say that my waking experience reveals to me that:

- ✎ "I" am a union of a physical body and a transphysical soul and
- ✎ my soul performs actions which are not dependent on matter.

This tells me that the disintegration of my body will not necessarily result in the demise of my soul. Knowing this, I can better evaluate claims of those who say they have encountered after-life-related persons or states.

We begin, then, in the middle of the action and end with a study of elements of our experience that tie in with the "action." This program is reflected in the sequence of the chapters (see text and following diagram).

The most appropriate starting point is what we might call the "smoking gun," the near-death experiences that have ripped a hole through the reigning myth of physicalism. The skeptics who deny the veracity of NDEs in knee-jerk fashion have retreated into a sulk mode and cannot be taken seriously. NDEs emerged suddenly and unexpectedly and in great quantity on the modern scene. In an NDE, an individual in a life-and-death situation claims to leave this world and enter another realm. As such, an NDE can be seen as a pre-after-life glimpse of the after-life rather than a "lived" experience of the after-life. The obvious follow-up question is whether we can know anything about the contours of the actual after-life.

Two potential sources are the collective experience of humankind and the domain of divine revelation. Hence in the next chapter we turn to the after-life testimony of the primordial religions. It is here that we find a remarkably unified universal account of a state of being beyond death. It is actually a matter of two potential states: either union with or separation from the divine.

Does this model of the after-life find echoes in subsequent human history? The fourth chapter reviews case-studies of reported communications between our present world and the world "to come." These ALVs (After-Life Visitations) range from visions of different after-life states that go beyond NDEs to interactions with individuals who have left this world for the next (in some cases centuries ago).

But these experiences of the after-life are not simply part of the historical record. In the fifth chapter, we explore contemporary after-life encounters that corroborate both the primordial models and historical case-studies. Some of the key encounters considered here involve skeptics who did not believe in a life after death.

So much for the action. Our next task is to step back and reflect on how this dramatic body of testimony, revelation, and observation relates to everyday experience. The sixth chapter therefore studies neuroscientific and other kinds of tangible data as it relates to the transphysical dimension of the human person. This takes us to the question of whether the transphysical dimension can survive separation from the physical. If there is survival, what form does it take—immortality, reincarnation, or resurrection? This is the topic of the seventh and last chapter.

The assumption throughout our inquiry is that progress is possible only with a global and historical perspective. But this perspective must be grounded in the raw data of immediate encounter and experience. We begin then *in medias res*.

Encounter/Experience/Paradigm

Near-Death Experiences

Primordial Paradigm of the After-Life

Historical After-Life Visitations

Contemporary After-Life Encounters

Pre-Death Experience— Conscious Self

Part 1

~

The Evidence of Encounter—
Visions and Witnesses

Chapter 2

~

The Smoking Gun

C laims about a realm that lies beyond death have been made almost from the dawn of human history. Strangely enough, these claims have been "born again" in the present day—this time seemingly custom-tailored to the new, more skeptical setting of the modern world. Millions of people who physically died and were then resuscitated have reported the reality of a world beyond death, a world that awaits all who die. These reports of near-death experiences have been taken seriously by everyone but the professional skeptics. This is not to say that the claims have been or should be accepted at face value. The skeptics, on the other hand, have either dismissed the claims as a priori impossible, or clutched at any straw to explain them away.

But despite three decades of onslaughts from the skeptics, the NDE phenomenon continues to pick up momentum. A 2007 story in *Time* magazine reported that "These are the best of times in the NDE field, with research gathering pace and new insights emerging."[1] More importantly, the worst that can be said about NDEs is that they have a 50/50 chance of being simply a product of brain biochemistry. But the features of certain NDEs (awareness of what is taking place at a distant location) make it unlikely that at least these NDEs are simply activities of the dying brain.

Defining Death and Near-Death

The term *near-death* is accurate because death itself is a process. "The process of dying occurs at different levels of organization from the organism to the organ, cellular, and sub-cellular levels," writes Dr. Linda Emmanuel, "And each set of systems can decline on a somewhat independent trajectory."[2] Dr. Michael Sabom applies this model to the NDE idea: "There is no definable moment of death, but only a process of dying which starts with life and eventually ends in death. The journey through a near-death experience may best be understood as an experiential counterpart to this physical dying process. And whether this journey ends in life or in death is determined not only by the physical factors at play but…by events unseen by all except the unconscious, dying patient."[3]

Dr. Sam Parnia, who is spearheading a major international study on NDEs, comments, "Contrary to popular perception, death is not a specific moment. It is a process that begins when the heart stops beating, the lungs stop working and the brain ceases functioning—a medical condition termed cardiac arrest, which from a biological viewpoint is synonymous with clinical death." As noted in an accompanying story, "Science has long struggled to define death, and to determine when the precise moment of death occurs. Now though, most doctors consider death more of a process than an event. A person is thought to have died when he stops breathing, his heart stops beating, and his brain activity ceases."[4]

For the purposes of the present study "near-death" concerns any state in which a subject is clinically dead. This, in turn, means there is a cessation of vital functions of the body such as breathing, the beating of the heart and, in some cases, brain activity.

Characteristics of Near-Death Experiences

The characteristics of the near-death experience—with occasional variations on the same general themes—have been thoroughly documented both by those who experienced them and by physicians and others who attended to them. In the book that launched the field of near-death studies, Dr. Raymond Moody listed some of the central characteristics of near-death experiences (while cautioning that no two NDEs are alike):

- ⤷ Ineffability.
- ⤷ Hearing spectators speaking of the subject's death.
- ⤷ Feelings of peace and quiet.
- ⤷ A strange noise during the occurrence.
- ⤷ The dark tunnel.
- ⤷ An out-of-the-body experience.

- Meeting deceased people.
- The being of light.
- The life review.
- The border or limit.
- Coming back.
- New views of death.[5]

In his foreword to this book, Dr. Moody has expanded further on these themes.

The Dutch cardiologist Pim Van Lommel, who did a 13-year study of NDE subjects, listed certain core attributes that emerged from his study:

- Out-of-body experience (OBE).
- Holographic life review.
- Encounter with deceased relatives or friends.
- Return to the body.
- Disappearance of fear of death.

Dr. Van Lommel writes, "Some people who have survived a life-threatening crisis report an extraordinary consciousness experience. A near-death experience (NDE) can be defined as the reported memory of a range of impressions during a special state of consciousness, including a number of special elements such as pleasant feelings, seeing a tunnel, a light or deceased relatives, or experiencing a life review, or an out-of-body experience with perception of one's own cardiopulmonary resuscitation (CPR)."

Dr. Van Lommel expands further on the kinds of events that give rise to NDEs: "Many circumstances are described during which related special and enhanced states of consciousness are reported. Such states include cardiac arrest (clinical death), shock after loss of blood, coma due to traumatic brain injury or intra-cerebral haemorrhage, near-drowning (mostly children) or asphyxia, but also in serious diseases not immediately life-threatening, during isolation, depression or meditation, or without any obvious reason. So an NDE can be experienced in a range of circumstances from severe injury of the brain as in cardiac arrest to continuum when the brain seems to function normally. What distinguishes a NDE is that it is a transforming experience causing enhanced intuitive sensibility, profound changes in attitude to life, and the loss of fear of death."[6]

NDE Case Study

Here is a typical NDE account published by the International Association for Near-Death Studies.

It was a Friday evening when I died. I was with friends, and we were all partying with drugs and alcohol.… As it turned out, that speedball turned out to be a lethal dose, causing me to overdose, I was clinically dead. When I crossed over, I had no idea that I was dead, I had no idea that I had lived on Earth, and had a family, there was no transition at all. I experienced the "light" while I was there. The light was not from a bulb, or in one area, it was everywhere. There is nothing on Earth that I have seen that could compare to the "light." One would have to truly experience it for themselves in order to fully understand. I can tell you that I felt love, peace, strength, and warmth from the light. I sensed that I was surrounded by hundreds of people, but I could not see their faces or bodies, since we were in the spiritual realm. We were all standing side-by-side on what was similar to an escalator, which was constantly moving. All of a sudden the "escalator" stopped, and I was now going to be shown a review of my life, and be judged for my actions.

I remember looking up and seeing, as if it were across the sky, my sister at 6 years old, and myself at 5. In the review, I was very mean and hateful to my sister, and calling her names and making her cry. As I stood in judgment, the "light" telepathically communicated with me and informed me of my hatred. At that point, I felt overwhelmed with guilt, shame, embarrassment, and humiliation. My feelings were very intense; I had never felt anything with that intensity before. I just wanted it to end, which it finally did, but it was not over!

The intense guilt and shame I experienced was the worst feeling I had ever known, but it was about to get worse. What I felt next was the worst pain I have ever experienced. Suddenly I realized that I had become my sister, I was "put" inside her so that I could now experience that gut-wrenching pain that she felt due to my actions. I have never felt any pain like the pain I was now experiencing. This was the worst feeling I have ever known, and I was begging for it to stop. I could not handle the pain anymore, and I would do anything to make it end, and suddenly it was over.

The "light" told me that the sins of a haughty spirit was the worst sin of all. At that point, the "escalator" started moving again, and it was moving in an upward motion. The "escalator" stopped again, and I was told that I am not to enter into the kingdom of heaven at this time. Instead, I was being given a second chance, I was being sent back to Earth in the physical realm. I was further told that I had to change my ways by loving instead of hating. The "light" informed me that I would not just be returned to Earth, but that I would bring the pain that I had experienced back with me. I was told that this pain would stay with me until my spirit had shed its earthly skin, that is, I would experience and carry this pain until the day that I would die.

I returned to Earth, and it would be about three weeks before I was on my feet again. It has been five months since my near death experience, and I remember everything as if it had just happened. And, yes, I did bring the pain back with me, this pain that I brought back was the pain my sister felt when I hurt her so bad. My sister's pain that I now carry, serves as a reminder of the importance of how we treat one another, and that we should love all, and hate none.

As a result of this experience, I am experiencing my spiritual awakening, and I can't wait to go out and heal and love the world."

NDEs in Other Cultures and Times

Millions of people in modern times have reported undergoing a near-death experience. But it should be noted that NDEs are not peculiar to the present day or Western society. They are both universal and transhistorical. "In nearly all cultures," writes Carol Zaleski, "people have told stories of travel to another world, in which a hero, shaman, prophet, king, or ordinary mortal passes through the gates of death and returns with a message for the living."[7]

Plato's Report on an NDE

These variants of NDEs have been documented from the time of the ancient Greeks. Plato has such a story in *The Republic*: "I will not however tell you a story of Alcinous, but rather of a strong man, Er, son of Armenius, by race a Pamphylian. Once upon a time he died in war; and on the tenth day, when the corpses, already decayed, were picked up, he was picked up in a good state of preservation. Having been brought home, he was about to be buried on the twelfth day; as he was lying on the pyre, he came back to life, and, come back to life, he told what he saw in the other world."[8]

Sixth-Century Experience

Zaleski cites a story told by a sixth-century holy man named Salvius, who had been lifeless for a night but was then sent back: "Four days ago, I died and was taken by two angels to the heights of heaven. And it was just as though I rose above not only this squalid earth, but even the sun and moon, the clouds and stars. Then I went through a gate that was brighter than normal daylight, into a place where the entire floor shone like gold and silver. The light was indescribable, and I can't tell you how vast it was."[9] We find carefully documented accounts of near-death experiences in medieval times.

NDEs in India

NDE research in India has shown interesting parallels: "Western studies of such experience indicate unusual cognitive and emotional outcomes when people experience a close brush with death and are revived. A comparison of Indian cases with American cases revealed some commonalities and some differences. The common features include seeing deceased relatives, "beings of light," and religious figures. Unlike their American counterparts, the Indian subjects felt that they were taken to the other world by messengers, that they went to a "man with a book," and that they were sent back because of a mistake. In a survey of near-death experiences in India, which consisted of interviewing 645 people in four villages in Karnataka with an estimated population of 6,430, Pasricha (1993) found 18 people who were revived after being close to death or even were believed to be dead. Of the 18 such people, NDEs were reported among 13."[10]

Chinese and Japanese NDEs

The *Time* story reports that NDEs in China center on estrangement from the body and that Japanese NDEs involve caves rather than tunnels. A researcher explains such differences by noting that expression is affected by culture, language, and learning.[11]

Differences and Similarities in Global NDEs

IANDS (The International Association for Near Death Studies) reports that, "some research has been conducted on NDE-ers outside the United States NDEs in western cultures such as Europe and Australia seem similar to those in the United States. Studies in non-western cultures have shown some differences but also some underlying similarities. For example, spiritual beings and encountering a border between the earthly and spiritual domains are common features in NDEs worldwide. A person's culture and personal experiences almost certainly influence the exact form that those features take and the experiencer's interpretation of them.

Children's NDEs

"Children's NDEs are especially interesting because the younger the child, the less the child's NDE has been influenced by culture. Young children's NDEs tend to be simpler than adults'. Perhaps this difference is due to children being mentally less developed in general than adults are. Childrens' NDEs do, however, have the same features as adults' NDEs—just in a simpler form. Child NDErs say they felt different from most other children while they were growing up."[12]

Negative NDEs

In most of the initially reported cases in the United States, the NDEs have been "positive," a pleasant experience where the subject feels reluctant to return to the "life before death." But ongoing research has shown that there are a significant number of "negative" NDEs as well. As leading NDE researcher Bruce Greyson put it, "Another interesting shift has been in the reports of hellish NDEs that leave people frightened; these were virtually unheard of for the first 10 or 15 years of research and have recently become far more common. Were they unreported in the beginning because of people's fears of revealing that experience?"[13]

In a book on negative NDEs, *Blessing in Disguise—Another Side of the Near-Death Experience*, Dr. Barbara Rommer observed, "By the time I had completed only 20 interviews, I realized that along with the pleasant near-death experiences came accounts that were very frightening. As I accumulated more and more of the frightening ones, certain patterns evolved. Profoundly positive life-altering changes occurred as a result of these frightening experiences. And those changes were sometimes even more significant and long-lasting than those that occurred after pleasant near-death experiences." She found that these changes were actually positive. "This very positive impact made the word *negative* (which has been applied to these events by other researchers) a misnomer. Therefore, I call them Less-Than-Positive near-death experiences or LTPs, and they are truly a 'Blessing in Disguise.'"[14]

Anti-NDE Dogmatists

In pursuing our inquiry, we should avoid three entirely different kinds of dogmatic preconceptions:

1. *Irrational skeptics*. The physicalist skeptic has determined on arbitrary grounds that an after-life is impossible and all evidence in its favor is simply dismissed without any attempt to study it.

2. *Conservative religionists*. Some conservative religionists have determined that the God of their religion could not possibly desire the salvation of all human persons and therefore any report that involves God's love for all is dismissed as a deception.

3. *New Age/Gnostic liberals*. On the other end of the spectrum are the New Age/Gnostic liberals who do not believe that our choices here can have consequences in the hereafter and that there is such a thing as evil. Any report that involves divine displeasure with human evil or the possibility of freely chosen endless separation from God (as revealed in a negative NDE) is suppressed or simply dismissed.

The Underlying Unity of Message in NDEs and the Primordial Religions

Now this willingness to consider both positive and negative NDEs is important because it helps locate the content of the NDEs within the collective experience of humanity. The after-life accounts of the ancient religions all see a direct correlation between our deeds in this life and our destiny in the next. And our ultimate destiny, as depicted in these religions, is that we can choose to be either united or separated from the Source of our being. The modern NDEs, when considered as a whole, give us the same message. Concerning the content of the after-life, it is true that NDEs cannot give us a definitive picture of the nature of life after death. Nevertheless, we should study all the available data given in NDEs and not just the elements that fit in with our own preconceptions. Many accounts of NDEs imply that all NDEs are pleasant experiences. As noted, this is not an accurate representation.

Focus on the Core, Not the Details

Of course not all the details laid out in NDE accounts can be taken as they stand. Much of what we are told is subjective interpretation or a reflection of cultural mores. As with any experience, the lens of interpretation is inescapable. But the more elaborate the account (especially if there is inference and speculation involved), the more suspect the details. It should be noted also that, as recounted, NDEs concern not our ultimate destiny as much as our immediate post-mortem experiences.

NDEs and Ultimate Destiny

But what about ultimate destiny? This highlights the issue of paradigm. The *Time* story observes, "While most researchers concede that there's a lot about NDEs we don't know, they reject the push to replace tried-and-tested paradigms with new (largely untestable) ones in an attempt to fill the gaps."[15] But the question is what is the "tried-and-tested" paradigm? Clearly what the unnamed researchers have in mind is physicalism —the dogma that matter is all there is. But physicalism is, at best, a blind belief which (as we show) is contradicted by the whole gamut of human experience. It does not pass any test other than of measuring whatever is quantifiable.

Reclaiming NDEs for the Wider Conversation of Humankind—A New Paradigm

Nevertheless this comment underlines the need for an adequate paradigm if we are to explain NDEs. The fact of the matter is that we do have a paradigm that makes sense of NDEs, and it is one that is testable in the realm we're dealing with, which is not the world of quantities. It is true that, for lack of a conceptual home, NDEs have been appropriated by the New Age carnival of psi, channeling, energies, crystals, astral bodies, OBEs, and the like. But in this book we seek to reclaim it for the wider conversation of humankind, the primordial paradigm of soul and body, and of insight into and interaction with the life after death. This paradigm is "tried-and-tested," and by infusing the data that comes to us from NDEs we renew it for the modern age. To that extent it is a new paradigm.

NDEs and the Soul

How does this paradigm relate to NDEs? We know within this paradigm that the human soul is immaterial and independent of the physical. The NDE, no matter what its provenance, is an experience of the soul. While the soul is in union with the body, the brain mediates most but not all of the self's actions. Because all monitoring devices are, by the nature of the case, physical, they can only "detect" what takes place in the brain. They cannot tell us anything about operations that are exclusive to the soul. To be sure, operations of the soul mediated through the brain will have physically measurable characteristics.

Now, as traditionally understood, the soul is the principle of life of the body. Does the soul leave the body in an NDE? If it does so for an extended period of time, the body ceases to exist, because there is nothing to unify the collocation of matter we call the body. Hence NDEs, if they involve a separation of soul and body, can only take place within a short window of time. The requirement for a lifeless body to come together after a few days is, from this standpoint, out of the question, because an extended separation of body and soul will mean that, in the absence of its integrator, the body dis-integrates—there would be nothing to which the soul can return. So under our paradigm an NDE can only be a short-term event.

How the Right Paradigm Helps Us Understand the Nature of NDEs

But we are left with the questions of whether, in an NDE, the soul actually "leaves" the body even for a short time and whether it has gotten a glimpse of the life after separation from the body—the after-life. The answer to both questions from the NDE-ers is yes. This is their claim. Can it possibly be true? Certainly "yes" in terms of our paradigm. Is it verifiable? Here the answer, by the nature of the case, is "no." But with the right paradigm, we can at least look for the right things. We can "confirm" rather than "verify."

Thus, if we recognize the fact of a soul and the fact that this soul does currently perform operations independent of the body, then this is our starting point. When presented with an NDE, we ask:

↪ Are the conditions such as required for the soul to leave the body? Absolutely. They are events that lead to death.

↪ Are the reports of the subjects what you would expect if the soul
   had left the body? Again, yes. The NDE subject is aware, from a
   different vantage point, of the body lying on the table, of the actions of people around the body and even of people in far away
   locations. The subject makes contact with deceased persons who,
   presumably, would be "found" in the after-life. There are also
   reports that fit in with traditional accounts: a life review, beings of
   light, and the like. Moreover, the accounts of how souls in the
   NDE state communicate—understanding without a sensory com-
   ponent—tally closely with St. Thomas Aquinas's description of
   the way in which a "separated soul" would operate.

Also to be noted is the fact that many NDE subjects report that there is a
threshold they do not cross, a point of no return. Hence, the possibility of return
is at least consistent with the rest of the account. But this also helps us see that
we are dealing with a transition state and not a permanent one. To the extent
that there are positive and negative NDEs, we hear an echo of traditional paradigm accounts of ultimate destiny, the choice between union and separation.

All these considerations indicate that we should modulate our expectations
as to whether or not we can "verify" NDEs. Remember that the separation of
soul and body would still be transitory at best. As such, it would involve all the
physiological changes that accompany the normal activities of the soul.

NDEs and the Occult

Many NDE books include a profusion of psychic and occultic claims. These
are clearly extraneous and peripheral add-ons that are like mushrooms sprout-
ing on fertile soil, but they are not the soil itself. In this inquiry, we take an
alternate path of remaining true to the universal experience of the human race.
Both New Age and physicalist perspectives fail the test of experience and universality. It should be pointed out also that we are not arguing for the ideas of an
astral body or ethereal energies and auras. Such claims, in any case, are quasi-
scientific in nature because they concern a physical reality. As such, they should
be tested scientifically, and science tells us that there is no evidence for their
existence.

Ultimately, then, there are two paths we can take in evaluating NDEs: either we restrict ourselves strictly to the physical, or we keep an open mind

concerning the reality of the intrinsically non-physical. The first path is physical-ism, the second is our paradigm of primordial-universal experience. Both paths will necessarily need to assemble the same hard facts that serve as evidence while ensuring that there are safeguards against fraud. But the expectations and criteria for inference vary, depending on the paradigm you adopt. If you believe (without proof) that there is nothing non-physical/transphysical, then any evidence in favor of the non-physical will be classified as a non-event to be explained as science progresses. If you do believe that the non-physical exists, then any evidence of non-physical realities or transactions will be taken on their own terms instead of being dogmatically dismissed.

Certainly reasonable people can disagree on the conclusions to be drawn from the existing evidence. Here we will give the pros and cons of the claim that NDEs are evidence of a state of being beyond the physical.

Pros

What is remarkable about NDE research is the number of highly special-ized doctors and distinguished scientists that (a) have conducted research on the phenomenon and (b) come away convinced that we are dealing with a non-physical phenomenon. This stands in contrast to the rarity of high-caliber re-searchers working on reincarnation and other New Age predilections.

The research that began with Raymond Moody has been carried on by others like:

- Van Lommel, who carried out a 13-year-study (previously refer-enced) with several hundred cardiac arrest survivors.
- The American cardiologist Michael Sabom, who performed a sys-tematic and carefully documented study of 160 patients of whom 47 had NDEs.
- The psychologist Kenneth Ring, who has studied NDE subjects since the 1970s.
- The pediatrician Melvin Morse, who has been studying NDEs in children for some 15 years.
- Dr. Bruce Greyson, a professor of Psychiatric Medicine, who has written some 60 peer-reviewed articles in scholarly journals on NDEs.
- Dr. Sam Parnia, who works with UK hospitals and Cornell University and just launched a study at the UN with 25 major medical centers.

↪ The British neuropsychiatrist Dr. Peter Fenwick, who has studied some 300 NDE subjects over four decades.

Results of the Van Lommel Study

The results of Dr. Van Lommel's 13-year study were published in the internationally known medical journal *The Lancet*. Van Lommel concluded:

> Our results show that medical factors cannot account for occurrences of NDE; although all patients had been clinically dead, most did not have NDE. Furthermore, seriousness of the crisis was not related to occurrence or depth of experience. If purely physiological factors resulting from cerebral anoxia caused NDE, most of our patient should have had this experience. Patients' medication was also unrelated to frequency of NDE. Psychological factors are unlikely to be important as fear was not associated with NDE.

He notes further:

> During cardiac arrest, the functioning of the brain and of other cells in our body stops because of anoxia. The electromagnetic fields of our neurons and other cells disappear, and the possibility of resonance, the interface between consciousness and physical body, is interrupted. Such understanding fundamentally changes one's opinion about death, because of the almost unavoidable conclusion that at the time of physical death consciousness will continue to be experienced in another dimension, in an invisible and immaterial world, the phase-space, in which all past, present, and future is enclosed. Research on NDE cannot give us the irrefutable scientific proof of this conclusion, because people with an NDE did not quite die, but they all were very, very close to death, without a functioning brain.... There are still more questions than answers, but, based on the aforementioned theoretical aspects of the obviously experienced continuity of our consciousness, we finally should consider the possibility that death, like birth, may well be a mere passing from one state of consciousness to another.[16]

Van Lommel holds that consciousness is not simply a bodily event. "In my view, the brain is not producing consciousness, but it enables us to experience our consciousness," he says. He compares the brain to a television, which receives programs by decoding information from electromagnetic waves. Likewise, he says, "the brain decodes from only a part of our enhanced consciousness, which we experience as waking consciousness. But our enhanced consciousness is different, and this is what is experienced during an NDE."[17]

Fenwick's Assessment of the Status of NDE Research

Fenwick, a senior Lecturer at the Institute of Psychiatry, Kings College, London, and Consultant Neuropsychiatrist at the Maudsley Hospital and at the John Radcliffe Hospital in Oxford, writes:

Four recent prospective studies suggest that 11-20% of cardiac arrest survivors report such experiences.... What causes these experiences? Chemical factors would seem to be important...but only 10% of patients have the experience, while the NMDA receptor is involved in every cardiac arrest with cerebral ischaemia. These experiences do not appear to be due to changes in serum electrolytes, PaO_2 and $PaCO_2$ or to treatment with sedative agents, as their incidence is less than 2% in intensive care unit patients. Psychological factors are unlikely and religious belief influences the content of the experience but not its occurrence.

The authors of these prospective studies conclude that the occurrence of lucid thought processes, with reasoning and memory formation, and an ability to remember events from the period of resuscitation, is a scientific paradox—paradoxical because studies of cerebral physiology during cardiac arrest suggest that lucid experiences should not occur or be remembered at a time when global cerebral function is severely impaired or absent. Cerebral localisation studies have indicated that complex subjective experiences are mediated through the activation of a number of different cortical areas, rather than any single area of the brain. A globally disordered brain would not be expected to support lucid thought processes or the ability to "see," "hear," and remember details of the experience. Any acute alteration in cerebral physiology leads to confusion and impaired higher cerebral function (Marshall et al 2001). Cerebral damage, particularly hippocampal damage, is common after cardiac arrest; thus only confusional and paranoid thinking as is found in intensive care patients should occur. The paradox is that experiences reported by cardiac arrest patients are not confusional. On the contrary, they indicate heightened awareness, attention, and memory at a time when consciousness and memory formation are not expected to be functioning.[18]

Cons

Despite these promising reports, the skeptics have been relentless in their rejection of other-worldly conclusions. NDEs in every case without exception, they claim, are induced solely by changes in brain chemistry, which in turn are caused by internal or external physial factors.

The *Time* story reports that no one denies that NDEs occur. But researchers are divided on whether this is entirely a physiological activity produced by a brain lacking in oxygen or if it is an instance of consciousness existing independent of a functioning brain.[19]

The skeptics do not just reject NDEs as evidence of an after-life. For the most part, they do not believe in a self or consciousness distinct from the physical. Obviously, these very assumptions preclude the possibility of survival.

Susan Blackmore

The best-known skeptic is the British psychologist Susan Blackmore whose *Dying to Live* is the source-book cited by most skeptics. She admits that her particular explanation may or may not be true: "I have not claimed that any of my work proves the Dying Brain Hypothesis. In fact no amount of research ever could," she said in a March 2001 debate with Greg Stone.[20] But Blackmore presents a brain-centered explanation for NDEs. She starts off by noting that the allegation that NDE are hallucinations explains nothing (since there has to be an explanation for why and how these particular hallucinations take place). She also agrees that Carl Sagan's theory that NDEs are simply a recreation of our childhood experience of birth is pitifully inadequate. The various phenomena associated with the NDE, in her view, are produced by chemicals in the brain. Neurochemistry, physiology, and psychology are sufficient to explain the well-known features of NDEs. Blackmore herself, during her drug-using days, had an out-of-body experience.

One explanation for the out-of-body, travel through the tunnel and euphoria experiences is lack of oxygen to the brain (hypoxia/anoxia). Pilots doing training in centrifuges, she remarks, sometimes lose consciousness due to lack of oxygen and report the same experiences. Three responses have been proposed to this criticism:

1. Studies with two groups of subjects who nearly died and who had similar amounts of oxygen in their blood showed that one group had NDEs while the other did not.

2. NDEs have been reported by subjects who did not have any depri-
   vation of oxygen to the brain (for example, those who fell from
   heights, had accidents, and so on).

3. The pilots in centrifuges (as we shall see) did not report the same
   experiences as those of NDE subjects.

In Blackmore's view, there are biochemical explanations for the different
NDE states. These explanations range from the stimulation of the NMDA receptors in nerve cell membranes and the level of endorphins in the brain to the
effect of serotonin. According to one theory she promotes, the brain releases
neuropeptides and neurotransmitters, particularly the endogenous endorphins, in
response to the stress of the near-death situation. These stimulate the limbic
system and associated structures. The life review is a result of seizures in the
limbic system and temporal lobe caused by the release of endorphins; stimulation of cells in the temporal lobe of the brain are known to cause experiences
that seem like a reliving of memories. The blissful state of the NDE is also a
product of the endorphins. Jeffrey Saver and John Rabin attribute NDEs to
"endorphin-induced limbic system activity or a blockade of NDMA receptors."[21]
Disruptions of neurotransmitters cause random firings of neurons and the resultant NDE states. Moreover, the illusion of entering new worlds is simply an
extension of our normal illusions that there exists a self and an external world.
The latter are creations of our own minds, as are the "worlds" experienced in
an NDE.

Blackmore's charges have been addressed by different NDE researchers.
What really happens to the pilots training in centrifuges? Michael Sabom writes,
"During the first six seconds of gravitational stress, subjects report tunnel vision
with contraction of the visual field from the periphery inward. Blackout, or
complete loss of vision, occurs next, and then unconsciousness. During the more
severe episodes of G-LOC, when the insult to the brain was the greatest,
'dreamlets,' or short dream interludes, occurred in some subjects. Typical near-
death experiences were not reported during G-LOC, leading the author, Dr.
James Whinnery, to conclude that symptoms 'unique to the NDE' are beyond
the scope of this type of experimentation and require longer forays into the
process of dying."

Temporal Lobe Seizures and Endorphins

About temporal lobe seizures and endorphins, Sabom writes:

The human brain is critically dependent on a rich supply of oxygen
and nutrients. Impairment of this supply, even for only a few seconds,

may lead to a myriad of electrical and biochemical events. Seizures are caused by abnormal electrical discharges within the brain and may occur immediately prior to death…. Endorphins and hypoxia (lack of oxygen) have both been proposed as triggers for temporal lobe seizures in the dying brain. Endorphins are morphine-like substances synthesized and released by the brain under conditions of stress such as anxiety, fear, or pain…. Whether endorphins cause seizures, however is unclear." Some researchers suggest "that endorphins may be effective in treating, not causing temporal lobe seizures. On the other hand, hypoxia has been shown to increase the brain's susceptibility to seizures, including seizures of the temporal lobe."[22]

Dr. Michael Persinger, who has mimicked temporal lobe seizures with electrical stimulation of the brain, has reported that these experiences were "fragmented and variable, whereas in NDEs these sensations are integrated and focused within a brief period." [23] Sabom comments that "this loss of mental integration is a key feature that separates seizure phenomena from the near-death experience."

Dr. Ernest Rodin, a major epilepsy researcher, says, "The hallmarks and nuclear components (of NDEs) are a sensation of peace or even bliss, the knowledge of having died, and, as a result, being no longer limited by the physical body. In spite of having seen hundreds of patients with temporal lobe seizures during three decades of professional life, I have never come across that symptomatology as part of a seizure."[24]

Sabom's conclusion is that "the 'dying brain hypothesis,' which attempts to explain the NDE on the basis of endorphins, hypoxia, and temporal lobe seizures, cannot adequately account for the near-death experience. To do so would be like confusing bronchitis and pneumonia—there may be similarities, but the trained medical observer knows that they are fundamentally different conditions with different symptoms and methods of treatment."[25]

IANDS has assembled various responses to the anoxia hypothesis: "Physicians have compared oxygen levels of cardiac arrest survivors who did and did not have NDEs and their findings discredit the anoxia hypothesis. In fact, in one study, the NDE-ers had higher oxygen levels than non-NDE-ers. People report near-death experiences from many situations when their brains are healthy—during childbirth, in accidents, in falls. People also report classical near-death-like experiences that have occurred during conversations or while holding a dying loved one. In those cases where anoxia is involved and monitored, such as in cardiac arrest, the effects are disorientation and poor memory. The opposite is true for those patients who report near-death experiences following their cardiac arrest."[26] It should be noted that even Dr. Daniel Carr, a prominent proponent of the endorphin theory, admits that there is no evidence that the brain creates a large quantity of endorphins in response to the stress of dying.

Interestingly, Blackmore announced a few years ago that she has discontinued research into NDEs.

OBEs and the Right Angular Gyrus

Another prominent critic of NDEs, a Swiss neuroscientist named Olaf Blanke, claims that out-of-body experiences naturally occur when activity in the right angular gyrus is suppressed for any reason. When people are in shock, say after an accident, a relative lack of blood flow to this region can easily produce sensations of floating outside one's body. The *Time* story observes that Blanke claims to have induced an OBE in an epilepsy patient by stimulating the temporoparietal junction of the brain.[27]

Now even if the illusion of an OBE can, in certain instances, be caused by a neurophysiological abnormality, this does not mean that all OBEs are the product of such an abnormality. But, in any case, Blanke's attempt to link OBEs to a certain brain function does not work for reasons pointed out by IANDS and others: "Haven't locations in the brain been found to produce an NDE? The right temporal lobe, the left temporal lobe, the frontal lobe attention area, the thalamus, the hypothalamus, the amygdala, and the hippocampus each have been suggested by different neuroscientists as linked to the near-death experience. Although different parts of the brain may be involved at some point before, during, or following some NDEs, there is no empirical evidence that any one of these, or a combination of them, manufacture the NDE. Every perception we have will be associated with activity in a specific part of the brain, but that doesn't mean the activity caused the experience. For example, as you read these words, there is increased electrical activity in your occipital lobe, but we don't conclude that these words are a hallucination caused by that brain activity. Swiss neuroscientist, Olaf Blanke, claimed that stimulation of the right angular gyrus can trigger out-of-body experiences (OBEs). However, the stimulated experience involved only one patient. That patient's experience was fragmentary, distorted and illusory, substantially different from OBEs occurring during NDEs."[28]

Other lines of criticism include Gerald Woerlee's claim that NDE subjects must be conscious even if they appear unconscious because they claim to have conscious experiences and Kevin Nelson's theory that NDEs are induced by dream-like states that are in turn caused by a crisis in the brain.

Regarding Woerlee we must say that his premise highlights the precise issue in dispute without breaking new ground. We admit that only a conscious subject can have a conscious experience. But this is not the issue: the issue is whether the subject in question can be conscious even if temporarily separated from the body? We want to find out if the human soul can leave the body on a temporary basis and be conscious even if separated from the body. These larger issues are not addressed by statements of the obvious, such as the fact that you have to be conscious to have a conscious experience. Such statements leave us neither here nor there.

NDEs Result From Sleep Disorders

With regard to Nelson, the proposal is "that NDEs occur in a dream-like state brought on when crisis in the brain trips a predisposition to a type of sleep disorder."

A laudatory article in *New Scientist* makes the case for Nelson's theory. Nelson, a neurophysiologist, argues that NDEs stem from "REM intrusions," a "glitch" in the brain that during periods of high stress "may flip it into a mixed state of awareness where it is both in REM sleep and partially awake at the same time." But the REM intrusion critique shares the flaws of the numerous biology-based hypotheses that have been floated to explain NDEs. It simply cannot deal with the multi-faceted nature of NDEs and simply piles on additional speculative hypotheses to "explain" each diverse element of the experience reported by survivors. It is speculation-based and not fact-based criticism.

Here is the line of "reasoning" in this particular framework:

↬ Narcoleptics have been known to have a propensity for OBEs.

↬ Nelson is told that a "fly in the ointment" with his explanation is the fact that REM intrusions are generally frightening in nature and cannot therefore be reconciled with the usual feelings of comfort accompanying NDEs. He responds that in the exceptional situation of an NDE "the REM intrusion happens in a crisis, when our fight-or-flight response has already dampened our normal fear." But just earlier Nelson himself had highlighted the fact that NDEs are not restricted to near-death situations, but take place in othe contexts such as a fainting fit.

- ↦ What about the peaceful feelings engendered by an NDE? According to the Nelson, this can be explained by the fact that the brain's limbic system that includes the amygdala lights up during REM sleep. But then how do you explain hellish or distress NDEs?
- ↦ Also why does an REM intrusion take place during an NDE? Again there is a resort to speculation. Nelson hypothesizes that the source of NDEs is the brainstem.

Bruce Greyson is critical of Nelson's recruitment methodology for subjects. In addition, he thinks that Nelson has reversed the cause-and-effect cycle. Those who have had NDEs may subsequently have REM intrusions. But this by no means is evidence that REM intrusions caused NDEs. Greyson points out that "It may be more plausible that NDEs played a role in subsequent REM intrusion." For instance, "people with post-traumatic stress disorder subsequently have more frequent REM intrusion—maybe because they sleep less soundly."[29]

Critics have also made the salient point that Nelson's own data argue against his hypothesis. Forty percent of the participants in his study reported that they have not had REM intrusions. So it can hardly be argued that REM intrusions underlie NDEs.[30]

As with all the other physicalist explanations, the REM intrusion hypothesis does not even try to account for the fact that NDE subjects have perceived actual events taking place in distant locations. There is no physicalist hypothesis that can explain such a phenomenon. Unintentionally perhaps, the *New Scientist* article includes two statements that could serve as an epitaph for all physicalist hypotheses:

- ↦ "But despite numerous attempts, no one has been able to scientifically explain all the elements of an NDE."
- ↦ "In fact, the list of explanations goes on and on. But many of them fail to account for the whole experience and are impossible to test scientifically."[31]

The Pam Reynolds Breakthrough

A major breakthrough in addressing the skeptics came with the Pam Reynolds NDE.

In 1991, Reynolds was found to have a basilar artery aneurysm in the brain that could not be operated on with conventional neurosurgical methods without the imminent risk of death. She was taken to the Barrow Neurological Institute in Phoenix where the neurologist Robert Spetzler had pioneered a new type of surgery called hypothermic cardiac arrest, nicknamed "Standstill." The patient first had to undergo induced clinical death, which would mean that the brain EEG would come to a stop (no cerebral cortex activity), there would be no response from the brainstem (hence no brain function), and bloodflow to the brain would cease. Reynolds's body temperature was brought down to 60 degrees, her heartbeat and breathing stopped, her brainwaves flattened with no electrical activity in the brain, and the blood drained from her head. Just when she was brought to this state and before the surgery commenced, Reynolds felt herself "pop" out of her body. She gave remarkably accurate descriptions of the unusual instruments used in the surgery, as well as the activities taking place in the operating room. This was followed by her encounter with deceased relatives.

As Reynolds recounts it:

The next thing I recall was the sound: It was a Natural D. As I listened to the sound, I felt it was pulling me out of the top of my head. The further out of my body I got, the more clear the tone became. I remember seeing several things in the operating room when I was looking down. It was the most aware that I think that I have ever been in my entire life. You're very focused and you have a place to go. The feeling was like going up in an elevator real fast. And there was a sensation, but it wasn't a bodily, physical sensation. It was like a tunnel but it wasn't a tunnel.

At some point very early in the tunnel vortex I became aware of my grandmother calling me. But I didn't hear her call me with my ears... it was a clearer hearing than with my ears. I trust that sense more than I trust my own ears.

The feeling was that she wanted me to come to her, so I continued with no fear down the shaft. It's a dark shaft that I went through, and at the very end there was this very little tiny pinpoint of light that kept getting bigger and bigger and bigger. The light was incredibly bright, like sitting in the middle of a light bulb. It was so bright that I put my hands in front of my face fully expecting to see them and I could not. But I knew they were there. Not from a sense of touch. Again, it's terribly hard to explain, but I knew they were there...I noticed that as I began to discern different figures in the light—and they were all covered with light, they were light, and had light permeating all around them—they began to form shapes I could recognize and understand. I could see that one of them was my grandmother. I don't know if it was reality or a projection, but I would know my grandmother, the sound of her, any-time, anywhere. Everyone I saw, looking back on it, fit perfectly into my understanding of what that person looked like at their best during their lives. I recognized a lot of people. My uncle Gene was there. So was my great-great-Aunt Maggie, who was really a cousin. On Papa's side of the family, my grandfather was there. They were specifically taking care of me, looking after me.

They would not permit me to go further. It was communicated to me—that's the best way I know how to say it, because they didn't speak like I'm speaking—that if I went all the way into the light some-thing would happen to me physically.

I wanted to go into the light, but I also wanted to come back. I had children to be reared. It was like watching a movie on fast-forward on your VCR: You get the general idea, but the individual freeze-frames are not slow enough to get detail. But then I got to the end of it and saw the thing, my body. I didn't want to get into it. It looked terrible, like a train wreck. It looked like what it was: dead. I believe it was covered. It scared me and I didn't want to look at it.

I felt a definite repelling and at the same time a pulling from the body. The body was pulling and the tunnel was pushing...it was like diving into a pool of ice water."[32]

Spetzler, Reynolds's neurosurgeon, commented that her recollections oc-curred shortly after surgery and were remarkably accurate. This was mystify-ing because, "The brain waves were completely gone. If you examine this patient with any of our techniques that we would normally use, EEG, pulse monitor, that patient would be dead. It's almost impossible to conceive that you would per-ceive through the brain itself what she has observed. To me it's completely perplexing. But I'm not arrogant enough, having seen so many things that I cannot understand and dealing with the brain day in and day out, to say that something isn't possible."[33]

So what do the skeptics say? In a contribution to a *Reader's Digest* article on the Reynolds case, Susan Blackmore wrote, "If the case you describe is true, the whole of science would need rewriting."[34] She thinks the account could not be as described: "I can only say that my expectation is that this case did not happen like that." Apart from this a priori rejection, Blackmore did not offer any detailed critique. Not so Gerald Woerlee who maintains that Reynolds must have been conscious in some way when she made observations of the operating room and that her NDE must have taken place before the flatline. His critique has, of course, been challenged.

Ian Lawton notes that Woerlee's claim is that Reynolds could have heard conversations through the speaker-plugs in her ears particularly when she was not totally anesthetized. Lawton points out that neither Woerlee nor other critics have been able to explain how Reynolds, "was able to 'see' the saw used to open up her skull. Remember that this had an unusual design that a non-expert could not be expected to guess at, and that Pam also described its accompanying 'interchangeable blades' in a 'socket-wrench case.'" Her eyes had been taped shut during the operation. Moreover, this distinctive saw was used on top of her head and thus would not have been visible to her.[35]

Kevin Williams engaged in an online debate on the Reynolds case-study with Woerlee and reached several conclusions after the discussion. Woerlee's theory is that Reynolds's NDE took place before the hypothermic cardiac arrest and not when her brain was flatline. But in fact her NDE account goes through the flatline phase. Woerlee hypothesizes that the VEP monitor and EEG machine may not have been fully reliable, and it is possible that she was conscious even though the machines reported no brain activity. Williams comments that that this would be "in the face of no heartbeat and her brain being drained of blood. If so, then she was conscious without a functioning brain, which would refute Woerlee's position!" [36]

Michael Sabom compared Spetzler's surgical transcript with Reynolds's account, and suggested that no brain activity may have occurred during the period when Reynolds was going through the tunnel. A dead brain cannot misfire or hallucinate. "She met all clinical criteria for death. She had no blood in her body. She had no vital signs at all," noted Sabom.[37] But none of this impresses the skeptics. As one wrote, "If she recalls things that took place while her brain was 'stopped,' then the obvious explanation is that it wasn't." My mind (or in this case "my" brain) is made up. Don't confuse me with the details.

Can We Know If NDEs Are Authentic?

So how do we know if an NDE is purely a function of the brain or, even more fundamentally, can we know? The *Time* story is inconclusive in its conclusion: "On balance, it's almost certain that NDEs happen in the theater of one's mind, and that in the absence of resuscitation, it's the brain's final sound and light show, followed by oblivion. Nonetheless, there's still no definitive explanation. There mightn't be a ghost in the machine. But it's a machine whose complexities remain well beyond our grasp."[38]

There can be no denying that biological structures are involved in NDEs. Certainly some aspects of an NDE could be replicated by physiological manipulation. But does this prove anything? If a certain out-of-body experience can be shown to arise purely from biochemical stimulation of some kind, does this prove that all OBEs have the same source? An analogy might help. Certain drugs might induce the sensation of your body floating in the air, but does this mean you cannot actually float in the air (say in gliding or skydiving)? If I have a hallucination that I am seeing an elephant, does this mean that every instance of my seeing an elephant is a hallucination? Sometimes our subjective experience corresponds to objective reality and sometimes it does not. Each claim should be examined on its own merits. When one person makes the extraordinary claim of having an OBE, a skeptical response is prudent. But if a number of people make the claim in the context of a certain paradigm, this claim is worthy of open-minded investigation. NDEs should be viewed as part of a package: it is not just a matter of OBEs, but a whole host of other phenomena.

For instance, another dimension that needs to be addressed is the profound change in the lives of most NDE subjects after the experience. The event seems to be transformative making them self-giving and hope-filled. They do not fear death because they no longer see it as the end. Mario Beauregard remarks that "there is no scientific evidence showing that delusions or hallucinations produced by a dysfunctional brain can induce the kind of long-term positive changes and psychospiritual transformations that often follow RSMEs. In fact, delusions and hallucinations usually constitute negative experiences from a subjective perspective."[39]

How do Thought Processes Co-exist With Severe Brain Dysfunction?

Sam Parnia, the leader of the largest international study of NDEs, asks:

How do the reports of NDE in cardiac arrest help the research into consciousness? Numerous studies have shown that thought processes are mediated by multiple areas of the brain and not just a single area. For this, brain cells need to communicate using electrical pulses. During cardiac arrest, there's a severe insult to the brain that causes either no blood flow to the brain or at best severely reduced blood flow. Either way, there's such a deficiency in blood flow that electrical activity in the brain ceases within a few seconds, and there remains a flatline throughout the period of the cardiac arrest and even afterward for some people. Nevertheless, some formal thought processes and consciousness appear to be present in a proportion of those who are in cardiac arrest.

In normal medical practice, it's well recognized that any alteration in the function of the brain leads to a clouded sense of consciousness, which is highlighted by a confusional state, and if the impairment is more significant, consciousness is lost. If such conditions are left untreated they can lead to a coma. However, in all these conditions, the insult is still not so great as to cause the brain waves to go flat. At worst they start to show changes in shape. How is it then that we have a clinical scenario in which there's severe brain dysfunction, the worst possible type, with an absence of electrical activity in the brain, but somehow thought processes, with reasoning, memory formation, and consciousness continue and are even heightened?

It might be suggested that the thoughts are arising from a small area of the brain that is somehow able to receive blood flow; however, numerous studies have demonstrated that thought processes are generated by global brain function. Also, it's almost impossible for one area to receive blood when there's hardly any blood flow to the brain. Scientifically speaking there should be no consciousness present at all. How then can we account for the findings of NDE research?

The most obvious explanation seems to be that perhaps the experience isn't occurring during the period of cardiac arrest at all. Dr. Susan

Blackmore and Professor Christopher French, two British psychologists, have suggested that it may be occurring just before the crisis, or even just after, when the individual is still in an unconscious state but blood flow is relatively normal and brain waves are present.

This is possible; however, there have been many individuals who have recalled details from the middle of the cardiac arrest when brain blood flow has been severely impaired.

Many thousands of people, including small children, have reported a fully functioning mind and consciousness and have been able to watch specific details that were happening during the cardiac arrest, the possibility is raised that mind and consciousness can exist separately from the brain and also during, and at least for some time, after death."[40]

Time Out

The academic community, on the whole, refuses to believe that NDEs constitute evidence either for a non-physical soul or a life after death. The philosopher Neal Grossman has written two penetrating critiques of the frame of mind of the "confirmed" skeptics.

When researchers ask the question, How can the near-death experience be explained, they tend to make the usual assumption that an acceptable explanation will be in terms of concepts—biological, neurological, psychological—with which they are already familiar. The near-death experience (NDE) would then be explained, for example, if it could be shown what brain state, which drugs, or what beliefs on the part of the experiencer correlate with the NDE. Those who have concluded that the NDE cannot be explained mean that it cannot be, or has not yet been, correlated with any physical or psychological condition of the experiencer.

I wish to suggest that this approach to explaining the NDE is fundamentally misguided. To my knowledge, no one who has had an NDE feels any need for an explanation in the reductionist sense that researchers are seeking. For the experiencer, the NDE does not need to be explained, because it is exactly what it purports to be, which is, at a minimum, the direct experience of consciousness—or minds, or selves, or personal identity—existing independently of the physical body. It is only with respect to our deeply entrenched materialist paradigm that the NDE needs to be explained, or more accurately, explained away. In this article, I will take the position that materialism has been shown to be empirically false; and hence, what does need to be explained is the academic establishment's collective refusal to examine the evidence and to see it for what it is. The academic establishment is in the same position today as the bishop who refused to look through Galileo's telescope. Why is this the case?

Before addressing this question, I'd like to say something about the kind and strength of evidence that refutes materialism. The materialist can, in principle, give no account of how a person acquires veridical information about events remote from his or her body. Consider, for example, the kind of case where the NDE-er accurately reports the conversation occurring in the waiting room while his or her body is unconscious in the operating room. There is no way for the relevant information, conveyed in sound waves or light waves, to travel from the waiting room, through corridors and up elevators, to reach the sense organs of the unconscious person. Yet the person wakes from the operation with the information. This kind of case—and there are lots of them—shows quite straightforwardly that there are nonphysical ways in which the mind can acquire information. Hence materialism is false.

Smoking Guns

Grossman thinks cases like those of Pam Reynolds are "smoking guns" when it comes to evidence for NDE.

A brain in this state cannot create any kind of experience. Yet the patient reported a profound NDE. Those materialists who believe that consciousness is secreted by the brain, or that the brain is necessary for conscious experience to exist, cannot possibly explain, in their own terms, cases such as this. An impartial observer would have to conclude that not all experience is produced by the brain, and that therefore the falsity of materialism has been empirically demonstrated. Thus, what needs to be explained is the abysmal failure of the academic establishment to examine this evidence and to embrace the conclusion: Materialism is false, and consciousness can and does exist independently of the body.

Our collective irrationality with respect to the wealth of evidence against materialism manifests in two ways: (1) by ignoring the evidence, and (2) by insisting on overly stringent standards of evidence, that, if adopted, would render any empirical science impossible.

My colleague believed in materialism not as a scientific hypothesis that, scientific hypothesis, might be false, but rather as dogma and ideology that "must" be true, evidence to the contrary notwithstanding. For him, materialism is the fundamental paradigm in terms of which everything else is explained, but which is not itself open to doubt. I shall coin the term "fundamaterialist" to refer to those who believe that materialism is a necessary truth, not amenable to empirical evidence.[41]

How Skeptics Prefer Their Philosophies Over the Evidence

Grossman's incisive comments help us get to the heart of the matter. The scientific skeptics are, to a great extent, skeptical because of their prior philosophical views. Blackmore, for instance, believes that we have no self and no consciousness or mind that is distinct from the processes in the brain. She is not even willing to trust the existence of the external world because this is simply a "model" created by our neurons (and if all our knowing is simply a matter of neural firings, she has a point). Such radical skepticism makes it impossible for her to take even the most exhaustively documented NDE as evidence for an after-life. There can be no survival because there is no such thing as a self that can survive.

This kind of skepticism ("fundamaterialism") is a paradigm and such a paradigm cannot be changed by one experiment or experience or event. Paradigms change only in the face of a diverse range of counter-evidence. This is, of course, what we will be trying to present in this book.

How the Skeptics Have Helped

Paradoxically, the skeptics may have played a useful role in separating the wheat from the chaff in NDE reports. The challenges issued by various skeptics have helped NDE researchers critically organize, analyze, and refine the data emerging from thousands of cases. And though scientific studies alone cannot answer the question of whether there is an after-life, they are certainly helpful in generating a body of data that can be tested against the primordial-universal after-life paradigm.

Fairness in One Scientific Forum

It should be said that not all scientific forums are dogmatically skeptical. Remarkably, *Discover* magazine recently carried a balanced and perceptive story on the questions posed by NDEs. The story considers the work of Greyson, Van Lommel, and Fenwick and notes that, on a scientific level, "the most significant aspect of many NDEs is that the individual's brain should not have been functioning at the time of the event." Greyson points out that "We have a lot of well-documented cases where we have EEG and other evidence that the brain is not functioning, and yet people will say, 'I was thinking clearer than I ever have before.'" Van Lommel observes that, at the moment of an NDE, "these people are not only conscious, their consciousness is even more expansive than ever. They can think extremely clearly, have memories going back to their earliest childhood, and experience an intense connection with everything and everyone around them. And yet their brain shows no activity at all." Fenwick remarks that "if it can be shown that people can acquire information when they are unconscious and out of their body, it would be indisputable evidence that consciousness is separate from the brain." The article concludes that, "If consciousness is the product of brain activity, near-death experiences should not happen. At the very least, the contrary evidence suggests that the standard understanding of consciousness is incomplete." [42]

Ground Rules

Certain clarifications must be made with regard to NDEs as it relates to a hypothesis of the after-life.

NDEs Are Not "Scientific" (That Is, Quantitative) Proof of the After-Life

It must be said that NDEs as such cannot scientifically "prove" the existence of an after-life. Life after death falls outside the domain of science simply because science is restricted to that which is quantitatively measurable. Whether there is a different dimension of being in which we continue to exist after physical death can be determined only on the basis of evidence of other kinds—not on the basis of scientific evidence. And it is precisely those kinds of evidence that we will study.

NDEs, by their nature, are always experienced by flesh-and-blood subjects with brains. Consequently, it is always possible for a skeptic to maintain that the experience is simply an activity in the brain. Now present-day science cannot show how the brain produces this experience.The skeptic will say that there is no reason why scientific research in the future may not do so. Moreover, the NDEs cannot, like most scientific experiments, be replicated at will. They emerge at random as anecdotes from certain individuals and not as the products of a systematic scientific study.

A Matter of Human Experience and Not Scientific Experiment

The only viable response to this line of thought is one that centers on human experience rather than scientific experiment:

- ↦ On a regular basis, we are conscious, we think, we experience the self. None of this can be denied without self-contradiction. If you deny it, you would have to say that *you* know that you do not exist! But none of this can be scientifically described—let alone replicated.
- ↦ If our self and conceptual thought fall outside scientific description (as we shall see), then they must be studied in a way that goes beyond the scientific method.

- If they are transphysical (although normally integrated with the physical), their destiny likewise has a transphysical dimension that cannot be discovered or demonstrated using methodologies and categories that apply only to the physical.
- It is, in this context, that NDEs can be taken seriously as possible pointers to a world beyond. But, by the nature of the case, science per se cannot show whether or not an NDE is evidence of an after-life.

Of course, even those who accept the reality of a transphysical soul do not necessarily have to accept NDEs as experiences of a different world. In its normal state the soul is integrated with the body (it "forms" matter into a body) and is therefore affected by it. We can, therefore, consistently believe in the soul while also believing that NDEs are purely the products of brain biochemistry. But let's say that:

- the evidence indicates that certain NDEs are unlikely to be triggered by the brain.
- the content of these NDEs matches universal beliefs concerning the after-life and body/soul separation.

If this is the case, there is good reason to move beyond the brain-alone hypothesis.

After all, if subjects are able to accurately report activities taking place hundreds of miles away during an NDE, then it is simply inane to suggest that this is just a currently unknown physical capability of the brain. NDEs involving visual observation of distant events have been reported. Any plausible explanation for this kind of NDE would entail the demise of physicalism and brain-alone explanations. Of course, these cannot be systematically replicated because NDEs by their very nature cannot be part of scientifically controlled studies (short of using the horrendous methods of Mengele).

Secondly, there is no necessary link between NDEs and alleged paranormal phenomena. Whether or not paranormal or parapsychological phenomena take place is a different question from whether or not NDEs are legitimate after-life experiences. In other words, our acceptance of the validity of NDEs does not mean that we are simultaneously accepting any claim of the paranormal. Likewise, we are not bound to accept any of the claims of spiritualists and mediums and others who claim to have esoteric knowledge of "the other side." These latter claims are highly suspect for various reasons not least of which is the fact that they are not spontaneous in the same fashion as NDEs.

The debate on whether paranormal phenomena such as telepathy take place is a legitimate one. But the jury is still out on this question as it was a hundred years ago.[43] There is, however, nothing paranormal about the transphysical human soul. It is a fact of experience that we are conscious, we think and we are aware of our self-identity, and that none of these capabilities can be described as having physical properties. Nevertheless, there is a seamless integration of physical and transphysical. This is "normal" not paranormal. A paranormal claim is one where it is alleged that, in this world, our transphysical dimension can act independently of the physical (in telepathy or telekinesis). Such a claim is obviously in a different class from that of an NDE claim, which is that the transphysical continues in being after death. Whether the latter is a valid claim has to be determined on its own terms.

NDEs Cannot Give a Definitive Picture of the After-Life

Next, there is the question of whether NDEs tell us what the after-life is like. Let it be said initially that neither NDEs nor alleged memories of past lives can serve as the basis of any definitive view of the after-life. We will deal with the past life hypothesis shortly, but here our concern is with NDE subjects. The content of the experiences reported by NDE subjects varies so dramatically that there's no logically consistent way in which we can accept all of them. The way you interpret your NDE reflects to a great extent *your* personality and existing tool-kit of beliefs. Most NDE accounts imply that the real action has yet to begin and that the subject will not be able to return to this world once the threshold of eternity has been crossed. It is reasonable, therefore, to assume that your account of the NDE reflects *your* way of seeing things in what is clearly a *transitional* state. It is *not* the actual nature of the *permanent* state you have yet to experience. Understandably NDE subjects present entirely different pictures of God and judgment and ultimate destiny. Simply on their own, we cannot tell which picture is true and which is simply a subjective projection, arbitrary representation, or self-deception.

Why There Are Differences in the NDE Narratives

Let us consider further the factors responsible for these differences. In the first place, the differences in the cultural and religious backgrounds of NDE subjects is such that their interpretations of their experiences are inevitably affected by their background.

Secondly, the era in which you live affects your way of viewing things. Both modern and medieval accounts tend to be "politically correct" in terms of the expectations of their eras.

Third, the danger of embellishment is ever present. When it comes to paranormal phenomena, self-proclaimed seers and seeresses report on experiences to which only they are privy. But, in the absence of overwhelming evidence from other sources, there is no reason why anyone should take these seriously. As for NDE reports, those subjects who have penned elaborate accounts of their experiences should be held to the same skeptical standards as seers and seeresses of the esoteric. After all, they are giving us personal reports that can only be provisionally accepted if it tallies with the primordial-universal paradigm of the after-life. We cannot rest any view of the after-life on one person's anecdote. This is so even if the subject claims to have heard this from God or Jesus.

Many apocryphal and gnostic gospels that are historically worthless rest on similar claims. Some of the elaborate NDE accounts seem very much like contemporary versions of the historically worthless private revelations of Gnostics and seers. To accept NDEs does not mean accepting the New Age spin applied by the subjects at the suggestion of mentors.

A leading NDE researcher, Dr. Kenneth Ring, noted recently that he now rejects the idea that NDEs somehow open the door to ultimate truth: "My views have changed quite drastically in some respects since I published *Heading Towards Omega*. In particular, I have foresworn my previous hypothesis about NDEs leading to Omega or anywhere else. I no longer think, and haven't for years now, that NDE-ers are part of a vanguard of folks leading us to the glory of higher consciousness. I won't deny that NDEs themselves can be transformative experiences for those who undergo them, but I do not think that such changes will spread like a kind of wildfire of consciousness to affect all of humanity.... The vision of a transformed humanity, shining like a golden promise just beyond the current historical epoch has been, like an ever-receding desert mirage, beguiling civilization almost from its beginnings.... History has shown the disappointment that comes when invariably the dream does not manifest as fact, and must be rationalized away.... I still believe in NDEs, though. They are the real thing, whatever else might be said."[44]

Fourthly, as noted, the NDE in most accounts is seen as an entrance point to the after-life and not the after-life itself; we are not shown what the permanent state will be like. You might call an NDE a pre-after-life experience.

Finally, it should be reiterated that the question of one's ultimate destiny is something that belongs to the domain of divine revelation if such there be: if there is a Creator of all human persons and if that Creator has prepared an ultimate destiny for each of these persons, then this destiny can only be known from a direct revelation of the Creator. Various religions claim to have received such a revelation, and if we wish to know the nature of our ultimate destiny (beyond the question of whether there is an after-life), it would be best to consider the claims of these religions. The collision of world-views represented by various religions cannot be resolved by appeal to NDEs because the detailed NDE reports themselves are shaped by the world-views of the recipients.

We should, of course, study all the available data given in NDEs and not just the elements that dovetail with our own preconceptions. Thus, we cannot simply study pleasant NDEs—such an unwarranted criterion would simply confirm the skeptics' charge of wish-fulfillment. To come to terms with the entire range of evidence, we have to also study the "negative" NDEs.

Having said all this, we should point out that NDEs are useful in their own right. They cannot tell us definitively what the after-life is like, but they can help us advance the discussion of whether or not there is an after-life. There are several things that are common to most NDEs, ancient and modern:

- A separation of soul from body.
- A departure to another state or world.
- A review of the deeds of one's life.
- Encounters with deceased souls and other beings.
- A realization of the supreme importance of loving one's neighbor.

The accounts given by the various survivors are colored by numerous factors:

- Their upbringing.
- Their psychological make-up.
- Their theological background.
- The shock of the experience and much else.

But for the most part they have this in common: *they are convinced there was a separation of soul and body and the soul entered a new state of being*. This is the core claim of an NDE that should be considered in any inquiry into the after-life. Moreover, when you compare the subtleties in the narratives of NDE subjects with the physicalist counter-explanations of the skeptics, it is evident that there is a thinness and artificiality about the skeptics' arguments. The skeptics simply do not engage with the depth and solidity of the NDE as an experience of another dimension of reality. The skeptics seem trapped in a one-dimensional world of their own and are therefore unable to grasp even the possibility of a three-dimensional state of being.

A Debate on NDEs Between Tweedledum and Tweedledee

Tweedledum: So-called near-death experiences are quite obviously events in the brain. There is no reason to believe that they have any reality outside the brain. Certainly no one can demonstrate that they took place in a world outside the brain.

Tweedledee: Tens of millions of people have experienced the journey through the tunnel, the being of light, the life review. In many cases this has been under situations of great trauma: cardiac arrest, flat-line, coma. Despite the life-threatening conditions, the narratives have been lucid, the lives of the subjects have been transformed. A mere brain event can't be responsible for such a radical effect. And the sheer quantity of these experiences, as well as the great diversity of the experiencers, indicates to me that the subjects were in touch with a reality outside their heads.

Dum: If the brain can produce a sound and light show for one person in a stressful situation, it will, of course, do the same for millions of others. No matter how diverse and how large the subject group, they all share the same biology. What we have here is simply the standard way in which the brain responds to traumas of certain kinds.

Dee: Essentially, any feature of the experiences I bring up, no matter how remarkable, you will simply dismiss as a product of the brain (albeit one which we may not understand at the moment). There is nothing I can bring to the table that you cannot cover under your "event-in-brain" umbrella.

Dum: True that! And if we're honest with each other, you can surely see that there's no way around the biology argument for you. Occam's Razor requires us not to multiply entities unnecessarily. In explaining any phenomenon we should use the fewest assumptions possible. Also science tells us to find a physical explanation for physical phenomena (I don't need to give you a history of all the problems that arose from trying to give supernatural explanations for obviously natural phenomena).

Dee: Heads you win, tails I lose. I see where this is going. As long as we're being honest with each other, let me point out what I think are your blind spots. Almost in knee-jerk fashion, right off the bat, you dismiss the veracity of the witnesses. Not for a second have you considered the possibility that they may really be experiencing something external to them. You've just taken it for granted that this is not even a remote possibility. You've also taken it for granted that there is no "world" beyond our space-time continuum—as is claimed by the NDE-ers. Finally, you assume that the human self is entirely its brain. These are the dogmas you embrace, but then you're begging the question. For it is the veracity of your dogmas that are being undermined by the NDE-er. There's no point in saying "My dogmas are true and so the NDE-er can't be right." You have to show how you can still hold to these dogmas in the face of the NDE-ers' experience. When someone tells you that they've seen a black swan, you can't simply say, "all swans are white and so you're wrong." You've got to examine the claim on its own merits and dismiss it only if you have clear evidence that the claimant is lying or deluded.

Dum: There is such a thing as the burden of proof. If someone tells me they saw Elvis at the local convenience store, I can confidently dismiss their veracity without producing an elaborate demonstration.

Dee: Okay, let's get back to the point at issue. Do you admit that there's a possibility that the NDE-er really experienced something real "outside" his head?

Dum: Of course it's a possibility. So are unicorns.

Dee: But no one (at least recently) has claimed to see unicorns. My second point is that if there is a life beyond death and if there is ever a possibility of us getting a glimpse of it, this is likely to happen at the verge of death. Is that acceptable?

Dum: Yes. It's as acceptable as the thesis that if there is an Abominable Snowman, he is likely to live in a snowy environment.

Dee: Your sarcasm is duly noted. Next point: if the content of the NDE as reported by subjects conforms to descriptions of the after-life in ancient traditions of humanity, we should give greater credence to the NDE-er.

Dum: Here I disagree. The same human brain produced both accounts. Biology is a sufficient explanation for the similarity of description.

Dee: But if there really is an after-life, the accounts given by NDE-ers and the ancient religious traditions would match.

Dum: Here we go again. If there are unicorns then…okay, go for it if this is the best you can do.

Dee: I've barely started, but I appreciate your cooperation. Now, if there is an after-life, and if living subjects become aware of it as they approach death, then NDEs make sense, since they take place at the precise time we would expect them to occur.

Dum: Now who's pushing everything under their own pie-in-the-sky umbrella!

Dee: Touche! But this tells you two can play at this game. What is sauce for the goose is sauce for the gander. If everything in an NDE can be "seen" as the expected outcome of a brain event, everything can also be "seen" as the to-be-expected outcome of an encounter with the after-life.

Dum: But which scenario is more plausible? We have made tremendous advances in our knowledge of the brain and will soon pinpoint the mechanisms that cause NDEs. Your after-life scenario is simply a matter of faith and hence inadmissible.

Dee: With respect to its advances, science has not and cannot pinpoint consciousness, thought, and the self. These are not quantifiable, observable, measurable realities. But they're nonetheless real—or else we wouldn't be communicating right now. Now if they fall outside scientific inquiry and observation, Occam's Razor is of no help. If you have a non-physical soul, it's a good idea to try to find out more about its nature before you pronounce on claims about its manifestations.

Dum: So you're saying you stay with your paradigm and I'll stay with mine. To each his own. I like apple pie and you like pecan. We each stay with our own pies and let the others do what they want.

Dee: Not so fast. I want to emphasize first that the cause of NDEs is either a phenomenon of the dying brain or a result of contact with the Other World. We are under no obligation to conclude at the start that NDEs are simply and solely manifestations of the brain at work. At the very least, we have to admit that NDEs are either entirely actions of the brain or interactions with the Other Side. I hold that the latter is not simply likely to be the case, but is actually the case.

Dum: And I hold that it is quite clearly the former. You obviously can't demonstrate the truth of your affirmation, which is simply an act of blind faith. I, on the other hand, can give you any number of examples of brains playing tricks on people in extreme circumstances.

Dee: Spoken like a true believer. You believe that the physical world is all that exists and therefore you think that only explanations in physical terms are acceptable. Anything that seems non-physical is swiftly dismissed as a mysterious manifestation of the physical. You say I can't prove the truth of what I'm talking about. Well, science has not explained the existence of consciousness, conceptual thought, or the self, which we experience on a daily basis. This hasn't stopped scientists for over a century from promising to "explain" these "within a decade." NDEs show that the human soul—which we know from experience to be intrinsically immaterial—survives the death of the body it animates. Far from being alien, the world described by the NDE-er ties in with what we know from everyday experience.

Dum: This "soul" you've started introducing is nothing but the regular activity of the brain. Any disorder of the brain affects your thinking and "self." That in itself proves the "soul" is just the brain.

Dee: The soul "organizes" and unifies the body and there is no split between bodily and "mental" operations: they are all actions of one person who IS a unity of body and soul. But there are some operations of the soul that have no bodily correlate. Conceptual thinking is one. Clearly you need neurons firing to perform any thought. But the thinking itself is quite obviously not the firing of the neurons. Rather these neurons perform the same function as paper and ink in manifesting a Shakespearean sonnet. The sonnet is obviously not just paper and ink. Nor is it a creation of the paper and ink.

Dum: As far as I'm concerned NDEs have not advanced the discussion on either the soul or survival one iota. Like everything else you folks bring up, these phenomena involve physical beings and changes in physical beings. Why you should appeal to a non-physical agency or reality is not a mystery. The primitives explained lightning as the wrath of God. But today we know the nature of lightning and what causes it.

Dee: That's hardly a good comparison. Yes, on many occasions, people mistakenly tried to explain physical phenomena in terms of a non-physical agent. That's not what we are talking about here. We are talking about a reality that is *experienced* as *non-physical* from the get-go, one that is experienced *by us*. You're making the same mistake as the primitives by trying to explaining what is clearly one kind of reality in terms of a totally different kind of reality—without any kind of evidence. And, because the non-physical reality that is the soul acts in union with the physical, we should expect a disorder of the physical to affect the functioning of the non-physical with which it is integrated. Correspondingly, when the non-physical soul begins the process of separation from the physical, then the kind of experiences reported by NDEers is precisely what we would expect.

Dum: But you can't prove that the NDE-er is actually entering a different world. For all you know they may be describing tricks played on them by their oxygen-deprived brains.

Dee: In theory, what you say is a possibility. But the lucidity of the NDE-ers and the transformation of their lives suggests the opposite. Those who suffer a cardiac arrest or brain death will, at best, be disjointed in describing their experiences if not entirely incoherent. Not so the NDEers. But what seems to me clear evidence of the reality of the NDE is the fact that some NDEers report events and situations taking place miles away while they are undergoing the NDE. Unless they were transported there (as they claim), there is no way they could have known these facts. So NDEs are real.

Dum: Well, your last point is anecdotal at best. There has been no systematic study of NDEers reporting long-distance events. So this tidbit has no bearing on the debate one way or another.

Dee: I think we're back where we started with no change on either side. My only suggestion is that anyone studying NDEs should first examine their assumptions and expectations. This applies especially to the questions of the possibility and implications of NDEs. In themselves NDEs cannot prove the existence of a life after death. But in tandem with a multitude of other phenomena that testify to a transcendent and transphysical reality, NDEs are especially relevant. In addition, the overall evidence for life after death includes elements that have an effect on events in this world. After-life visitations have real-world consequences!

Chapter 3

~

The Dead Are Alive—
The Universal Testimony of
Humanity

We have said repeatedly that the question of whether there is an afterlife cannot be studied in isolation from either the hard facts of our everyday experience or the view of the world that we bring to the table. This is especially the case because a life after death is a life that lies beyond the physical as such. It cannot be studied with the methodologies and tools that work in the tangible, measurable world. Hence it falls outside the domain of science. The physicalist will say that the idea of being conscious without a physical brain or seeing without a visual cortex is nonsensical, and so the notion of an afterlife is an oxymoron. This is clearly where one's world-view kicks in. The same physicalist can neither demonstrate that consciousness is produced by the brain (rather than transmitted through it) nor begin to explain the phenomena of the self and conceptual immaterial thought. All that the physicalist offers is a dogmatic declaration that matter is all there is.

Pretty much the entire human race, however, has taken a different view of the matter (and of matter!). From the dawn of human history, societies and cultures have been united in one common conviction: the human person is not simply a physical being, and something of the person subsists after the death of the body. There is, of course, a diversity of belief concerning the questions of what survives death and what happens to the "survivor." But the earliest "developed" communities with their own holy books have proclaimed two possible destinies for those who leave this world: one is separation from the divine which results in misery, and the second is eternal union with the divine, and corresponding ecstasy. Strangely enough this was apparently the world-view taken also by the primordial hunter-gatherers who populated the planet for 95 percent of human history. Belief in an after-life, and an after-life that involves the Supreme Being, has been the default position of humanity.

The Divine Dimension

The introduction of the divine is not something welcomed by certain after-life claimants—spiritualists, mediums, channelers, New Age reincarnationists. But the after-life as understood by the human race in general was seen within the context of the divine. Buddhism is an obvious exception, but Buddhism is historically and conceptually a later-stage tributary of Hinduism. At any rate, the background framework of all the primordial religions conceived of the after-life in relation to the divine and more specifically a supreme Being, namely God.

So is there a God and did that God create us for a life that continues after physical death? As noted earlier in this book, my answer to the first question is "yes" for reasons I have laid out in two previous books. The existence of consciousness, conceptual thought, and the self can only be explained by reference to an infinite-eternal Mind. Further discussion on this question will have to be taken "offline," because it calls for more extensive discussion than is possible here. But if we affirm the existence of God we recognize that anything concerning an after-life would have to be part of a divine blueprint. In terms of a background framework, the existence of God makes the possibility of our posthumous existence much more credible.

Entering the Realm of God

God is a pure Spirit who nevertheless acts in the physical world and, in fact, brought the physical into being. The realm of the Divine is non-physical. There is no reason why the human soul cannot operate in such a non-physical realm after surviving its separation from the physical. The evidence brought to bear in this work suggests that we do survive. Such being the case, we are then led to ask whether we have any idea of God's plans for our future either through our own intuitions or through a direct revelation.

The answer to this question is one that we ultimately have to find on our own. But a quick survey of the universal beliefs of humanity indicates that we do have some idea of what God had in mind for us. Every major society, culture, and religion has proclaimed the reality of an after-life. Now this could be attributed to one of three sources: wish-fulfillment, innate intuition, and divine revelation.

The first option, wish-fulfillment, hardly serves as an explanation, because the after-life was not always greeted with joy: it was often considered a state of misery. We could even argue that the atheist's rejection of an after-life is purely a product of fear-fulfillment; so such psychological charges get us neither here nor there.

The second option, innate intuition, can actually be seen as a "revelation," one that is implanted in the human heart by the divine Mind. So the second and third options (innate intuition and divine revelation) merge. The evidence indicates that the affirmation of a life after death can only be called a universal insight that is articulated and amplified by the first religious texts of humanity. A study of this universal message is essential for us to "place" the idea of survival and destiny in the larger context of the human story.

Accordingly, we will embark on a brief study of the after-life beliefs of primitive humanity and the earliest developed religions. The primordial religions of humanity that go back some 4,000 years and that are undergirded by written texts and ritual practice are Judaism, Vedic Hinduism, and Zoroastrianism. Christianity, as a "continuation" of Judaism, belongs to this pantheon. We will consider these religions as well as the religious life of the hunter-gatherers, Mesopotamians, Greeks, Egyptians, Chinese, and Africans. (As for Buddhism, we will consider reincarnation and rebirth in a later chapter.)

The Hunter-Gatherers

In his survey of world religions, Ninian Smart observes that the remnants of ancient burial sites indicate belief in an after-life even among the earliest hominids: "Some of the burial rites suggest too a kind of ceremonial to somehow ensure safe passage to the next world.... All this suggest some belief in life beyond death."[1]

Walter Burkert, the great historian of the ancient world, points out that it is an "indisputable fact, namely, that the age of the hunter, the Paleolithic, comprises by far the largest part of human history...between 95 and 99 percent." In contrast, "the period since the invention of agriculture—10,000 years, at most—is a drop in the bucket."[2]

How Can We Find Out What They Believed?

What did the hunter-gatherers believe about the after-life? Because no written records are available, only a study of primeval peoples who have lived on into the modern world can give a clue. The most exhaustive such study was carried out by the linguist-ethnographer Wilhelm Schmidt in his 12-volume study, *The Origin of the Idea of God*. Although there are limitations to the comparisons between primeval societies today and in the past, there is a rationale for it as well. David Rooney observes that the two time-consuming tasks of hunting and gathering left little opportunity for technological breakthroughs. Consequently societies could persist for many generations with no appreciable progress in material sophistication. He cites the example of the Yamana tribe in Tierra del Fuego, the southernmost tip of South America: "Archaeological finds indicate that the Yamana were the first to people their region around 2,000 years ago, and artifacts excavated in the 20th century show no sign of advance in tool-making over that timespan."

Schmidt's research, carried out in the early 20th century, was done just in time. He was able to collect a comprehensive range of data now no longer available. Rooney notes that the field work done by Schmidt in the 1920s cannot be replicated today given that "many of the primitive tribes have since disappeared from the face of the earth due to a combination of disease, dispersion, and intermarriage with other tribes."[3]

This is Schmidt's summary of the after-life beliefs of the primeval peoples:

All primitive peoples without exception believe in another life. As to what it is like, they cannot all say; for instance, the Yamana declare that they do not know, and give that as the reason why they are so sad when any of their relatives die.... The great majority of them recognize such a distinction of good and bad in a future life. Their most definite opinions concern the future lot of the good; as to the fate of the wicked, they are often uncertain or vague. The good usually go, in cases concerning which we have any information, to the sky, where the Supreme Being lives. In many instances they enjoy his own company; there they live a life free from death, sickness and pain, full of all manner of happiness.... In some cases there is a regular judgement to decide the fate of the good and the bad, the souls having to appear before the Supreme Being. This is the belief perhaps of the South Andamanese, certainly of the Halkwulup of Tierra del Fuego, where the soul presents an account of its life. The lot of the wicked is often described expressly as one of painful punishment, by fire and heat, as among the Ajongo negrillos and the Southern Wiradyuri; but it may also be by cold, or by wanderings without rest. In other cases it consists simply in exclusion from the happiness of the good, or in an empty shadow-life.[4]

Numerous other field researchers have confirmed Schmidt's findings. For instance, in his "The Afterlife Among Hunter-Gatherers," Anthony Zimmerman talks of the Delaware-based Lenape Indians who were convinced that, after death, good people would go to the beautiful land of the living and the Australian aborigines who believed that "when a person dies, his soul goes to meet Daramulun [the Supreme Being] who welcomes it and takes care of it. The Supreme Being dwells in heaven, where He rewards all who lived a good life."[5] Rooney describes the Selknam, a primitive tribe in Tierra del Fuego, who held that "after death the soul travels to heaven and remains there, in the abode where God dwells and to which his first man, K'enos, was summoned. Souls can never return to earth."[6]

Mesopotamia, Egypt, Greece

The after-life played a prominent role in the beliefs of ancient Mesopotamia, Egypt, Greece, and Rome.

Gilgamesh

The Mesopotamians believed that the dead live on as ghosts or "shades" and descend to an underworld where they are judged. The Epic of Gilgamesh recounts the conditions beheld there by the hero's deceased friend: "To the house which none may leave who enter it, on the road from which there is no way back, to the house where its inhabitants are bereft of light, where dust is their fare and clay their food. They are clothed like birds, with wings for garments. They see no light, residing in darkness. In this House of Dust which I entered, I beheld rulers, their crowns now put away, and royal princes who had ruled the land in days gone by."[7] The living have an obligation to bury the dead and provide them sustenance—and in failing their ghosts would roam the earth.

Odysseus

The Greeks, of course, propounded various philosophies. But their image of the after-life is best captured in Homer's *Odyssey*. Here too (as in Gilgamesh) we are given a glimpse of a dreary region ruled by Hades, the brother of Zeus and Poseidon. When the hero Odysseus reaches there, "the ghosts came trooping up from Erebus—brides, young bachelors, old men worn out with toil, maids who had been crossed in love, and brave men who had been killed in battle, with their armour still smirched with blood; they came from every quarter and flitted round the trench with a strange kind of screaming sound that made me turn pale with fear."

Especially moving is Odysseus' encounter with his mother Anticlia:

Then she knew me at once and spoke fondly to me, saying, "My son, how did you come down to this abode of darkness while you are still alive? It is a hard thing for the living to see these places."

Then I tried to find some way of embracing my mother's ghost. Thrice I sprang towards her and tried to clasp her in my arms, but each time she flitted from my embrace as it were a dream or phantom, and being touched to the quick I said to her, "Mother, why do you not stay still when I would embrace you? If we could throw our arms around one another we might find sad comfort in the sharing of our sorrows even in the house of Hades; does Proserpine want to lay a still further load of grief upon me by mocking me with a phantom only?"

"My son," she answered, "most ill-fated of all mankind, it is not Proserpine that is beguiling you, but all people are like this when they are dead. The sinews no longer hold the flesh and bones together; these perish in the fierceness of consuming fire as soon as life has left the body, and the soul flits away as though it were a dream. Now, however, go back to the light of day as soon as you can, and note all these things that you may tell them to your wife hereafter."[8]

The Heaven, Hell, and Purgatory of the Greeks

In Greek belief, the journey to Hades begins with a ferryride across the River Styx. Three judges, Aeacus, Minos, and Rhadamanthus, would decide your eternal destiny based on the kind of life you led on earth. The superior souls are sent to the Elysian Fields, a place of joy: "The deathless ones will sweep you off the world's end, the Elysian Fields…where life glides on in immortal ease for mortal men; no snow, no winter onslaught, never a downpour there but night and day the Ocean River sends up breezes, singing winds of the West refreshing all mankind."[9] The evil are sent to Tartarus, a dark region of eternal punishment. Those who are neither evil nor virtuous are sent to the Fields of Asphodel, a sort of limbo. A proper burial is required for the dead to cross Styx. Women visited the graves of the dead with cakes and libations.

Egypt

As pyramids and mummies show, the after-life was taken seriously in ancient Egypt. The Egyptians believed in the importance of the body for full participation in the after-life; hence the attempts to preserve it after death. Upon death, they believed that the soul is judged by 42 judges along with Osiris. The evil were consumed by the Devourer of Souls whereas the good went to the Field of Rushes. According to a Reuters April 27, 2009 story, 4,000-year old Pharonic-age mummies, recently discovered near the Lahun Pyramid, were inscribed with prayers intended to help the deceased.

China

Shang Di—God

For 4,000 years, the Chinese have consistently believed in the Supreme Being, God, whom they call Shang Di. They have been equally consistent in their affirmation of an after-life. They said of an emperor, "may the Son of Heaven live forever." About one of their kings they said, "King Wen's soul is active and he lives in the presence of Shang Di."[10] Respect for ancestors, and sometimes worship of ancestors, was common and "reverence for the powerful dead and the invoking of their *mana* for the sustenance of the clan became part of Chinese social mores, and filial piety a central Confucian teaching."[11]

Connecting the World of the Dead and the World of the Living

The world of the dead was closely connected to the living. "In traditional China, the idea that personal continuance after death could be found in the lives of one's descendants has been closely linked to practices rooted in mutual obligations between the living and the dead: those who had moved on to the ancestral state of existence…. The nature of ancestral existence was relatively undefined. Generally speaking, the world of the ancestors was conceived as a murky, dark realm, a "yin" space (*yinjian*). While not clear on the exact details, Chinese considered the world of departed spirits similar to the world of the living in key ways."[12]

The Taoist religion (as opposed to the philosophy of Taoism) taught that a devotee could "by piety, by confession and atonement acquire the necessary merit by which, at death, after a stay in the underworld, he or she could be saved and escorted to paradise. Similarly, by pious observances and by attending special services for their redemption, the faithful could pray for the souls of the dead, who, through the merit of the living, might finally gain release from the underworld and entrance to paradise."[13]

Africa

As with other regions across the globe, the after-life is a present reality in the traditional religions of Africa. Parrinder points out that "everywhere belief in the survival after death is unquestioned and many rituals are performed."[14]

The living and the dead are members of the same community. "The importance of ancestors results from the fact that they are considered to be ever present and alive members of the community although through their death they actually left this community," writes Henryk Zimo.

The living as well as the dead are members of the African community. The African peoples both recognize and question the destructive work of death. A human being dies but he still lives; he is 'a living dead,' using the term introduced by Mbiti. Ancestors, as mediators between the Supreme Being and the living, take an active part in the community life and they affect the fate of the living. They create the strongest bond linking people with the spiritual world. It is just through them the spiritual, invisible world becomes close and personal to people. Ancestors accompany their living relatives in all more important moments of individual and social life. They interfere into the existence of an individual, a family and a lineage, a tribe and a people (ancestors of rulers). Ancestors are guardians of family matters and the clan-tribe tradition….

The importance of ancestors is reflected in funeral rituals, which express the bond between the dead and the living and make it possible for the dead to pass to the land of ancestors and to reach the status of ancestors.[15]

Vedic Hinduism

Although most people associate Hinduism with the doctrines of karma and reincarnation, neither idea is found in the Vedas, the wellspring of Hindu belief. Instead, the Vedas, the oldest work of literature in any Indo-European language, speak of a final judgment after death. Those who lead good lives are taken to the "World of the Fathers" where they enjoy bliss while the evil suffer punishment in the "House of Clay." Even the later Upanishads speak of the World of the Fathers: "Now, there are, verily, three worlds, the world of men (Manushyaloka), the world of the fathers (Pitriloka), and the world of the Gods (Devaloka)." (*Brihadaranyaka Upanishad*, Verse 1.5.17).

World of the Fathers and the House of Clay

There is no notion in the Vedas of continuous rebirth—only of a permanent state after death. "Varuna sits in the palace of heaven and oversees the world below. As the guardian of the moral order, both earthly and cosmic, Varuna punishes the sinner with disease, or for all time by condemning them to the House of Clay following death. Aryans who practiced right deeds, or performed the proper ritual would forever celebrate happiness after death....

"The cosmic order of the Aryan universe remained fairly simple. The heavens served as the residence of the major gods and the souls of the righteous. The region between heaven and earth was called the *antariksa*. This region, where the birds flew and the clouds crossed the sky, was also home to the demigods. Below the earth, in the darkness of the House of Clay, dwelled the spirits of the unrighteous and the demons that sought to disrupt *rta*. The concept of birth and rebirth had not yet become part of the Indian cosmology that would later be indicative of all Indian religion."[16]

The Upanishads

The Upanishads and later writings introduced the idea of reincarnation, the claim that every person undergoes a cycle of birth and rebirth. Intrinsically related to this latter notion are the ideas of karma and the caste system. Your status after death is determined by your karma, the sum of your actions in this life. Your caste in this life (whether of priest or warrior, merchant, laborer, or "untouchable") is the result of your actions in a previous life. To make progress, you must overcome the desire for earthly pleasures and fully recognize the truths taught in the scriptures. Significantly, the idea of Nirvana, of escape from the cycle of rebirth through the dissolution of the self in the Absolute, is not found in the Upanishads. This idea was introduced nearly 1,000 years later by Sankaracharya (eighth century AD) under the influence of the then-dominant Buddhism. But long before the emergence of reincarnation and other beliefs, the Vedas had been centered around the tenets of one Supreme Spirit and the urgency of sacrifice in expiation for sin.

The Rig Veda

"The hymns of the Rig Veda focus on pleasing the principal gods Indra (war, wind, and rain), Agni (the sacrificial fire), Surga (the sun) and Varuna (the cosmic order) through ritual sacrifices. Along with governing important matters of life such as rain, wind, fire, and war, the Vedic gods also forgive wrongdoing (5.85.7) and mete out justice in the afterlife (1.97.1).

"Deceased ancestors are able to influence the living (10.15.6), so they are also appeased with rituals (10.15.1-11). The afterlife of the Rig Veda is eternal conscious survival in the abode of Yama, the god of the dead (9.113.7-11). It is the gods, not karma, that are responsible for assuring justice in this life and the next (7.104)."[17]

Heaven and Hell in the Vedas

In a famous passage in the *Rig Veda* (Mandala 7, Verse 89), the seer Vasishta, who is dying of thirst, asks Varuna not to let him go into the house of clay.

1. Let me not yet, King Varuna, enter into the house of clay:

Have mercy, spare me, Mighty Lord. …

5. O Varuna, whatever the offence may be which we as men commit against the heavenly host,

When through our want of thought we violate thy laws, punish us not, O God, for that iniquity. [18]

The *Atharva Veda* has a prayer for deliverance from the House of Clay:

1. From near thy vicinity, from near thy distance (do I call): remain here, do not follow; do not follow the Fathers of yore! Firmly do I fasten thy life's breath....

14. Unite him, Agni, with breath and sight, provide him with a body and with strength! Thou hast a knowledge of immortality: let him not now depart, let him not now become a dweller in a house of clay! [19]

The *Atharva Veda* also speaks of Heaven, a place of joy and wholeness:

Where men of goodwill and good deeds rejoice,
Their bodies now made free from all disease,
Their limbs made whole from lameness or defect—
In that heaven may we behold our parents and our sons![20]

The Living and the Dead

Quite unlike the reincarnationists, the Vedas require a close relationship between the living and the dead. The dead are now seen as moving to a different state of being while retaining their earthly identity. Geoffrey Parrinder points out that the Aryan householder was "obliged to perform three times daily what is called the 'Five Great Sacrifices.'" In addition to "the worship of Brahman, the world-spirit," he must present "the fathers with offerings of food and water for their nourishment."

"The ancestors confer blessings and benefits on their living descendants by conferring prosperity, progeny, and the like. Thus, the *shraddha* [ceremony] is the point of meeting between the living and the dead, the expression of their interdependence. But this relationship may be inverted if the proper funeral rites are not performed for the deceased; for until installed in the World of the Fathers, the ghosts of the dead are liable to visit misery on the heads of descendants who do not nourish them with offerings or secure their passage to the proper sphere."[21]

The entire religious life of Vedic Hindus required them to affirm the continued existence of their ancestors in a different realm. This is obviously different from the later reincarnationist view.

Persia

At one time, Zoroastrianism was the most influential religion in the world, because it was the state religion of the Persian empire under the Achaemenid kings who ruled the known civilized world before the Romans. There were three phases in the growth of the religion of Persia before the onset of Islam. Initially, there was the religion of pre-Aryan inhabitants of the land. Then came the Aryan immigrants with their new religious system. Finally there was Zoroaster's reform of the Aryan religion. Zoroaster was the great prophet of monotheism. There is no consensus as to when Zoroaster was born and where he lived, as the libraries of Persia were burned down by later invaders. Estimates range between 628–551 BC to 1000 BC and before. He is believed to have received a divine revelation and his teachings are believed to be preserved in 17 hymns called the Gathas. The central tenet of Zoroaster's religious reform was his assertion that there is only one God, Ahura Mazda.

The Aryans of India and Persia

The linguistic and theological similarities between the writings of the Aryans of India and Persia become evident from a study of their scriptures. The holy books of India are called the Vedas, those of Persia Zend Avesta (very few of the latter have survived). Vedic deities are found in the Avesta. The central idea of a cosmic and moral order, *rtá*, in the Vedas has a counterpart in the Avesta called *Asha*.

The After-life in Zoroastrian Religion

With regard to the after-life, Mary Boyce, one of the leading authorities on the Zoroastrian religion, notes, "From the evidence of both the *Vedas* and the most archaic *Avestan* texts, the continuance of life after death was something taken for granted as self-evident and not open to question."[22] Zoroaster's *Gathas*, in fact, constantly talks of the after-life and the relation between every thought, word, and deed in this life and one's destiny after death.

Farhang Mehr explains that "in Zoroastrianism, the Eternal Law of Asha determines the consequences of an individual's acts and the fate of the soul after the individual's physical death. Asha is God's will. The individual's thoughts, words, and deeds in this world, through the exercise of one's free choice, set the consequences (*Mizhdem*) into motion and condition one's life and future according to the Law of Asha. Hence there is no predestined fate; the acts have predestined consequences....

> According to the *Gathas,* the souls of the righteous people go in a state of perfect happiness, referred to as the Abode of the Song (*Garo Demana*), also called the Abode of the Good Mind (*Vangheush Demana Manangho*) or the Abode of Endless Light (*Anghra Raosha*). The souls of the evildoers go to the Abode of Wickedness (*Druji Demana*), also referred to as the Abode of the Worst Mind (*Aschishtahya Daena Manengho*), and Worst Existence (*Achishta Ahu*). These terms confirm that in Zoroastrianism heaven and hell are states of consciousness and not concrete geographical regions."[23]

Judgment

There is a life-review/judgment dimension:

> "Three days after death, the soul meets three judges," writes Paula Hartz. "They judge the soul on its actions in life. It then passes on to the Chinvat Bridge, the Bridge of the Separator. There it meets its Daena, the guide who will take it across. She represents the person's conscience in life. If that life has been righteous, Daena is beautiful beyond all imagining and is accompanied by a sweet-smelling breeze. If the life has been one of ignorance and evil, the guide is an ugly hag with a foul odor.

> The two move across the bridge. For the righteous, the bridge is wide and flat, and leads into eternal joy. For the wicked it becomes narrower and narrower until it is a knife-blade, and the wicked soul falls off, into the pit of hell.

> During this time, priests and the family continue with special prayers for the dead. Mourners may continue to recite the Patet, a prayer of repentance, and other prayers in honor and remembrance of the dead person daily for a month or even longer. Their prayers cannot, however, change the fate of the soul, which has been decided according to the dead person's behavior in life."[24]

Resurrection

Zoroaster also taught the resurrection of the body in the after-life. Among Zoroaster's "most revolutionary concepts [is] that of the savior, the 'bringer of benefit' or the benefactor known in the Gathas as the Saoshyant. It is this savior figure—also referred to in the plural—who will bring about the renovation of the world."[25] "The purpose of punishment is to reform so that on the day of resurrection all may be raised by the saviour to face the final judgment."[25] Of the three saviors predicted by Zoroaster, the last, named Saoshyans, will dispense final judgment, bring about the resurrection of the dead, and inaugurate a new world.

Judaism

The common idea that Jews deny the existence of an after-life is a misconception. Orthodox Jews affirm not simply our continued existence after death, but also a resurrection of the body for the righteous at the end of time. The Amidah prayer that is to be recited thrice every week day includes the phrase, "Faithful You are to revive the dead. Blessed are You, O Lord, who revive the dead." But was it always thus? The question rises because the Hebrew Bible does not begin with a clear-cut presentation of the life to come and the idea of a resurrection of the righteous emerges only in later biblical texts (Daniel in particular). Consequently critics have been quick to charge that the affirmation of resurrection in what is called Second Temple Judaism is a product of influences from the Greeks with their idea of the immortality of the soul and Zoroastrians with their notion of a resurrection.

In his masterly work, *Resurrection and the Restoration of Israel – the Ultimate Victory of the God of Life*,[26] the Jewish scholar Jon Levenson has conclusively addressed these charges while drilling down to the heart of Jewish belief on human destiny.

Seven Features of the Jewish Understanding of the After-life

Seven things emerge from a study of Judaism as it relates to the after-life:

- ⊷ Like the Mesopotamians and other neighbors, the Jews believed that the dead descend to a shadowy underworld that they called Sheol.

- Unlike their neighbors, the Jews believed that God can deliver them from this realm (and has done so in certain cases).
- It is forbidden to make sacrifices to the dead or to communicate with them through mediums.
- Resurrections from the dead were described in Jewish texts long before the Jews came under Persian rule.
- The Jews were concerned less with life after death than life with God; those who were faithful would be redeemed by him.
- The Jews saw humans as irreducibly psychophysical beings and only a bodily resurrection could qualify as an after-life.
- The immortality of the soul could not fit into this picture.
- There will be a resurrection of all human beings at the end of history. But it is a resurrection that differs significantly from the Zoroastrian world-picture. It is instead organically integrated with earlier themes that began in the Book of Genesis and continue throughout the Bible.

Misconceptions About Jewish After-life Beliefs

Levenson points out that many of the misconceptions about Jewish beliefs on the life to come spring from misconceptions about Judaism in general. For instance, Judaism is not concerned with the continuation of the world, but its redemption. In rabbinic Judaism, resurrection is an event "that is expected to occur in history but also to transform and redeem history and to open onto a barely imaginable world beyond anything that preceded it." This prophetic vision entails the "expectation that God will redeem the tragedies of history, not just for the few who will survive till the end but for all who lived, or have lived rightly. The expectation of an eschatological resurrection coexists easily with immortality so long as the latter is defined as the state of those who have died and await their embodiment, that is, into full human existence."

Sheol

The first books of the Bible speak of the dead existing in Sheol, a gloomy state not unlike that of the Mesopotamian underworld. But there is a big difference in that the Hebraic is not a Land of No Return. As Levenson puts it, "God's miraculous intervention can avert this fate and turn around the failing fortunes of the doomed. As one psalmist puts it: 'He lifted me out of the miry pit, the slimy clay, and set my feet on a rock, steadied my legs.' (Ps 40:3). Nothing in the nature of death, however, guarantees this happy reversal.... When such a movement occurs, it does so because of God's surprising grace and in defiance of the way of all flesh, in defiance of death, in defiance of Sheol." Such a miraculous rescue from Sheol is seen in 2 Samuel 22:8-19.

Contact With the Dead

Some have said that the Israelites had a cult of the dead (albeit a prohibited one). Levenson finds the evidence to be flimsy while admitting that there is archaeological evidence that the dead were offered food. On the other hand, it is clear that verbal communication with the dead was practiced—and prohibited. It was for (successfully) contacting the dead prophet Samuel that Saul was punished. "The eerie meeting of Saul and Samuel—the rendezvous of the doomed and the deceased—contributes further evidence that in ancient Israel the dead were not always thought to have passed into oblivion," says Levenson.

Heaven in the Hebrew Bible

Levenson emphasizes that "in the Hebrew Bible, there is no place that serves as the binary opposite of Sheol in the sense that the blessed go there to enjoy a beatific afterlife that is the reverse of the miserable existence in the God-forsaken netherworld."

Certainly there are instances of people who leave the earth without having first died such as Elijah, who went up to heaven in a chariot (2 Kings 2:1-12). Prior to that, in the Book of Genesis, we had Enoch who was "taken" by God. Psalm 49:16 proclaims that "God will redeem my life from the clutches of Sheol, for He will take me." Psalm 73:24-5 says "You guided me by your counsel and will receive me with glory. Whom else have I in heaven? And having You, I want no one on earth." Levenson remarks that these instances are more consistent with a resurrection of the body than with immortality of the soul: "They speak of an active intervention of God, snatching up to the sky the person found worthy (Elijah), taking him before his time and still in his innocence (Enoch), redeeming him from the power of Sheol (Psalm 49), or receiving him with glory, in contrast to the wicked whom God annihilates (Psalm 73). [27]

Between Death and Resurrection

Rabbinic Judaism does see a state of existence between death and resurrection. "The survival of the deceased even before their resurrection becomes a staple of rabbinic thought," says Levenson. However, if a person "is to return 'as a psycho-physical organism,' it will have to be not through a reincarnation of his soul in some new person but through the resurrection of the body, with *all* its parts reassembled and revitalized. For in the understanding of the Hebrew Bible, a human being is not a spirit, soul, or consciousness that happens to inhabit this body or that—or none at all. Rather, the unity of body and soul…is basic to the person." At the same time, it should be remembered that "resurrection is still only the prelude to something greater and more permanent. This is 'eternal life,' as the book of Daniel puts it (12:2), or, to use the familiar rabbinic expression, life in the World-to-Come."[28]

Resurrection in Kings and Ezekiel

Resurrection does not appear out of the blue in Second Temple Judaism. In the second book of Kings, we see the prophet Elisha miraculously bring a deceased boy back to life. "Long before the apocalyptic framework came into existence, the resurrection of the dead was thought possible—not according to nature, of course, but through the miraculous intervention of the living God." But it is in the vision of the prophet Ezekiel (Ezekiel 37:1-14) that we see resurrection taken on a national scale: "The hand of the LORD came upon me. He took me out by the spirit of the LORD and set me down in the valley. It was full of bones…I prophesied as He commanded me. The breath entered them, and they came to life and stood up on their feet, a vast multitude. And He said to me, 'O mortal, these bones are the whole House of Israel.' Thus said the Lord GOD: I am going to open your graves and lift you out of the graves." Levenson comments that this vision (dated to 600 BC or so) is "the best approximation that we have yet seen to the developed doctrine of a general resurrection that one finds in Second Temple and rabbinic Judaism (and, of course, early Christianity)." This is not a vision simply of revivification, but of transformation and re-creation as well.

Eternal Life in Daniel

There is an organic progression in the idea of resurrection as it appears in the Hebrew Bible: "Death is universal in the Hebrew Bible and seldom, reversed, but God promises, offers, and prefers life and saves his chosen people from annihilation. He even saves some individuals (in extraordinarily rare and therefore especially noteworthy circumstances) from a death that is impending

or one that has already occurred." This process, which began in pre-exilic Israel reaches a climax in the prophecy of the resurrection of the dead in the
Book of Daniel: "Many of those that sleep in the dust of the earth will awake,
some to eternal life, others to reproaches, to everlasting abhorrence." (Daniel
12:1-3). What is striking, among other things, is the note of finality. Daniel "en-
visions no second death for those resurrected, only 'eternal life' for the faithful
and 'everlasting abhorrence' for the desecrators of the covenant." Resurrection, as understood here, "is thought to yield a transformed and perfected form
of bodily existence and thus a state of being both like and unlike any we can
know in the flesh." What is also new here is that "the condemnation of the
wicked no longer involves their simply ceasing to exist or their being dispatched
to Sheol, never to rise from there. Now both groups awake from death, but to
different verdicts."

It should be noted that these elements "existed, at least germinally, in earlier
stages of the religion of Israel, though their combination and fusion are relatively
new and distinctive. They point forward to the Pharisaic and rabbinic doctrine
of resurrection (and to their Christian counterpart) as much as they recall their
biblical forbears."[29]

Resurrection in Zoroastrianism and Judaism

Authors like Alan Segal have charged that Zoroastrian influence gave birth
to the Jewish idea of resurrection. Levenson has this to say about such claims:
"In the case of resurrection...any such influence seems to have been quite
distant, a matter of milieu rather than of direct borrowing." For one thing, "the
Zoroastrians neither buried their dead nor spoke of resurrection in the language
of waking." More important, Judaism's belief in resurrection is "both an innovation
and a restatement of a tension that had pervaded the religion of Israel from the
beginning, the tension between the LORD's promise of life, on the one hand,
and the reality of death, on the other. In the case of resurrection, the last word
once again lies not with death—undeniably grievous though it is. Given the
reality and potency ascribed to death throughout the Hebrew Bible, what over-
comes it is nothing short of the most astonishing miracle, the Divine Warrior's
eschatological victory." (216). The resurrection doctrine of Second Temple was
thus "the end product of a centuries-long process by which these old
traditions...coalesced."[30]

Healing in the After-life

Two other ideas concerning the after-life that were prominent in Second Temple Judaism should be mentioned. The first is that "people will first be resurrected with their infirmities and then healed of them." Deuteronomy 32:39 makes this point: "I deal death and give life; I wounded and I will heal." The rationale for the two stages is clear. "On the one hand, were the dead to come back already healed and transformed, they would no longer be the same persons—the same inextricable combination of body and soul—that they were in this life. On the other hand, were they to come back with their same defective, mortal bodies and morally ambiguous souls, they would be unfit for the eternal life in the World-to-Come for which they are to be resurrected. The schema of two stages —first resurrection, then healing—navigates the paradox brilliantly. It both preserves the continuity of personal identity and subjects the risen dead to a process of re-creation that renders them fit for life after death."[31]

Prayers for the Dead

The second idea is outlined in the inter-testamental book of Maccabees. "Judas Maccabees and his men went to gather up the bodies of the slain (after the battle) and bury them with their kinsmen in their ancestral tombs. But under the tunic of each of the dead they found amulets sacred to the idols of Jamnia, which the law forbids the Jews to wear. So it was clear to all that this was why these men had been slain...He then took up a collection among all his soldiers, amounting to 2,000 silver drachmas, which he sent to Jerusalem to provide for an expiatory sacrifice. In doing this he acted in a very excellent and noble way...it was a holy and pious thought. Thus he made atonement for the dead that they might be freed from sin." (2 Maccabees 12:39-40, 43).

Both ideas, it might be said, served as the seedbed from which sprouted the notions of purgatory and prayers for the dead in early Christianity. Moreover, the New Testament scholar Joachim Jeremias has noted that the Jews believed in the intercession of the prophets, especially at their gravesites. The posthumous intercession of the prophets is documented in the book of Maccabees: "Then in the same way another man appeared, distinguished by his white hair and dignity, and with an air about him of extraordinary, majestic authority. Onias then said of him, 'This is God's prophet Jeremiah, who loves his brethren and fervently prays for his people and their holy city.'" (2 Maccabees 15:13-14).

Christianity

Similar to other religions, Christianity affirms the after-life and a correlation between our deeds here and our destiny hereafter. Some Christians might say that only faith is required, but the act of faith is itself a deed—in fact a deed that helps determine your destiny (we consider the question of faith and works below). Unlike other religions, Christianity anchors its claims in the identity and acts of its founder, Jesus of Nazareth, whom it acclaims as God incarnate. Moreover, the Christian understanding of the after-life is grounded in its claim that Jesus physically rose from the dead. Any study of the Christian vision of life-after-death, therefore, has to consider the claim that Jesus rose from the dead.

It should be noted, in addition, that the notion of "eternal life" already present in the Book of Daniel takes on central importance in the Christian dispensation. The focal point of the central teachings and acts of Jesus—most especially the climactic Last Supper—were the fulfillment of the Covenant, the proclamation of the Kingdom, and the invitation to eternal life. Eternal life and salvation, in Jesus's teaching, concerns not an endless period of time in the hereafter, but a new state of being acquired here and now—that of being divinized. All men and women are called to be divinized, to share in the divine nature, to participate in the life of God. Jesus himself is proclaimed to be both God and man. He had said, "I am the life" (not "I have the life"). To live in him is to live with the life of God, "to share in the divine nature." (2 Peter 1:4) God took on a human nature so that humans may take on the divine nature. God "humanized" himself so humans could be divinized. "For the Son of God became man so that we might become God," said the Church Father Athanasius. Hence St. Paul could write, "We are the offspring of God" (Acts 17:39). It should be clarified here that we are not talking of a human person "becoming" God or the finite becoming the infinite. To be divinized is to live with the Life of God and to know and love with the Power of God. To know like God and to love like God is to become *like* God. But you cannot *be* God.

Heaven, Hell, and Resurrection

The saga of divinization, begun in this world, reaches a climax in the world to come. The glorification that comes with direct union with God—Heaven—is the divine desire and blueprint for all humanity. But, if we are free beings, it is possible to reject the divine invitation and hence the state of separation popularly called Hell remains a possibility. Another essential element of the Christian message was the idea of the resurrection of the body. The eternal destiny of humanity was unthinkable without a bodily life albeit in a glorified state. Thus, we see here not a doctrine of the immortality of the soul, but a celebration of all dimensions of our being in tune with our deepest intuitions. It should be said here that the New Testament, while teaching that the resurrection of the body only takes place at the end of history, also affirms a continued existence in the period between our physical death and the resurrection. Thus Jesus tells the thief on the cross, "Today you will be with me in Paradise" and St. Paul tells his audience that his desire is to depart and be with Christ.

Which Christianity?

Our objective is to begin with an overview of the Christian claim about the resurrection of Jesus, because it is one of the direct sources of Christian afterlife beliefs—and then review the ideas of Heaven, Hell, Purgatory, the intercession of the saints, and the resurrection of the body. One obvious issue we confront at this point is *which* Christian view we should consider. Granting that no answer will please everyone, I submit that a study of the beliefs of the undivided Church of the first millennium is reasonable, because these are the beliefs closest to Jesus and his Apostles (much as Vedic Hinduism is the primordial repository of Hindu doctrine and devotion).

The issue of true doctrines and the correct interpretations of the Bible is a contentious one for Christians. How should the narratives, expositions, and letters of the Bible be authoritatively understood and interpreted? (Without an authoritative interpretation, any passage can be interpreted according to any individual's predilection.) In practice, in the first millennium of Christianity, the definitions of Church Councils certified by the papal magisterium were considered normative. Also, any doctrine taught unanimously by the Fathers of East and West, the ancient interpreters of Scripture, was considered authoritative by that very fact. Finally, the truest witness to the faith of the believing community was the language of their prayer and liturgical celebration. These were the different sources that created the body of doctrine and interpretation that is today called Christian. Even if one's contemporary reading of Scripture is cited as the source, any interpretation or doctrine that rejects what was believed by these first Christians can be called many things: novel, original, creative. But it cannot be called definitive or binding for Christians. The New Testament, in fact, says that the church is the pillar and foundation of truth (1 Timothy 3:15).

The Resurrection of Jesus

From the beginning of the Christian Church, one of its central claims was the resurrection from the dead of its founder. Three primary arguments have been offered in support of this claim: the empty tomb of Jesus, his posthumous appearances to his disciples, and the origin of Christianity. Recent years have seen an intellectual resurrection of the Resurrection claim as these arguments have been placed back on the agenda of scholarly inquiry by three pathbreaking works:

- ↦ "The Events of Easter and the Empty Tomb" by Hans von Campenhausen who in 1952 defended the historical basis of the empty tomb claim.

- ↦ *Jesus—God and Man* by Wolfhart Pannenberg, one of Germany's leading theologians, who argued in 1968 that based on the evidence for the empty tomb and the appearances of Jesus it is possible to rationally conclude that Jesus's resurrection from the dead took place in history.

- ↦ *The Resurrection of the Son of God* by N.T. Wright, whose epochal 2003 work ties together the historical arguments in favor of the bodily resurrection of Christ. Wright notes that the question to be answered is, "Why did Christianity emerge so rapidly, with such power, and why did believers risk everything to teach that Jesus really rose?" The best explanation, in his view, is that "Jesus's tomb was discovered empty on Easter morning" and "Jesus then appeared to his followers alive in bodily form."

A Jewish Scholar on the Resurrection of Jesus

This is not the forum to discuss the claim of the resurrection. But it is worth considering that the transformation of the dispirited disciples and the explosion of the Christian movement in first-century Palestine cries out for an explanation. So much so, the Jewish theologian Pinchas Lapide is critical of *Christian* attempts to explain away the resurrection: "Such a post-Easter change, which was no less real than sudden and unexpected, certainly needed a concrete foundation which can by no means exclude the possibility of any physical resurrection. One thing we may assume with certainty: neither the Twelve nor the early church believed in the ingenious wisdom of theologians!"

Lapide concludes:

I cannot rid myself of the impression that some modern Christian theologians are ashamed of the material facticity of the resurrection. Their varying attempts at dehistoricizing the Easter experience which give the lie to the four evangelists are simply not understandable to me in any other way. Indeed, the four authors of the Gospels definitely compete with one another in illustrating the tangible, substantial dimension of this resurrection explicitly. Often it seems as if renowned New Testament scholars in our days want to insert a kind of ideological or dogmatic curtain between the pre-Easter and the risen Jesus in order to protect the latter against any kind of contamination by earthly three-dimensionality. However, for the first Christians who thought, believed, and hoped in a Jewish manner, the immediate historicity was not only a part of that happening but the indispensable precondition for the recognition of its significance for salvation.[32]

Another Jew, the famous philosopher Ludwig Wittgenstein, poignantly considers the resurrection of Jesus in the context of the meaning of life: "What inclines even me to believe in Christ's resurrection? It is as though I play with the thought—If he did not rise from the dead, then he is decomposed in the grave like any other man. He is dead and decomposed. In that case he is a teacher like any other and can no longer help; and once more we are orphaned and alone. So we have to content ourselves with wisdom and speculation. We are in a sort of hell where we can do nothing but dream, roofed in, as it were, and cut off from heaven. But if I am to be really saved—what I need is certainty—not wisdom, dreams or speculations—and this certainty is faith. And faith is what is needed by my heart, my soul, not my speculative intelligence. For it is my soul with its passions, as it were with its flesh and blood, that has to be saved, not my abstract mind. Perhaps we can say: Only love can believe the Resurrection. Or: It is love that believes the Resurrection."[33]

Heaven

In the teaching of Jesus, human beings have to make a choice between one of two possible ultimate destinies: union with God, which is Heaven, or separation from God, which is Hell.

The essence of Heaven is total union with God. In its fullest sense, Heaven is understood as the Beatific Vision, the closest possible union between finite and Infinite, creature and Creature. It is to see God as he is in himself and to enjoy the everlasting Vision of God, the vision that makes us happy ("beatificus" is Latin for "making happy"). This talk of "seeing God" comes straight out of the New Testament where the key term used in talking of Heaven is "seeing." "We shall see him as he is" (I John 3:2). "Now we see through a glass, darkly; but then face to face." (I Corinthians 13:12). Jesus says of the angels, "their angels do always behold the face of my Father which is in heaven." (Matthew 18:10). "Seeing" here denotes "knowing," and thus Corinthians 13:12 continues, "now I know in part; but then shall I know even as also I am known." This knowing does not come either through our minds or the creatures of God: we are in unmediated contact so that "we shall be like Him" (I John 3:2). God becomes present in us in the same way as our innermost thoughts. All our capacities and potentialities are fulfilled to the utmost. The two primary capabilities of every human person are knowing and loving and to be united with the infinite Mind and Will is to fulfill both capabilities to their utmost, because we will directly and forever know perfect Truth and love perfect Goodness. This fulfillment is simultaneously for us supreme and eternal happiness because all our potentialities are actualized. All the instances of knowing and loving we experience in this life give us a foretaste of what could happen if we choose union with God.

It might be said, in fact, it has been said, that these ideas are all well and good, but they don't exercise the imagination. They are meaningless abstractions at best, pious pie-in-the-sky at worst. There's nothing concrete here, nothing that excites Mind and Will. Heaven is hardly mentioned in modern times (as opposed to Hell and "damn," which have been recycled as handy expletives). And conceptions of Heaven have see-sawed between theocentric and anthropocentric poles.

The renowned philosopher of science Sir Karl Popper rejected belief in life after death while noting that the accounts of mediums and spiritualists are positively unattractive. "Most terrible of all prospects appears to be the prospect which the people who believe in psychical research and spiritualism seem to offer. That is to say, a kind of ghostly semi-existence after death, and one which is not only ghostly, but which seems to be intellectually on a particularly low level—on a lower level than the normal level of human affairs. This form of semi-survival is probably the most unpleasant form which has so far been conceived. I do think that if there is anything in the idea of survival, then it would have to be different from anything we can imagine in order to be tolerable."

Significantly Sir Karl added that any viable idea of life after death must be qualitatively different from life before death: "If there is anything in the idea of survival, then I think that those who say that this cannot be just in space and time, and that it cannot be just a temporal eternity, have to be taken very seriously."[34]

Beyond Space and Time

Many of the great theologians who explored the Christian picture of Heaven had always conceived it in terms that went beyond the spatio-temporal. St. Paul had laid down the ground rules when he wrote, "Eye hath not seen, nor ear heard, neither have entered into the heart of man the things which God hath prepared for them that love him." (I Corinthians 2:9)

Tedium?

About the fear of tedium, John Haldane writes,

In finding what they have always craved—absolute, unconditional and everlasting love—their minds [those of the blessed in Heaven] are themselves made loving, but now without prospect of relapse, for the wound from which their darkness and disturbance issued as a consequence of wilful disobedience has now been healed, and their lives transfigured. The idea that this state might induce tedium is a product of too low an expectation of what the transformation of human life in Heaven might involve. God knows infinities by creating them; created minds know unending depths by exploring them. Even given eternity, that exploration will not be completed: as with the number series, however long one continues, and however far one reaches, there is still an infinity ahead. Those who find no attraction in the prospect of unlimited exploration of a reality that is at once *significant* (in the manner of a meaning-endowing narrative), *pleasing* (after the fashion of an aesthetically engaging composition), and *sustaining* (as in a loving friendship) are, I suggest, gravely wanting in imagination.[35]

Garth Hallett suggests six conceptions of Heaven that address the boredom problem: timeless beatitude, heavenly continuation, indefinite progress, subjective timelessness, eternal youthfulness, and creative contentment.[36]

Martin D'Arcy points out that Heaven is loving as much as it is knowing. "In eternity all joys and all loveliness meet in a Person who has first loved us and thinks of us as the light of His own countenance. There is no ending to it, no past and no more loss."

It is love that is the answer to concerns about tedium. "A thousand years could be as a moment to one who has been caught up in an ecstasy of love, whereas to a man in prison a few days can seem an eternity.… If we meet an object or a person in the next life of a kind to absorb all our attention, draw out the best in us and completely capture our love, time would be no more, or rather all the scattered moments of our life would be gathered up into a single and perpetual now; nothing could distract us, give us pause or weary us."[37]

It is recognized, of course, that all the believer can really know about Heaven in this life is its essential nature. Everything else is speculation or extrapolation. Those concerned with the tedium of immortality are thinking simply of an endless extension of life as we know it today and this is unattractive at best. But Heaven is understood as not just quantitatively different from our present life, but also qualitatively so.

At the same time, even while saying that Heaven is indescribable in terrestrial terms, it is acknowledged that there will be continuity between life on earth and in Heaven. Remove the concrete and all you have are pale abstractions.

Yet speculation about Heaven in purely human terms is pointless because, by its very nature, the immediate knowledge and love of God is something man cannot enjoy in this life and hence cannot describe or grasp. But the Christian believer does know that Heaven is a union with the Creator of this immense universe, with the Author of all the love, goodness, and joy around him, with the One in Whom all these are found in perfection. He does know that such union cannot but bring him the highest possible satisfaction and happiness. All physical and spiritual pleasures in this world derive from God, who is the Source of all joy, and are only hints and harbingers of the final and direct union with Him at "Whose right hand there are pleasures forevermore." There is an almost terrifying ecstasy, a fearful joy, in the thought of union with the Creator, the Inventor, of galaxies and pine trees, sunsets and smiles, babies and giraffes, angels and the Alps.

As Christians understand it, the everlasting vision of God does not exclude loving communion among those in Heaven. The New Testament includes various instances of recognition in the after-life. Heaven includes the fullest satisfaction of all pure human loves rather than impediments to them. And though Heaven is not primarily supposed to be a place where one meets one's dear ones again (as the spiritualists seem to think)—it is the mode of one's everlasting union with God—one can nevertheless be certain that God will not fail to give the joy of final fruition to one's relationships with those whom one loved most. In Heaven, we will know and love others as we have never known or loved anyone on earth. The love and friendship we bore for our brothers and sisters in this life will be infinitely ennobled and intensified in Heaven where we are united and indwelt by God, who is the source of all love and joy. It may be said that such concern with other people seems to cause too much distraction from the vision of God. But his followers believe that when Jesus said, "Love your neighbor," he meant this for all eternity. Our God-given attachment and love for our dear ones will reach a glorious flowering in Heaven as a facet of our boundless enjoyment of the presence of God Himself, for to love one another, even in Heaven, is to appreciate the variety of God's glory. "He does not snatch away our mortal joys because He gives to us the bliss of Heaven."

D'Arcy holds that God will also "restore the experiences which made us what we are and bound friends to us by affection and vow. Nor will those experiences be just memories, for memories mean that something has been lost and that we are spiritual orphans. 'I will not leave you orphans: I will come to you.' … In the day of the reward we will not have to ask for anything, for all things, all joys and all loves will be ours. Memories will give up their dead and the past will live again in this fullness of life."[38]

A Question of What and Not Where

So where is Heaven? With regard to "where" we have to make it clear that it is in no respect physical in the sense we currently experience the physical. Then again, neither God nor the angels are physical. They are present "where" they act. To enter Heaven is not to enter a new material dimension. Rather it is said that we will experience a new state of being that infinitely surpasses all that we have encountered in our current state. It may seem here that we are slowly backing into abstractions leaving in our wake a trail of tortuous verbiage. But there is only so far you can go with an imagination formed entirely by our three-dimensional world. Of course Christianity claims that human beings will be fully reconstituted with the resurrected body, but this "body" will be entirely different in capability from our present bodies. Moreover, humans will commune with angels and God who are bodiless by nature. The question here should be "what" rather than "where."

Happiness and Heaven

In conclusion, we return to the question of how knowing and loving God can make one happy. God is he who has no limitation of any kind: he knows all things, he is all-powerful, he is not limited by space or time. He is the plenitude of perfections. All that is good and beautiful is found in him in an unlimited degree such that he is himself Goodness and Beauty. If you know and love him with his own power and energy, then your intellect and will, which are the sources of your happiness, will be fulfilled to the maximal degree. If you find joy in admiring a work of art, or reading a work of literature or entering into a romantic relationship, then you will have some idea of the endless ecstasy that comes in uniting yourself with the One who is the summit and source and perfection of all that is good and beautiful. Echoes of the Ecstasy that is God are heard in the splendor of every sunset, melodies that rush you out of space and time, kindly faces and family fellowship, fairy tales and folklore, the pursuit of truth, carnivals and sport, laughter and humor, thunderstorms spent indoors, sunspecked lakes, and the roar of ocean waves.

In speaking of Heaven, the Christian affirms that Jesus descended to the uttermost depths of the human heart, assuring us that our deepest yearnings have a home, that the transient and the contingent will become enduring, and that our wildest dreams can come true. But there is no element of wishfulfillment in this story of glory. For the darkness of sin stands between the human heart and its heavenly destiny. And the only way to overcome the darkness is the Way of the Cross.

Christianity has always taught that God desires the salvation of all men and women. The Church, from its earliest days, has preached this doctrine of the universal salvific will of God. We exist to love him who is Love itself. And it is our duty to draw those around us to this love.

Christians hold that if one accepts the truth about God revealed by Christ with both intellect and will, with our thoughts and actions, then we are taking the path that God has ordained for our salvation. But not all people will have the opportunity of understanding this truth about God, this way to God, this life in God. Nevertheless, God's intent to save them, to save all humanity, does not change, and the salvific effects of the death of Christ applies to all. Both Old and New Testaments resound with this message of a Creator who wishes that no creature perish, a Holy of Holies who invites the wicked to turn from evil, an infinite lover who seeks eternal union with every human person.

> ✤ "Do I indeed derive any pleasure from the death of the wicked? Says the Lord God. Do I not rather rejoice when he turns from evil way that he may live." (Ezekiel 18:23).

- ⮵ "The hour is coming when the dead will leave their graves at the sound of his voice; those who did good will rise again for life; and those who did evil, to condemnation." (John 5:28-8).

- ⮵ "This is good and pleasing to God our savior, who wills everyone to be saved and to come to knowledge of the truth." (1 Timothy 2:3-4).

Hell

According to Christianity, if Heaven is one possibility for the human person, Hell is the other. By Hell we mean a total separation from God, as Heaven is the most total possible union with him. "These will pay the penalty of eternal ruin, separated from the presence of the Lord and from the glory of his power," (2 Thessalonians 1:9). In this lies the essential suffering of Hell: it is separation from God and therefore the separation from everything that is required by human nature. Ultimately, the choice is between God and self, and if we choose the self we are left with the self—and only the self. And because our entire being is made for God, the suffering experienced by the self left to itself is the greatest imaginable. It is worse than unending hunger or thirst in a desolate wilderness or endless separation from one's loved ones. These cause suffering, because the needs of our nature are not met. But God is the greatest need of human nature and total separation from him—a separation unmitigated by sleep or death—causes us the greatest possible suffering.

For those who truly understand the nature of Hell, it is too dreadful a thought to contemplate without recoiling in horror. So dreadful is it that some have eliminated the doctrine of Hell from their beliefs about the after-life, or simply rejected any belief in an after-life.

But these escapist options are not available for those who take their own freedom seriously or consider the Christian proclamation to be divine revelation. If talk of life-after-death was simply a wish-fulfillment, we could dispense with the idea of Hell simply by refusing to think about it. But reality cannot be adjusted to fit into our comfort zone. A loving God would want to warn his creatures of the consequences of the freedom that makes them human. And certainly, the Jesus of the Gospels was emphatic about the possibility and danger of Hell.

The tragic logic of Hell can be understood even by those who do not accept it:

- ⮵ The first point to grasp is that God does not wish anyone to go to Hell.

❧ Secondly, God has created us for Heaven and will do everything coherently possible to take us there.

❧ Third, happiness can only be enjoyed by free beings and not machines or puppets, and Heaven is therefore a result of a free choice. But this freedom implies the equal possibility of saying no, which means that the very possibility of Heaven inescapably leads to the possibility of Hell. Love means Hell is possible. No way around it.

❧ Fourth, those who are in Hell (if there be any) are there only because they have (against the divine will) chosen Hell. The puzzle of Hell is not a puzzle about God's love, but about the nature of human freedom. We cannot be rational creatures capable of true happiness if we were not free, and we cannot be free without the option of saying no.

There is much more to all this and many questions that arise, but the essential predicament is laid out here.

Hell Is Our Creation

"God never 'created' hell," says theologian Zdzislaw Kijas. "Hell is something *we* create. Whether in this life or the next, hell is always our own doing, our own creation, because hell is 'self-exclusion from God'—it is not God who excludes us, it is we ourselves who freely choose to exclude ourselves from him.… Love is either free, or it is not love at all. Hell is the logical consequence of the use of that freedom outside of the realm of love, who is God.…

"God never condemns or sentences anyone. When we appear before God on the day of Judgement, it is not God who sentences us, but we ourselves. This is because on that Day we will see ourselves as we really are in the mirror of God, and in that faithful mirror we will have the right criteria for judging ourselves."[39]

Every choice at its root is a choice for self or God. We form our whole character and being through our choices. If we ask why the soul in Hell should not be annihilated, we do not realize that the self-love of such a soul is so great that it would not want annihilation. Only such a soul would choose Hell.

A student of Ludwig Wittgenstein once expressed regret that the Church had condemned Origen's idea of God eliminating Hell. To this Wittgenstein replied, "Of course it was rejected. It would make nonsense of everything else. If what we do now is to make no difference in the end, then all the seriousness of life is done away with."[40]

Where Is Hell?

To the question, "Where is Hell?," Kijas responds that Hell "is a location, a place, only in the metaphorical sense; it would be more appropriate to define it as a psychological condition in which those who die in mortal sin are forever contemplating the horror of their deeds and, moreover, are painfully aware of that which they have lost for all eternity—communion with God, the source of all true happiness."[41]

According to Peter Geach, because separated souls and lost angels "are *ex hypothesi* immaterial, no place can be straightforwardly ascribed to them; and their damnation is in any event a state not a place. As Mephistopheles said to Faustus's question 'How comes it then that thou art out of Hell?' 'Why, this is Hell, nor am I out of it.'"[42]

This insight is well captured in a line from the movie *Lord of War*. The conscientious lawman is ultimately out-maneuvered by the ruthless and venal gunrunner. As the latter gloats in triumph, the lawman comments that he would like to say "go to hell," but doesn't have to because "I think you're already there."

"For the damned," writes Geach, "all love and joy and peace are things that were once, and were once going to be, but now will never be, never any more. For them, the Blessed and God's grace have disappeared from the world forever. With no hope of death, they are left forever with their own dreadful company." [43]

A Second Chance?

It might be asked whether the person who chooses Hell might be given a second chance. To this, the philosopher Eric Mascall responds that in seeing God at death we are given "all conceivable and possible chances at once." Mascall shows too that it is precisely God's love that makes Hell necessary.

> ↬ "If all that God was prepared to confer on us was a state of impersonal or merely animal beatitude, he might easily give it to us all, quite regardless of our attitude to him or to our fellow creatures." But true union "by its very nature requires free and irrevocable choice on both sides.... And it is such a choice that confronts us, when, at the moment of death, we come into the sheer presence of God himself, as created spirits face with uncreated Spirit. It is no longer, as in this life, a choice between lesser goods and greater...it is simply a choice between accepting God and rejecting him."

- ✧ "Hell, as Christianity conceives it, is not incompatible with God's love; it is a direct consequence of it. For love can be received only in a free response of love; and, God's love being pure self-giving, we must receive it as such or not at all."

- ✧ "If it is suggested that God will surely give us an indefinite number of second chances, the answer is very simple. It is that this is precisely what he is continually doing while we are in this life, but, when at death we see him in the fullness of his glory and love, he is giving us all conceivable and possible chances at once."

- ✧ "We may indeed find it difficult to imagine that anyone whom we know or of whom we have heard will *in fact* reject God under these conditions; but in order to recognize the *possibility*, we have only to reflect on the nature of God and man and love, or, better still, to look into our own souls."[44]

Purgatory and Prayers for the Dead

Most Christians accept Heaven and Hell as the two ultimate options for every human person. But, ever since the Reformation, some have rejected the whole idea of an intermediate state for those who have been "saved" and still need to be "purified." This is the state often called "purgatory" ("purge" meaning "purify"); it is further affirmed that the souls in Purgatory can be assisted, by the prayers of the living. As controversial as these ideas is the notion of the intercession of the saints.

Before considering these notions in more detail, we should recognize the following:

- ✧ Both ideas were taken for granted as true by Christians from the very beginning in their faith and applied in their devotional practices and liturgies.

- ✧ Both were taught by the Fathers of the Church.

- ✧ The New Testament does not formally pronounce a position on these teachings, although proponents and opponents have cited various verses in support of their positions. But this is hardly an objection, given that the New Testament does not formally "teach" such fundamental Christian doctrines as the doctrine of the Trinity.

- ✧ Eminent Protestant Christians like C.S. Lewis have accepted Purgatory and prayers for the dead.

What the First Christians Believed

The belief that many of the dead undergo a purifying process before entering Heaven was instinctively adopted by the first Christians. Accordingly they prayed for their deceased friends. Catherine Marshall, a well-known Protestant writer, has chronicled this historical detail that is unknown to many today:

"Did Christians then [in the first centuries of Christianity] know something about personal contact across the dividing line of death that we do not know today?

The first fact I uncovered was that, from the establishment of the church after Pentecost to the Protestant Reformation in the sixteenth century, *prayer for and with the dead had been universally practiced by Christendom.* This followed naturally from two bedrock beliefs of the Apostolic Church: (1) that of immortality, that Christ—through His resurrection, to which the earliest Christians claimed to be eyewitnesses had for ever conquered death; and (2) that the unity of the church—the Body of Christ—was such that death could not dismember it.

The prayers of the first Christians for the dead were not mere petitions that the departed from some state of eternal punishment. To them, prayer was as natural as breathing. It was the life of the spirit; it was their lifeline with the Risen Lord. He had taught them that they were 'members one of another' of an organic fellowship. To them it was unthinkable that the incident of death should sever their communion with each other and with the living Christ....

The writings of the earliest church fathers who came after the apostles—such as Tertullian and Cyprian—also bear unanimous testimony that the fellowship of prayer with those in the next life was taken for granted. Then in Augustine's Confessions we have his prayer for his mother Monica, written after her death."[45]

Freedom and Salvation

The question is, why did the Christian community believe in this, and how did the belief fit in with their scriptures and doctrines? On the question of faith, we should point out that free choices are critical to salvation. The standoff between those who proclaim that faith alone is sufficient for salvation, and those who allegedly point to faith and works or works alone as the path to salvation rests on a false dilemma. The New Testament clearly teaches that freewill is involved in salvation.

The Gospels teach that one's free decisions determine one's eternal destiny: "For the Son of Man is going to come in the glory of his Father with his angels, and, when he does, he will reward each one according to his behavior." (Matthew 16:27). This is a teaching that is reiterated in the rest of the New Testament. Says St. Paul, "Your stubborn refusal to repent is only adding to the anger God will have toward you on that day of anger when his just judgments will be made known. He will repay each one as his works deserve. For those who sought renown and honor and immortality by always doing good there will be eternal life; for the unsubmissive who refused to take truth for their guide and took depravity instead, there will be anger and fury." (Romans 2:5-8).

But is the choice we make for God a kind of work and does this mean that salvation comes from works? The reality is that God is omnipotent and sovereign. The only real power that humans have, a power not shared by animals, is a negative power—the power to say no to God. The human person can reject the divine offer of salvation. But the person who chooses *not* to say no is not performing a work. In not saying no, you are simply choosing not to exercise the negative power at your disposal.

So what of faith? In the Christian account, faith means surrendering your will to Jesus, trusting him, and following him however imperfectly. In the Christian view, this is the ordinary way to salvation, but (as noted), God is not limited by his ordinary way in bringing his creatures to salvation.

Purgatory and the New Testament

As for Purgatory, the New Testament says clearly "nothing defiled" shall enter Heaven. (Revelation 21:27). Most people who die have some defilement or other when they leave this world. Does this mean they go to Hell? Some Christians might say that their faith in Christ will save them no matter what their imperfections. But here it is not a question of salvation, but of whether you can enter Heaven while defiled. Even those who have faith in Christ cannot claim to be fully transformed as persons. Even if you had the made the choice for Heaven, you soul still has to be remoulded to live in Heaven.

The New Testament hints that there is a possibility of some kind of punishment after death that is not final. St. Paul writes, "For no one can lay a foundation other than the one that there is, namely, Jesus Christ. If anyone builds on this foundation with gold, silver, precious stones, wood, hay or straw, the work of each one will come to light, for the Day will disclose it. It will be revealed with fire, and the fire will test the quality of each one's work. If the work stands that someone built upon the foundation, that person will receive a wage. But if someone's work is burned up, that one will suffer loss; the person will be saved, but only through fire." (1 Corinthians 3:11-15). The person is saved, but only through fire.

In his book *Eternal Security*, the well-known Baptist writer Charles Stanley has an interpretation of this verse that is of interest here. He asks us to visualize the believer standing before God.

> Picture yourself watching saint after saint rewarded for faithfulness and service to the King—and all the time knowing that you had just as many opportunities but did nothing about them. We cannot conceive of the agony and frustration we would feel if we were to undergo such an ordeal; the realization that our unfaithfulness had cost us eternally would be devastating. And so it will be for many believers. Just as those who are found faithful will rejoice, so those who suffer loss will weep. As some are celebrated for their faithfulness, others will gnash their teeth in frustration over their own shortsightedness and greed. We do not know how long this time of rejoicing and sorrow will last. Those whose works are burned will not weep and gnash their teeth for eternity. At some point we know God will comfort those who have suffered loss (see Rev. 21:4). On the other side of the coin, we can rest assured that none of our good deeds will go unnoticed, either.[46]

As a Baptist, Dr. Stanley does not, of course, believe in Purgatory. But clearly his interpretation of this verse in Corinthians entails the idea of some kind of "loss" after death for those who still end up in Heaven.

Other verses have been used in support of the doctrine. These include Jesus's reference to a sin that "will not be forgiven either in this world or in the next" (Matthew 12:32) (which implies some kind of restitution in the next world) and Matthew 5:25: "Amen, I say to you, you will not be released until you have paid the last penny."

None of these verses formally teach Purgatory, but they certainly make sense in the light of the doctrine. It should be remembered that such fundamental doctrines of Christianity as the Trinity were developed not by assembling proof-texts, but by interpreting the teaching of Christ through the lens of the Fathers, Councils and liturgies. This is the true birth-place of Purgatory and other basic beliefs of the early Christians.

We illustrate this by reference to the teachings on Purgatory and prayers for the dead that emerged from the Fathers.

Cyprian

It is one thing, tortured by long suffering for sins, to be cleansed and long purged by fire; another to have purged all sins by suffering. It is one thing, in fine, to be in suspense till the sentence of God at the Day of Judgment; another to be at once crowned by the Lord (Letters 51[55]:20 [AD 253]).

Cyril of Jerusalem

Then we make mention also of those who have already fallen asleep: first, the patriarchs, prophets, apostles, and martyrs, that through their prayers and supplications God would receive our petition, next, we make mention also of the holy fathers and bishops who have already fallen asleep, and, to put it simply, of all among us who have already fallen asleep. For we believe that it will be of very great benefit to the souls of those for whom the petition is carried up, while this holy and most solemn sacrifice is laid out. (Catechetical Lectures 23:5:9 [AD 350]).

Augustine

Temporal punishments are suffered by some in this life only, by some after death, by some both here and hereafter, but all of them before that last and strictest judgment. But not all who suffer temporal punishments after death will come to eternal punishments, which are to follow after that judgment (The City of God 21:13 [AD 419]).

Purgatory as Part of Sanctification

Much of the revulsion for Purgatory is a result of misconceptions about the teaching. As the Anglican theologian John Macquarrie has said, Purgatory is "one aspect of that process of sanctification, whereby we are conformed to Christ." It is a completion of earthly penance and of conversion. The pains of Purgatory, as Francis Mannion puts it, are pains not of punishment, but of growth and transformation, of putting on a new self. In Macquarrie's words, it is "the painful surrender of the ego-centered self that the God-centered self of love may take its place." The fire of Purgatory is a cleansing fire.

Purgatory is also a recognition that God always respects our freedom. Let's say we freely choose eternal union with God. Next, we have to address the self-created impediments that come in the way of consummating our union with him. The state of the soul cannot be transformed by a magic wand: it has to be cleansed with our full consent. The soul has to be "straightened out," rehabilitated, detoxified. And this is what is meant by Purgatory. It is a detox facility, a rehab center. As with any such facility, depending on the degree of the patient's problem, the kind and duration of the therapy will vary. The patients cannot help themselves, but they can certainly receive assistance from outside.

Dr. Johnson helped clarify some of the misconceptions about Purgatory to his biographer Boswell: [Christians who affirm Purgatory] "are of the opinion that the generality of mankind are neither so obstinately wicked as to deserve everlasting punishment, nor so good as to merit being admitted into the society of the blessed spirits; and therefore that God is graciously pleased to allow of a middle state, where they may be purified by certain degrees of suffering. You see, Sir, there is nothing unreasonable in this."

Perhaps the most memorable Protestant defense of Purgatory came from C.S. Lewis:

> Of course I pray for the dead. The action is so spontaneous, so all but inevitable, that only the most compulsive theological case against it would deter me....
>
> I believe in purgatory....
>
> Our souls *demand* purgatory, don't they? Would it not break the heart if God said to us, 'It is true, my son, that your breath smells and your rags drip with mud and slime, but we are charitable here and no one will upbraid you with these things, nor draw away from you. Enter into the joy?' Should we not reply, 'With submission, sir, and if there is no objection, I'd *rather* be cleaned first.' 'It may hurt, you know'— 'Even so, sir.'
>
> I assume that the process of purification will normally involve suffering. Partly from tradition; partly because most real good that has been done me in this life has involved it. But I don't think the suffering

is the purpose of the purgation. I can well believe that people neither much worse nor much better than I will suffer less than I or more…. The treatment given will be the one required, whether it hurts little or much.[47]

The Pains of Purgatory

In what consists the pain of Purgatory as traditionally understood? Frank Sheed writes, "We cannot pretend to know what the suffering of a disembodied soul is, but for the souls we are considering there can be no question what the principal element is. They long to see the unveiled face of God, yet they could not bear to see it while any uncleanness remains in them. They suffer from the anguish of their desire and the clear vision of the taint of self still in their own will. By accepting God's will, they find healing for their own will…. When the cleansing is complete, they are at last fully human. The evil they have done is purified and they can face God and both those who have wronged them and those they have wronged."[48]

Intercession of the Saints

Also in the same domain of discussion is the so-called communion of saints. According to the Christian narrative, the Holy Ones in Heaven, also called saints, are spiritually united with all living Christians. So also are those being purified in preparation for Heaven (that is, the souls in Purgatory). The Epistle to the Hebrews talks of the faithful on earth being "surrounded by so great a cloud of witnesses" and exhorts them to approach without fear the "heavenly Jerusalem" where they find "the assembly of the firstborn enrolled in heaven." For those who live in Christ, death is not thought of as a barrier, and the Church itself is a communion of those in Heaven (the Church Triumphant), Purgatory (the Church Suffering), and the present-day world (the Church Militant). There are no borders or barriers other than sin. Consequently, millions of people throughout history have claimed to have miraculous answers to prayers addressed to various saints in Heaven. These range from medically inexplicable cures to more mundane forms of help. This is what is called the intercession of the saints.

Saints in the Book of Revelation

Today some Christians frown on belief in the saints, claiming that it is unbiblical or incompatible with faith in God's total sovereignty. Catholic, Orthodox, and many Protestant Christians, however, do accept the role of the saints. Such disdain would have been incomprehensible to the early Christians (even the catacombs have prayers to the blessed dead). It also flies in the face of the biblical narratives. The Book of Revelation is a classic instance of the saints in Heaven intervening in earthly affairs. "When he took it, the four living creatures and the 24 elders fell down before the Lamb. Each of the elders held a harp and gold bowls filled with incense, which are the prayers of the holy ones." (Revelation 5:8). The elders in this instance are Christians in Heaven. "The smoke of the incense along with the prayers of the holy ones went up before God from the hand of the angel." (Revelation 8:4). "I saw underneath the altar the souls of those who had been slaughtered because of the witness they bore to the word of God. They cried out in a loud voice, 'How long will it be, holy and true master, before you sit in judgment and avenge our blood on the inhabitants of the earth?' Each of them was given a white robe, and they were told to be patient a little while longer until the number was filled of their fellow servants and brothers who were going to be killed as they had been." (Revelation 6:9-11).

God Is Glorified in His Angels and Saints

The New Testament texts show saints who are dead appear on earth as when Moses and Elijah appear and commune with Christ or when certain saints rose from their graves at the death of Jesus. Other examples abound. Does such intercession or intervention compromise God's power? If it does, then there is no basis on which Christians can ask others to pray for them or believe that their prayers for someone else has any effect. And yet the Bible expressly teaches the importance of both. In fact, it is pointed out that "The fervent prayer of a righteous person is very powerful" (James 5:16)—and anyone in Heaven is righteous. The glory of God comes not from puppetry, but the free and coopera- tive activity of his creatures. That's why he created a world of angels and human persons with powers of reason and freewill! Moreover, as seen in the Book of Revelation, the intercession of the saints pertains to earthly matters. Is this communing with the dead? The answer is no, because the central Christian belief is that those who accept God are alive in him, living with the divine life, active in the affairs of God. In fact, this is precisely what we see in the Book of Revelation. And Jesus expressly says, "Have you not read what was said to you by God, 'I am the God of Abraham, the God of Isaac, and the God of Jacob?' He is not the God of the dead but of the living." (Matthew 22:31-32).

Polytheistic Paganism?

It is often assumed that devotion to the saints is simply a Christianized version of the paganism and polytheism of ancient Rome, Egypt, and so on. Simply as a matter of history this is utterly mistaken as shown by the Oxford scholar Peter Brown. [49] The pagans looked at the Christian devotion to the saints with repugnance. Julian the Apostate said that the Christian celebration of the dead was an ill-omened sight that displeased the pagan gods. The Egyptian pagans were horrified by contact with the bones of criminals (relics of martyrs). The pagan and polytheistic worlds assumed an unbridgeable gulf between the realms of the dead and the divine.

The invasion of the Christian view of reality overturned this map of the world bringing about (as Brown puts it) a joining of heaven and earth. The holy dead were with God and were more active now in the affairs of their fellows than when alive. They were powerful expressly because of their union with God (an unthinkable idea to the pagans). Their tombs became pilgrimage sites where exorcisms were performed and healings took place. Whereas cemeteries of the pre-Christian past were kept outside the city centers, the tombs of the saints became the centers of the new Christian communities. Graves became un-graves. The pagans who paid fearful homage to their nature spirits were now invited to discard such superstitions and turn instead to their friendly fellow humans, who were now with God. This tender devotion to the saints and awareness of their intercessory activity was embedded in the mental infrastructure of all Christians, learned, illiterate, rich, poor. If anything, says Brown, the devotion to the saints was a liberation from savage superstition and a triumph of incarnational and resurrection-centered Christianity. It is this, in fact, that sealed the fate of paganism and polytheism.

The Role of Mary

It should be noted also that the role of Mary in salvation history is now getting a second look in the Protestant world. An article in *Time* titled "Hail Mary," notes, "In a shift whose ideological breadth is unusual in the fragmented Protestant world, a long-standing wall around Mary appears to be eroding.... A growing number of Christian thinkers who are neither Catholic nor Eastern Orthodox (another branch of faith to which Mary is central) have concluded that their various traditions have shortchanged her in the very arena in which Protestantism most prides itself: the careful and full reading of Scripture. Arguments on the Virgin's behalf have appeared in a flurry of scholarly essays and popular articles." [50]

The contemporary outlook on Mary was also reviewed in the Protestant publication *Christian Century* in an article entitled "Protestants and Marian Devotion—What about Mary?" The article cites the works of the prominent Protestant theologian Robert Jenson—in particular his noted two-volume *Systematic Theology* (1997, 1999) and his *Mary; Mother of God* (2004). "[Mary's] womb was the physical site of the enfleshment of God. This leads Robert Jenson to a conclusion that may sting Protestant sensibilities—we ought to ask Mary to pray for us. Jenson argues that death does not sever the bonds of the body of Christ. To ask for a departed saint's prayer, then, is not in principle different from asking another Christian for her prayers. We hold that the saints are not simply gone, but are ever alive to God, and so we ought also consider them to be available as intercessors, and powerful ones at that. Jenson insists that 'the saints are not our way to Christ; he is our way to them.' Each saint's particular graces can be seen as reflections of the grace of Christ." [51]

Resurrection of the Body

Christians hold that the bodies of all humans will be resurrected at the end of time, because this was taught by Christ both in his preaching and in his own resurrection from the dead. The model for the resurrection is Christ's Risen Body, as described in the New Testament accounts. Of course, resurrection was already a familiar idea in Judaism. But there was no notion of a specific individual rising from the dead before the General Judgment.

It might be said that the doctrines of the resurrection and the Beatific Vision are both required if a life after death is to be a life worth living. The human person is a union of spirit and matter, of body and soul, and to exist as a separated soul is to remain in an unnatural state. Christianity tells us that we become "whole" when history has run its course.

John Haldane considers St. Paul's idea of a "spiritual body":

Paul had it in mind that the life of the world to come should involve a recognisably personal form of existence. Thus he would rightly think in terms of animation: of sights and sounds, of action and communication. On the other hand if the triumph over death is to be permanent, not just life *after* death but life *without* death, then the natural causes of decline and decay must be absent.... Accordingly, in whatever sense the future life is 'bodily' it cannot involve the sort of material processes that sustain life in this world. It may be spatial, it may involve movement, it may be characterized by features such as sights and sounds, but it must also be non-material to the extent of not involving privation or entropy—and on this account one might think of its occupants as having, in some sense, 'spiritual bodies.'"[52]

Conclusion

This overview of the religious history of primordial humanity, as it relates to the after-life, makes it abundantly clear that the ancient world as a whole believed in a life after death. It was also generally believed that the kind of life we lead on earth will determine the state of our continued existence. What warrant did the ancients have for such confident belief in things unseen? This was not like a belief that the world is flat, because the latter belief was reached on the basis of observations. The after-life, on the other hand, lies entirely beyond our ken. And yet our ancestors centered their entire lives around their particular understanding of the after-life.

Clearly, if there is a life after death and we are aware that it is related to our actions in this life, then it makes sense to synchronize our behavior accordingly. To that extent, after-life centered actions make sense. But what is especially amazing is the fact that—unaffected by constraints of era and culture, ethnicity and geography—humanity affirmed the reality of an after-life in which our choices determine our destiny beyond death. We know that their religious texts and traditions portrayed this same insight in different ways. But what gave birth to the beliefs enshrined in these texts and traditions? Was it a special insight into the nature of reality? Was it a thought implanted in the human mind by the divine Mind? Was it a result of encounters with eternity?

If indeed the after-life is a part of reality, and if God is not simply Creator but Lover and Revealer, this is the kind of subtle but unmistakable guidance that we would expect. No society, no group, no human would be left without a celestial compass. Moreover, these hints complement the glimpses of "the other side" given through other sources, as well as what we know from our own experience of being human.

When it comes to our own precise conception of ultimate destiny, we turn to the religion or view of the world that we hold to be true. But whatever our view, we cannot but marvel at the commonality of the testimony of humanity as it pertains to a life beyond death. To believe in an after-life is the natural train of thought of the normal human. To deny it is…well, let me stop here!

Chapter 4

The Hereafter Here and Now—Visions of Heaven, Hell, and the Grateful Dead

NDEs first introduced the serious possibility of the after-life to the modern mind. NDEs, as typically understood, involve a brief round-trip journey to "the other side." But for centuries, there have been reports of an entirely different class of phenomena. In these cases, the after-life "visits" the here and now! Out of the blue. These are what we have we have called After-Life Visitations or ALVs. Reports of ALVs, in fact, have persisted into modern times.

How credible are such reports and how relevant are they to our study? Strictly speaking, the reports concern one-of-a-kind sorts of phenomena. By the nature of the case, this is all they could be. Because they involve a state of being that lies beyond our space-time realm, these phenomena cannot be "scientifically" studied (in terms of observation and measurement), and can only be experienced on a "one-of-a-kind" basis. Minimally, their credibility rests on two pillars:

- ✧ The credibility of the witness who provides the account.
- ✧ The consistency of this account with what has been said about the after-life by other sources.

But there are other criteria as well that can be deployed:

- ⤍ Has there been any concerted attempt to "authenticate" these reports?
- ⤍ Are they spontaneous or "induced" as in the case of hypnotic regressions or mediums?

Even if a report passes these "tests" we cannot know them to be true in the same way we know that there is a force of gravity. We would have to make our own judgments as to the veracity of the witnesses and the accuracy of their accounts.

Which leads to another question: are these kinds of phenomena relevant to this study? They are certainly helpful as concrete illustrations of the content of traditional beliefs. But this begs the question of whether they can function as evidence. Here we can say that they are as useful as evidence as NDEs. Both NDEs and ALVs rest on the reliability of the witnesses concerned and the coherence of their reports with what we know from other sources.

Both NDEs and ALVs can be explained away as tricks played by the brain or plain fraud. Certain of the narratives in both cases can be traced to psycho-physical abnormalities and willful fraud. But this does not mean that they can all be classified under these twin categories. Counterfeit notes do not prove the non-existence of real currency. So, at the end of the day, we are left with claims of certain phenomena that may give us new insights into the nature of the after-life. We can see them either as mirages in a dreary wilderness or lights in the darkness. They cannot bear the whole load of "proving" the actuality of the after-life or even their picture of the after-life. They are simply one more array of dots we can connect as we piece together a picture of the life to come.

Three Varieties of ALVs

Three varieties of After-Life Visitations are of importance here:

1. The intercession of the saints and their interaction with the living.
2. Prayers for the dead and visits of the Poor Souls.
3. Visions of Heaven and Hell.

All three varieties are familiar to millions of people, but are curiously absent in most books on the after-life. This is possibly because certain aspects of these phenomena are peculiar to Christianity although, at a fundamental level, they embody themes present in the primordial religious traditions. In particular, some critics are turned off by the idea of Hell. But the ideas of Heaven and Hell are present in most of the world religions. Consequently, they have to be taken seriously by all investigators into the after-life, no matter what their ideological preference.

Christians and Non-Christians

Granted, these ALVs are reported in the context of certain beliefs about Jesus of Nazareth. But there are non-Christians who can and do affirm the reality of an after-life and the possibility of separation or union with God. For them these accounts can be just as instructive and moving as for a Christian considering the after-life accounts in the *Odysseus* and the Zoroastrian Book of *Arda Viraz*. This is not to say that Christians should disavow their claims about Jesus or put them on hold. A Christian is committed to the belief that Jesus is not only God incarnate, but that his redemptive death was required to make Heaven possible and acceptance of him as the Lord is the ordinary path to salvation. But Christians also hold that we cannot limit either God's unconditional love for all humans or his ability to go beyond this ordinary path. God desires the salvation of every person. In any case, a discussion on the identity of Jesus is a quite different discussion from one on whether or not we survive physical death.

Two Objections

Two other objections must be addressed. Those who pursue investigations into mediums and spiritistic communications will demand a seat at the table, pointing to their investigations as legitimate inquiries into the hereafter. At the other end of the spectrum, certain Christians will condemn all discussions involving Purgatory, saints, and visions as prohibited by Christianity because, according to these critics, such phenomena are nothing but investigations into mediums and spiritistic communications! This is as clear-cut an example of not being able to please everyone as you can get.

Via Medium

Concerning the first charge it should be said that our investigation has restricted itself to phenomena that are spontaneous by their very nature, because there is less chance of deception in such instances. The world of mediums and spiritualists and ouija boards is built around the premise of inducing, even manipulating, the dead to manifest themselves. So these phenomena are not spontaneous. Neither can they be considered more "scientific" because it is impossible to determine with scientific precision who (if anyone) is being made present.

For good reason, these kinds of attempts have been looked on with disapproval by most of the major religions. This is because of the perceived dangers of freelancing with the supernatural.

Now let's consider the opposite objection. The critics in this instance point to Deuteronomy 18:10-11, which says, "Let no one be found among you...who is a medium or a spiritist or who consults the dead." We have already pointed out that the Christian understanding is that all those who live with the life of Christ, whether here or in the hereafter, are alive. The Transfiguration account in the New Testament, of course, shows Jesus communicating with Moses and Elijah, and the Book of Revelation shows the saints in Heaven concerning themselves with earthly affairs. There is no question of idle curiosity in any of this because all are focused on reconciling all things through Christ, "everything in heaven and everything on earth." (Colossians 1:19-20). There is also no question of questioning the sufficiency of Christ's work. The followers of Christ are called to disseminate his message and participate in his mission: "It makes me happy to suffer for you, as I am suffering now, and in my own body to do what I can to make up all that has still to be undergone by Christ for the sake of his body, the Church." (Colossians 1:24).

Assessing and Authenticating One-of-a-Kind Claims

What about the viability of "authenticating" the reports and claims considered here, given that they belong to the "one-of-a-kind" category? Here we should note that there is only one body that has historically sought to investigate and "certify" claims of this kind, namely the Catholic Church. There is no comparable body among the other Christian denominations that studies and pronounces on claims relating to the appearances of saints and the extraordinary in general. Whatever one thinks of the judgments made by this body, it has at the very least put in place a system and mechanism to weed out obvious fraud. Its investigative infrastructure has been especially refined in the last two centuries. With the aid of scientists, physicians, and theologians, it has rigorously examined witnesses, testimonies, and assorted kinds of evidence relating to alleged supernatural phenomena. In general, it follows a guilty until proved innocent approach, and tends to be highly skeptical. Moreover, the Church has consistently stated that no one is obliged to believe any claim relating to a "private" revelation of the kind it examines—even those it has judged "worthy of belief."

The Saints Come Marching Down

We have seen earlier that the intercession of the saints in Heaven on behalf of their brothers and sisters still on earth was not simply a peripheral phenomenon. Its reality was embedded in the Christian consciousness. Many of the saints, while alive on earth, were noted for their virtue and sometimes their miraculous powers. Saint Padre Pio of Pietrelcina, for instance, was reputed to bilocate (be in two places at the same time), read souls, prophesy, heal, and much else. He was also known for the stigmata. The five wounds associated with the crucifixion of Christ manifested themselves on his body for a period of 50 years until his death. In some 100 cases, the bodies of those acclaimed as saints have not decayed throughout periods of decades and centuries. Although, this could be attributed to prior embalming or to environmental conditions in some instances, it certainly does not serve as an explanation in several notable cases. This is especially true of the bodies on public display. The most famous instance is that of St. Bernadette of Lourdes who died in 1879. Her body was not only found to be incorrupt, but the internal organs were found to be supple (with the liver being "soft and almost normal in consistency" when the body was opened at the third exhumation).

Extraordinary as these kinds of phenomena may be, the Christian faithful were more interested in the intercessory activity of the saints. There have been many volumes written on the miracles and favors rendered by saints in response to petitions. In fact, saints have been named patrons of different professions, ailments, cities, peoples, and a whole host of other things for particular kinds of miracles associated with them. St. Peregrine is the patron for cancer patients, St. Anthony for lost articles, St. Joseph of Cupertino for pilots (he was known for his levitation), and St. Jude for impossible causes and the like. Any further study of these kinds of claims and phenomena would take us too far afield from the central theme of this book. More significantly, it would require a work of many volumes. For our immediate purposes, it is enough to state that the intercessory activity of the Holy Ones of God has been taken for granted by millions of people for nearly 2,000 years.

The Appearances of the Faithful Departed

Beyond the intercessory activity of the faithful departed we encounter also their "return" to this world. Throughout centuries we have had innumerable claims of "separated souls" appearing to the living, some of these souls claiming to be in Purgatory, others in Heaven. A frequent motif is a soul in Purgatory coming to a holy person asking for assistance through prayer. The saints in

Heaven have also been believed to manifest themselves. St. Anthony of Padua, St. Teresa of Lisieux, St. Padre Pio of Pietrelcina, and St. Philomena, the ancient child-martyr, are the saints most commonly reported to have appeared to those seeking their intercession. Also notable were the glimpses of Heaven, Hell, and Purgatory that were imparted either through visions or journeys to the "places" concerned.

The Mother of Jesus

An integral element of the celestial-terrestrial interaction in Christian history was the role of Mary, the Mother of Jesus. Her reported appearances across centuries involved miracles, exhortations, and visions of the after-life.

These reports and claims are relevant to our understanding of the nature of the after-life. Suppose it is true that the holy ones of God (those who led holy lives) really do interact with our everyday world and the lives of the faithful. Such being the case, we are able to get a fairly robust picture of activities that can be performed by human persons after death.

What These Visitiations Mean for Our Understanding of the After-life

Granted, we cannot provide scientific or philosophical proof for such interaction. But then again we are dealing with something that falls entirely outside the techniques and tools of science and philosophy. The activities of a "separated" soul cannot be monitored by any method or system that works only with the quantitatively measurable. In fact these tools cannot even detect the non-separated soul (that is, the soul in everyday experience)! Likewise, the rules and axioms of logic and metaphysics cannot determine the veracity of the empirical claims that are inevitably involved in ALVs. Take the case of one person claiming to have had an encounter with another person who says she is the Virgin Mary (while offering such additional evidence as was found in Lourdes or Fatima). Or consider a scenario in which a terminally ill patient is cured and claims that the apparent miracle was a fruit of seeking the intercession of a particular saint. Neither science nor philosophy can prove or disprove the claims made in either of these instances.

The reasonable thing to do in this situation is to study as much of the evidence as is available. What we find is that there are thousands of people who have reported appearances of the saints and the souls in Purgatory. Likewise, millions have claimed experiences of the intercessory activity of saints.

Remarkably all of these reports and claims form a coherent whole that is consistent with at least the Christian understanding of the after-life. But the key point for our purposes is this: Interaction with the after-life world was and is considered so normal that it is not even thought of in terms of life-after-death!

We will begin our survey with the visions of the after-life presented in three famous appearances of Mary, those said to have taken place at Fatima, Portugal; Medjugorje, Bosnia; and Kibeho, Rwanda. Following these we chronicle the after-life visions of two famous saints (St. Faustina Kowalska and St. Catherine of Genoa) and end with observations and insights from a veteran of visitations from the other world. The three reported appearances of Mary occurred in the 20th century (with one of them reputedly still continuing). Of the other three accounts, the first (Faustina) belongs to the 20th century, the second (Catherine) to the 15th, and the third (Maria Simma), again, to the 20th. Although there are hundreds of accounts of this kind, the ones referenced here give us a feel for what is being claimed.

Fatima

Three shepherd children, Lucia dos Santos and Francisco and Jacinta Marto, claimed to have seen the Virgin Mary between May 13 and October 13, 1917, in Fatima, Portugal. Thousands of observers held that they witnessed a miracle of the sun during the last encounter. The Fatima Secrets have since become an international sensation and various prophecies made at Fatima were subsequently said to have been fulfilled. But what is relevant to our purposes is the vision of Hell said to have been given during one of the appearances. The account below is taken from Lucia's Third Memoir (August 31, 1941).

> Our Lady showed us a great sea of fire which seemed to be under the earth. Plunged in this fire were demons and souls in human form, like transparent burning embers, all blackened or burnished bronze, floating about in the conflagration, now raised into the air by the flames that issued from within themselves together with great clouds of smoke, now falling back on every side like sparks in a huge fire, without weight or equilibrium, and amid shrieks and groans of pain and despair, which horrified us and made us tremble with fear. The demons could be distinguished by their terrifying and repulsive likeness to frightful and unknown animals, all black and transparent. This vision lasted but an instant. How can we ever be grateful enough to our kind heavenly Mother, who had already prepared us by promising, in the first Apparition, to take us to heaven. Otherwise, I think we would have died of fear and terror.

"We then looked up at Our Lady, who said to us so kindly and so sadly: "You have seen hell where the souls of poor sinners go.""[1]

Medjugorje

Medjugorje, Bosnia, is without doubt the most influential apparition since Fatima. More than 30 million pilgrims including 50,000 priests and hundreds of bishops and cardinals have come to Medjugorje. Hundreds of thousands have claimed that their lives were changed by Medjugorje. Admirers of Medjugorje included Pope John Paul II, Mother Teresa, and Fr. Gabriele Amorth, the world's dean of exorcists.

Six children, now adults, Marija Pavlovic-Lunetti, Vicka Ivankovic-Mijatovic, Ivan Dragicevic, Mirjana Dragicevic-Soldo, Ivanka Ivankovic-Elez, and Jakov Colo reported witnessing appearances of Mary on a daily basis since June 1981.

During the course of these appearances, Vicka and Jakov said that they were taken by Mary to Heaven, Hell, and Purgatory, while the others said they were shown these "places" as in a movie. They have spoken about their experiences on numerous occasions. Here we provide excerpts relating to Heaven, Hell, and Purgatory from their interviews with the author Janice Connell.[2]

Vicka

Is it true that you yourself have personally seen Heaven, Hell, and Purgatory?

Yes. The Blessed Mother has shown me Heaven, Hell, and Purgatory.

Why?

Many people today do not believe there is a place or state of life after death of the body. They believe that when we die, life is over. The Blessed Mother says no; on the contrary, we are only passengers on earth. She has come to remind us of the eternal truths of the Gospel.

Are Heaven and Hell actual places?
Yes. I saw them.

How?
Two ways—I saw with my eyes—

A vision?

Yes. And then I visited these places. Jacov and I were taken there by the Blessed Mother.

Tell us about Heaven.

Heaven is a vast space, and it has a brilliant light, which does not leave it. It is a life which we do not know here on earth.... When God has filled you with His love, bored is a word that has no meaning. People in Heaven know the absolute fullness of a created being....

Did the people talk to you?

It was very unusual. They were speaking, but I could not understand them.

What about Hell— is it a place too?

Yes.

Do many people go there today?

Yes. We saw many people in Hell. Many are there already, and many more will go there when they die.

Why so many?

The Blessed Mother says that those people who are in Hell are there because they chose to go there. They wanted to go to Hell.... They deny Him [God], even when it is time to die. And they continue to deny Him, after they are dead. It is their choice. It is their will that they go to Hell. They choose Hell.

Describe Hell as you remember it.

In the center of this place is a great fire, like an ocean of raging flames. We could see people before they went into the fire, and then we could see them coming out of the fire. Before they go into the fire, they look like normal people. The more they are against God's will, the deeper they enter into the fire, and the deeper they go, the more they rage against Him. When they come out of the fire, they don't have human shape anymore; they are more like grotesque animals, but unlike anything on earth. It's as if they were never human beings before.

Can you describe them?

They were horrible. Ugly. Angry. And each was different; no two looked alike.

After they came out of the ocean of fire, what did they do?

When they came out, they were raging and smashing everything around and hissing and gnashing and screeching.

You said that God condemns no one, that people choose Hell for themselves. Would it be fair, then, to say that if you can choose Hell, you can also choose Heaven?

There are two differences: the people on earth who choose Hell know that they will go there. But nobody is sure on the earth if they are going to Heaven or Purgatory. Not one of us is sure.

Can you be sure that you are not going to Hell?

Yes. Follow God's will. The most important thing is to know that God loves us.

How does this knowledge help us to go to Heaven?

When we know for sure that God loves us, we try to love him in return—to respond to God's love for us by being faithful in good times and bad.

Has seeing Hell changed how you pray?

Oh, yes! Now I pray for the conversion of sinners! I know what awaits them if they refuse to convert.

What about Purgatory? Is it near Hell?

First is Heaven, then Purgatory, then Hell. It, too, is a very big space. We couldn't see people in Purgatory, just a misty, gray fog. It looked like ashes. We could sense persons weeping, moaning, trembling, in what seemed like terrible suffering. The Blessed Mother said: "These people need your prayers, especially the ones who have no one to pray for them." And that is why we have prayed so much for these poor souls; they desperately need our prayers to go from Purgatory to Heaven.

The only time they can see us on earth is during those moments we pray for them—is that true?

Yes. They can see us on earth when we pray for them, by name. Please tell people to pray for their own family members who are dead. Please tell people to pray and forgive each other, the living and the dead.

Jakov

Did you see Hell?
Yes.

Can you tell us about it?
Very seldom do I talk about Hell.

Why?
I choose not to think about Hell. The self-chosen suffering there is beyond your ability to comprehend.

Does it cause you pain?
More than you can understand.

Why?
Because no one needs to go to Hell. It is the ultimate waste.

What can people do to keep from going to Hell?
Believe in God, no matter what happens in a lifetime.

Mirjana

I saw Heaven as if it were a movie. The first thing I noticed was the faces of the people there; they were radiating a type of inner light that showed how immensely happy they were. Heaven is beautiful beyond anything I know on earth.

Do the people you saw have bodies?
Yes.

What ages were they?

They were different from what we are like now. Perhaps they were all around 30 years of age.

Did you see Purgatory?

Yes. There are several levels in Purgatory. The more you pray on earth, the higher your level in Purgatory will be.

How many levels are there?

The lowest level is the closest to Hell, where the suffering is the most intense. The highest level is closest to Heaven, and there the suffering is the least. What level you are on depends on the state of purity of your soul. The lower the people are in Purgatory and the less they are able to pray, the more they suffer. The higher a person is in Purgatory and the easier it is for him to pray, the more he enjoys praying, and the less he suffers.

How long do people stay in Purgatory?

I don't know. I do know that the Blessed Mother has asked us to pray for the souls in Purgatory. They are helpless to pray for themselves. Through prayer, we on earth can do much to help them.

Ivanka

Did you see Heaven, Hell, and Purgatory?

I saw Purgatory and Heaven as a picture. I told the Blessed Mother I did not want to see Hell.

Heaven?

Everyone I saw was filled with a happiness I can't explain—and I can't forget! God made us for Heaven. If you pray, you will know that.

What was Purgatory like?
Only darkness.

Why did the Blessed Mother show you Heaven and Purgatory?
She wants to remind her children of the results of their choices on earth.

Does God love unbelievers too?
God loves everybody in the whole world. He made everyone. He loves everyone. God is the Creator. He loves what He creates.

Ivan

Will you tell us about Heaven?
Heaven is worth any cost! Jesus showed us that with His death on the Cross. His death was not the end. He rose from the dead, glorified, to put an end to death forever for God's children. People in Heaven are happy. They live in the fullness of God. You'll have to experience it to know. It is better than anything you can imagine!

Marija

Would you tell us about Purgatory?
Yes. Purgatory is a large place. It is foggy. It is ash gray. It is misty. You cannot see people there. It is as if they are immersed in deep clouds. You can feel that the people in the mist are traveling, hitting each other. They can pray for us, but not for themselves. They are desperately in need of our prayers. The Blessed Mother asks us to pray for the poor souls in Purgatory, because during their life here, one moment they thought there is no God, then they recognized Him, then they went to Purgatory where they saw there is a God, and now they need our prayers. With our prayers we can send them to Heaven. The biggest suffering that souls in Purgatory have is that they see there is a God, but they did not accept Him here on earth. Now they long so much to come close to God. Now they suffer so intensely, because they recognize how much they have hurt God, how many chances they had on earth, and how many times they disregarded God.

Have you ever seen Hell?
Yes, it's a large space with a big sea of fire in the middle. There are many people there. I particularly noticed a beautiful young girl. But when she came near the fire, she was no longer beautiful. She came out of the fire like an

animal; she was no longer human. The Blessed Mother told me that God gives us all choices. Everyone responds to these choices. Everyone can choose if he wants to go to Hell or not. Anyone who goes to Hell chooses Hell.

How and why does a soul choose Hell for himself for all eternity?

In the moment of death, God gives us the light to see ourselves as we really are. God gives freedom of choice to everybody during his life on earth. The one who lives in sin on earth can see what he has done and recognize himself as he really is. When he sees himself and his life, the only possible place for him is Hell. He chooses Hell, because that is what he is. That is where he fits. It is his own wish. God does not make the choice. God condemns no one. We condemn ourselves. Every individual has free choice. God gave us freedom.[3]

Kibeho

The Marian apparitions of Kibeho in Rwanda took place from 1981 to 1989. As in some other apparitions, the Virgin announced impending bloodshed on a horrific scale. The warnings issued in the apparitions turned out to be prophetically accurate. As in Medjugorje, the apparitions themselves took place in the very region that would shortly become synonymous around the world with genocide and systematic butchery. The apparitions were officially approved by the Vatican in 2001. Several of the visionaries were given glimpses of Heaven, Hell, and Purgatory. Their accounts of these visions are excerpted from *Our Lady of Kibeho* by Immaculee Ilibagiza.

Alphonsine

"The first place Mary took me was dark and very frightening. It was filled with shadows and groans of sadness and pain. She called it 'the Place of Despair,' where the road leading away from God's Light ends. Our travels were many…we moved across the stars until we arrived in a place of golden light filled with happiness and laughter and songs sung by so many joyous voices that I thought the souls of all the people who once had lived were floating around singing praises to God."

Anathalie

Anathalie was taken to three different worlds, "each of which was bathed in its own unique color and light." In the first she saw "millions of people dressed in white. All seemed overwhelmingly happy." Mary told her "that this was Isenderezwa z'byishimo, the place of the cherished of God."

From here they moved on to "a world where the light was as dim as dusk. Below us were people dressed in clothes of dreary and duller colors in comparison to the other worlds we'd seen. Most of them seemed content, but many seemed quite sad and were even suffering. Mary said, 'This is Isesengurwa, a place of purification; the people you see are Intarambirwa, those who persevere.'

"The last place we visited was a land of twilight where the only illumination was an unpleasant shade of red that reminded me of congealed blood," testified Anathalie. "The heat that rose from that world was stifling and dry—it brushed my face like a flame, and I feared that my skin would blister and crack. I couldn't look at the countless people who populated that unhappy place because their misery and anguish pained me so greatly. Mary didn't have to say the name of this place...I knew I was in hell."

Explaining the three worlds further, Mary told her, "The first place, the happy world of the cherished of God, was reserved for people whose hearts are good, who pray regularly, and who strive always to follow God's will. Our second visit to the place of purification was for those who called on God only during times of trouble, turning away from Him when their troubles were over. The last place of heat and no name was for those who never paid God any attention at all."[4]

St. Faustina Kowalska

St. Faustina Kowalska (1905–1938) was a Polish nun who claimed to be the recipient of visions and revelations of Jesus and was known for such gifts as prophecy and the reading of souls. She was canonized a saint by John Paul II in 2000. Her experiences are chronicled in *Diary: Divine Mercy in My Soul*. The central theme of the messages she received was the Mercy of God and the divine desire to save all souls. She was shown both the consequences of refusing God, as well as the overwhelming love of God for every person.

Among her visions was the visit to Hell recorded below:

I, Sister Faustina Kowalska, by the order of God, have visited the Abysses of Hell so that I might tell souls about it and testify to its existence...the devils were full of hatred for me, but they had to obey me at the command of God. What I have written is but a pale shadow of the things I saw. But I noticed one thing: That most of the souls there are those who disbelieved that there is a hell (741).

Today, I was led by an angel to the Chasms of Hell. It is a place of great torture; how awesomely large and extensive it is! The kinds of tortures I saw:

- ✧ The First Torture that constitutes hell is: The loss of God.

- ✧ The Second is: Perpetual remorse of conscience.

- ✧ The Third is: That one's condition will never change.

- ✧ The Fourth is: The fire that will penetrate the soul without destroying it. A terrible suffering since it is a purely spiritual fire, lit by God's anger.

- ✧ The Fifth Torture is: Continual darkness and a terrible suffocating smell, and despite the darkness, the devils and the souls of the damned see each other and all the evil, both of others and their own.

- ✧ The Sixth Torture is: The constant company of Satan.

- ✧ The Seventh Torture is: Horrible despair, hatred of God, vile words, curses, and blasphemies....

I am writing this at the command of God, so that no soul may find an excuse by saying there is no hell, or that nobody has ever been there, and so no one can say what it is like...how terribly souls suffer there! Consequently, I pray even more fervently for the conversion of sinners. I incessantly plead God's mercy upon them. O My Jesus, I would rather be in agony until the end of the world, amidst the greatest sufferings, than offend you by the least sin (741).

Against this backdrop of the possibility of rejecting God, she presents a series of messages from God in which mercy is proclaimed as the greatest divine attribute:

✧

"Proclaim that mercy is the greatest attribute of God. All the works of My hands are crowned with mercy." (301).

✧

"As often as you want to make Me happy, speak to the world about My great and unfathomable mercy." (164)

✧

"Let the greatest sinners place their trust in My mercy. They have the right before others to trust in the abyss of My mercy. My daughter, write about My mercy towards tormented souls. Souls that make an appeal to My mercy delight Me. To such souls I grant even more graces than they ask. I cannot punish even the greatest sinner if he makes an appeal to My compassion, but on the contrary, I justify him in My unfathomable and inscrutable mercy. Write: before I come as a just Judge, I first open wide the door of My mercy."(1146).[5]

Saint Catherine of Genoa

Catherine of Genoa (1447–1510) was a mystic who worked with the sick and the poor. She is considered one of the great authorities on Purgatory and the following is an excerpt from her account of visiting Purgatory:

Catherine found herself "while still in the flesh, placed by the fiery love of God in Purgatory, which burnt her, cleansing whatever in her needed cleansing, to the end that when she passed from this life she might be presented to the sight of God, her dear Love. By means of this loving fire, she understood in her soul the state of the souls of the faithful who are placed in Purgatory to purge them of all the rust and stains of sin of which they have not rid themselves in this life. And since this Soul, placed by the divine fire in this loving Purgatory, was united to that divine love and content with all that was wrought in her, she understood the state of the souls who are in Purgatory. And she said:

The souls who are in Purgatory cannot, as I understand, choose but be there, and this is by God's ordinance who therein has done justly. They cannot turn their thoughts back to themselves, nor can they say, 'Such sins I have committed for which I deserve to be here,' nor, 'I would that I had not committed them for then I would go now to Paradise,' nor, 'That one will leave sooner than I,' nor, 'I will leave sooner than he.' They can have neither of themselves nor of others any memory, whether of good or evil, whence they would have greater pain than they suffer ordinarily. So happy are they to be within God's ordinance, and that He should do all which pleases Him, as it pleases Him that in their greatest pain they cannot think of themselves. They see only the working of the divine goodness, which leads man to itself mercifully, so that he no longer sees aught of the pain or good which may befall him. Nor would these souls be in pure charity if they could see that pain or good. They cannot see that they are in pain because of their sins; that sight they cannot hold in their minds because in it there would be an active imperfection, which cannot be where no actual sin can be.

Only once, as they pass from this life, do they see the cause of the Purgatory they endure; never again do they see it for in another sight of it there would be self. Being then in charity from which they cannot now depart by any actual fault, they can no longer will nor desire save with the pure will of pure charity. Being in that fire of Purgatory, they are within the divine ordinance, which is pure charity, and in nothing can they depart thence for they are deprived of the power to sin as of the power to merit.[6]

The Grateful Dead

Mary Simma (1915–2004) was an Austrian mystic who reported receiving visits from souls in Purgatory starting in 1940. She was well known all over Europe for her experiences, often receiving visits from leading Church officials. Below are excerpts from an interview she granted to Sr. Emmanuel.

One night, around 3 or 4 o'clock in the morning, I heard someone coming into my bedroom. This woke me up: I looked to see who on earth could have walked into my bedroom. Well, I saw a complete stranger. He walked back and forth slowly. I said to him severely: 'How did you get in here? Go away!' But he continued to walk impatiently around the bedroom, as if he hadn't heard. So I asked him again: 'What are you doing?' But as he still didn't answer, I jumped out of bed and tried to grab him, but I grasped only air. There was nothing there. So I went back to bed, but again I heard him pacing back and forth.

I wondered how I could see this man, but I couldn't grab him. I rose again to hold onto him and stop him walking around; again, I grasped only emptiness.

Puzzled, I went back to bed. He didn't come back, but I couldn't get back to sleep. The next day, after Mass, I went to see my spiritual director and told him everything. He told me that if this should happen again, I shouldn't ask, "Who are you?" but "What do you want from me?"

The following night, the man returned, definitely the same man. I asked him "What do you want from me?" He replied: "Have three Masses celebrated for me and I will be delivered."

So I understood that it was a soul in Purgatory. My spiritual father confirmed this.

He also advised never to turn away the poor souls, but to accept with generosity whatever they asked of me."

Maria, do the souls in Purgatory have, nevertheless, joy and hope in the midst of their suffering?

Yes. No soul would want to come back from Purgatory to the earth. They have knowledge which is infinitely beyond ours. They just could not decide to return to the darkness of the earth.

Can you tell us if it is God who sends a soul into Purgatory, or if the soul itself decides to go there?

It is the soul itself which wants to go to Purgatory, in order to be pure before going to Heaven.

Why does one go to Purgatory? What are the sins which lead most to Purgatory?

Sins against charity, against the love of one's neighbor, hardness of heart, hostility, slandering, calumny—all these things.

Who are those who have the greatest chance of going straight to Heaven?

Those who have a good heart towards everyone. Love covers a multitude of sins.

I would like to ask you: at the moment of death, is there a time in which the soul still has the chance to turn towards God, even after a sinful life, before entering into eternity—a time, if you like, between apparent death and real death?

Yes, yes, the Lord gives several minutes to each one, in order to regret his sins and to decide: I accept or I do not accept to see God. There, we see a film of our lives.

I knew a man who believed in the Church's teachings but not in eternal life. One day, he fell gravely ill, and slid into a coma. He saw himself in a room with a board on which all his deeds were written, the good and the bad. Then the board disappeared as well as the walls of the room, and it was infinitely beautiful. Then he woke up from his coma and decided to change his life.

At the moment of death, does God reveal himself with the same intensity to all souls?

Each one is given knowledge of his life and also the sufferings to come; but it is not the same for everyone. The intensity of the Lord's revelation depends on each one's life.

Are there different degrees in Purgatory?

Yes, there is a great difference of degree of moral suffering. Each soul has a unique suffering, particular to it; there are different degrees.

What is the difference between how you are living with the souls of the departed, and the practices of spiritism?

We are not supposed to summon up the souls—I don't try to get them to come. In spiritism people try to call them forth.

This distinction is quite clear, and we must take it very seriously.... It is forbidden, strictly forbidden, to call up the dead. As for me, I have never done so, I do not do so, and I never will do so. When something appears to me, God alone permits it.[7]

Going Forward

The accounts presented here are simply headline stories. There are numerous other such reports of the after-life as witnessed by those who claim to have had visits from Heaven or Purgatory. We have said that these belong to the realm of private revelation and each account should be studied on its own merits.

What these accounts highlight are the following claims:

- ↩ There is an after-life.
- ↩ There are three states of being in the after-life.
- ↩ The kind of after-life we enter depends on the kind of life we lead on earth.

This, of course, is also the overall message of the primordial-universal religions and of NDEs. Life after death can hardly be seen as wish-fulfillment when we consider the fact that not all accounts are pleasant (either in visions of Hell, of hellish NDEs, or of the accounts of Hell in the various religions).

There is a fourth message highlighted here as well: We fail the dead by forgetting about them. Life after death is not simply an individualistic affair. It is a state that affirms the solidarity of those who departed this world with their families, friends, and all other humans in the here-and-now.

Chapter 5

Contemporary Encounters With Eternity

We have discussed NDEs, accounts of the after-life in ancient religions, and visions of the hereafter delivered in the here-and-now. We now complement these three kinds of phenomena with a personal touch.

Below are excerpts from recent visits to the after-life that each have their own distinctive dynamic. These involve:

- ➴ Sir Alfred Ayer, the Oxford atheist who caught a quick glimpse of a possible hereafter. Although he later reinterpreted the experience, his first comment to the attending physician was that he had seen God.

- ➴ The popular Christian author C.S. Lewis, who is reported to have paid a posthumous visit to a theologian friend.

- ➴ An atheist academic.

- ➴ A dentist from Colombia.

The encounters, partially recounted here, changed the perspectives of the recipients not just on the hereafter, but on their lives here and now.

Sir Alfred Ayer

I had the pleasure of meeting Sir Alfred before his NDE and discussing the existence of the soul. Ayer did not believe in a subsistent soul, but confirmed to me that, in his view, the mental was distinct from the physical. Although I remained in touch with him after his NDE, we never discussed his experience.

In a public discussion with Dr. Raymond Moody soon after the event, Ayer did say that his experience led him to believe in the after-life. In a later article for the London *Times* titled, "What I Saw When I Was Dead," Ayer was noncommittal with regard to the after-life. The attending doctor, however, later revealed that Ayer was much more forthcoming immediately after his experience. Excerpts from both accounts are given here.

Ayer's Account

In his article, Sir Alfred said, "The only memory that I have of an experience, closely encompassing my death, is very vivid.

"I was confronted by a red light, exceedingly bright, and also very painful even when I turned away from it. I was aware that this light was responsible for the government of the universe. Among its ministers were two creatures who had been put in charge of space....

"On the face of it, these experiences, on the assumption that the last one was veridical, are rather strong evidence that death does not put an end to consciousness.

"Does it follow that there is a future life? Not necessarily. The trouble is that there are different criteria for being dead, which are indeed logically compatible but may not always be satisfied together.

"So there it is. My recent experiences have slightly weakened my conviction that my genuine death, which is due fairly soon, will be the end of me, though I continue to hope that it will be."[1]

A Report from the Attending Doctor

A recent news story disclosed the report of the doctor who attended to Ayer.

"I haven't told this to anybody before," said Dr. Jeremy George, senior consultant in the Department of Thoracic Medicine at London University's Middlesex Hospital. On the table in front of him were the official hospital notes of "Sir Alfred Ayer, date of birth 29/10/10, of 51 York Street, London, W1."

We were discussing the incident of June, 1988, when the eminent 77-year-old British philosopher, arguably the most influential 20th-century rationalist after Bertrand Russell, famously "died" in London University Hospital. His heart stopped for four minutes when he apparently choked on a slice of smoked salmon smuggled in by a former mistress....

In the early evening of June 6, Ayer later wrote, he "carelessly tossed" a slice of salmon down this throat. Choking as it went the wrong way down, he was clinically dead for four minutes. The hospital notes state: "cardiac arrest with bradycardia and asystole, but was resuscitated....

In order to ascertain whether Ayer had suffered any brain damage, Professor Spiro, the senior consultant, and Dr. George then had to subject Ayer to a general knowledge quiz to test his brain.

"I think we asked him who the prime minister was, and what day was it," said Dr. George. "The answers quickly shut us up. They were all correct. He blew us out of the water. There was absolutely no brain damage. He was very lucid. I think he wanted to be asked more questions, such as the name the players of the winning football team of the First Division. We had no idea if he was making them up or not, we just assumed he got them right."

That same day, having finished his rounds, Dr. George returned to Ayer's bedside. "I came back to talk to him. Very discreetly, I asked him, as a philosopher, what was it like to have had a near-death experience? He suddenly looked rather sheepish. Then he said, 'I saw a Divine Being. I'm afraid I'm going to have to revise all my various books and opinions.'

"He clearly said 'Divine Being,'" said Dr. George. "He was confiding in me, and I think he was slightly embarrassed because it was unsettling for him as an atheist. He spoke in a very confidential manner. I think he felt he had come face to face with God, or his maker, or what one might say was God.

"Later, when I read his article, I was surprised to see he had left out all mention of it. I was simply amused. I wasn't very familiar with his philosophy at the time of the incident, so the significance wasn't immediately obvious. I didn't realize he was a logical positivist...."

Despite declaring himself a "born-again atheist," his friends and family noticed that Freddie—like the 63 patients interviewed for last week's report—certainly seemed to change.

"Freddie became so much nicer after he died," said Dee. [Ayer's wife]. "He was not nearly so boastful. He took an interest in other people." Ayer also told the writer Edward St. Aubyn in France that he had had "a kind of resurrection" and for the first time in his life, he had begun to notice scenery. In France, on a mountain near his villa, he said, "I suddenly stopped and looked out at the sea and thought, my God, how beautiful this is...for 26 years I had never really looked at it before."

"What is also undeniably true—and has never been reported on—is that at the end of his life, Freddie spent more and more time with his former BBC debating opponent, the Jesuit priest and philosopher Frederick Copleston, who was at Freddie's funeral at Golders Green crematorium.

"They got closer and closer and, in the end, he was Freddie's closest friend," said Dee. "It was quite extraordinary. As he got older, Freddie realized more and more that philosophy was just chasing its own tail."[2]

C.S. Lewis

The biblical scholar J.B. Phillips reported a vision of C.S. Lewis shortly after Lewis's death:

Many of us who believe in what is technically known as the Communion of Saints must have experienced the sense of nearness, for a fairly short time, of those whom we love soon after they have died. This has certainly happened to me several times. But the late C. S. Lewis, whom I did not know very well and had only seen in the flesh once, but with whom I had corresponded a fair amount, gave me an unusual experience. A few days after his death, while I was watching television, he 'appeared' sitting in a chair within a few feet of me, and spoke a few words which were particularly relevant to the difficult circumstances through which I was passing. He was ruddier in complexion than ever, grinning all over his face and, as the old-fashioned saying has it, positively glowing with health. The interesting thing to me was that I had not been thinking about him at all. I was neither alarmed nor suprised nor, to satisfy the Bishop of Woolwich, did I look up to see the hole in the ceiling that he might have made on arrival! He was just *there*—'large as life and twice as natural.' A week later, this time when I was in bed, reading before going to sleep, he appeared again, even more rosily radiant than before, and repeated to me the same message, which was very important to me at the time. I was a little puzzled by this, and I mentioned it to a certain saintly bishop who was then living in retirement here in Dorset. His reply was, 'My dear J—, this sort of thing is happening all the time.'[3]

What makes this appearance significant is the context. Loy Mershimer narrates that J.B. Phillips was in a life-threatening depression at the time. He would not leave his room and refused proper food and exercise. Although a Christian writer, he had begun to doubt God's love for him. It was during this time that Lewis made his sudden appearance, sitting in front of Phillips despite the fact that the chambers were closed. In this vision, writes Morsheimer, "Lewis only spoke only one sentence to Phillips: 'J.B., it's not as hard as you think.'" The meaning of this sentence has been debated but not its effect. "It snapped Phillips out of his depression. After Lewis spoke that cryptic sentence, he disappeared. Phillips came out of his chambers only to find that Lewis had died…miles away."[4]

Howard Storm

Howard Storm, a professor of art, described himself as a selfish man who not only did not believe in God, but detested those who did. While on a trip to Paris he passed out in a hospital with a perforation of his intestines. His NDE, partially recounted here, changed his beliefs and his life. He is now a minister.[5]

On June 1, 1985, I was concluding a three-week art tour of Europe with my wife and a group of students. At 11 that morning, which was a Saturday, without any warning I had the most severe pain I have ever experienced in my life right in the center of my abdomen, which knocked me to the ground screaming and kicking and yelling. It was terrifying, because there was no warning. It just happened. I actually thought I had been shot by a bullet. That was the only thing I could think of. My wife called the hotel desk and they called an emergency medical service and a doctor arrived. He got me off the floor and examined me and said that I had a perforation of the duodenum. He called an ambulance and they came and took me across Paris to a hospital, to an emergency room. And I was examined by two more doctors. They confirmed the first diagnosis and told me I had to have surgery right now, immediately.

I was sent to a surgical hospital. Unfortunately at the surgical hospital there was no doctor available to do the surgery, but I didn't know

that at the time. I found out much later. So I was put in a room to await
the arrival of a surgeon. But because it was a Saturday they had, unbe-
knownst to me, no luck in finding a surgeon willing to come in to do the
surgery. So I was left in that room and not seen by a doctor. I was not
given any medication and I was begging for relief from the pain. But
the nurse couldn't do anything because there was no doctor available
and they can't give any medication at all. So I wasn't given anything.
Nobody took my blood pressure or my pulse or my temperature. I had
a sheet on the bed, I didn't have any pillow. I was just put in this room
to wait for someone to do something. But with no doctor nothing happened at all. Every few hours the nurse would come by and ask how
we were doing. I would tell her that I was dying because I felt like I
was. And I had a roommate who was a very kind 68-year-old retired
Frenchman who had a good position in the French Government in avia-
tion. He was sympathetic. He was trying to intercede for me. But he
was powerless to do anything either.

At 8:30 that night—this had begun at 11 in the morning and I had
come to the surgical hospital by noon—the nurse came into the room
and said they were very sorry. There were unable to locate a doctor to
do the surgery and they would try to find one the next day. My doctors
in the United States, this was of course weeks later, told me that my life
expectancy was five hours from the beginning. It is like having a burst
appendix. What happens is that the stomach acid, and the bacteria and
the enzymes migrate through the perforation in the stomach into your
abdominal cavity and you become very septic and extreme peritonis
sets in and then you die. And that's what was happening to me. The
hydrochloric acid which is the primary ingredient in your digestive juices
was actually trying to digest me. It was leaking out of the stomach into
my abdomen and then migrating all the way up into my shoulders and
down into my pelvis. The sensation of burning was very real.

After the nurse announced that there would be no more doctors
she left. And I told my wife that I was going to die. And the reason why
I could make that declaration is that for hours and hours and hours I had
been trying to fight with all of my will, all of my ever declining might.
This sense of death was overcoming me. I was an atheist and I didn't
believe in God obviously and didn't believe in life after death or anything. So to me death was the conclusion of my life. I was 38 years old

and I was an artist and I had a wife and children and family and career and lots of ego. It seemed like a disappointment that I wasn't ready to deal with—all of it just coming to an end and such an ignoble end. There wasn't anything heroic about it; it was just lying on a metal bed in a hospital. No importance, no consequence, just fading away into oblivion. I didn't want that to happen, but I couldn't take the pain any more. At this point I was approaching 10 hours and I wasn't survivable any more. The doctors in the United States were [later] surprised I was still alive at 10 hours.

So I closed my eyes and went into oblivion. It's very easy to do, just let it run its course and stop breathing. And I did stop breathing and went unconscious.

Then I wasn't unconscious any more. Not only was I conscious, but I was more conscious than I had ever been in my entire life. My sense of sight, taste, touch, hearing, hot and cold, smell, were all greater than they had ever been. And I was absolutely amazed that my senses were so heightened. I was standing up by my bed and I could feel the texture of the floor at the bottom of my feet so intensely that it was almost overwhelming. The tactile sense where I could feel the air move-ment in the room on my skin. I could smell myself, I could smell my roommate, I could smell all the smells in the room like never before. I could taste my mouth—awful, terrible, bitter, stale. I hadn't had any-thing in my mouth for more than 10 hours.

One of the things I noticed, because I was interested, was that I had total focus, total depth of field. I could see clearly everything near and far simultaneously. I was also aware that my field of vision was greater than it had ever been. The normal field of vision is 160 degrees and my field of vision was way bigger than that. And I was kind of troubled: Why could I see so well? Now [there was] one thing that was counteracting all of this positive sensation of hyper-life. I was trying to communicate with my wife and with my roommate. My impression was they were ignoring me; they refused to respond to me. Of course, they couldn't see me, they couldn't hear me at all. What they were aware of was the body in the bed which I was also aware of, which I refused to believe was me, although I recognized it as resembling me.

Then I heard people calling me outside the room. I went over to the doorway of the room and they were saying to me in English, plain simple

English, "Hurry up, let's go. We've been waiting for you." And I said, "Who are you?" And they said, "We don't have time for your questions. We know all about you. We've been waiting for you a long time." I assumed by the things that they were saying that they were hospital personnel sent to take me to the surgery. I said to them, "You're here for my operation." They [responded], "We know what's wrong with you. We know everything about you. Let's go." I said, "Well, that would be an affirmative." And I left the room.

I had a very bad feeling when I left the room. It was nighttime, but the room was well lit. It was very bright and clear. We left the room and went to the hall. It was quite the opposite. It was very dank, very gray, and lacking in definition. Kind of like a fog, a lot like a very very bad TV picture, what one would describe as snow on a TV picture. And the people were unclear. This group of people that were commanding me to come with them. Not asking me. Commanding me. They were very authoritative.

I presumed that they were hospital personnel, because they didn't contradict my question/statement that they were hospital personnel.

So we proceeded into this unclear space and walked and walked and walked. Over this journey, I became aware that my sense of timing was gone. Having been a teacher, I had acquired over my career an innate sense of time. As a matter of fact, one of my weird things was, since I didn't wear wristwatches and I didn't have clocks in the classrooms that I taught in, I could judge time very well. I always had an ability with time, a sort of sixth sense about time. You could say to me what time is it and I would say, Oh, it's 2:30, and I would be within a few minutes. [But here] I had this acute sense that there's no time. I didn't know what time it was. So when I say I walked on this long journey, people say, "How long was it?" And I say, well, kind of like walking a couple of hundred miles. They say, "What are you talking about?" It just went on and on and on.

One of the things that I became aware of was that I was never tired, although I had been so sick that I was dying and wasn't even able to lift my head. I couldn't even lift my hand to scratch my nose. I was weak. Now I was up and walking with these people and I had no fatigue. The pain that I was experiencing before was gone. I was very aware that I was sick and was theoretically in a hospital, walking with these people and going to have surgery. But I didn't have pain any-more. I was exceedingly happy about that.

So we're going along and I'm trying to ask these people questions and they wouldn't answer any questions. They kept saying, "We don't have time. Don't ask questions." Eventually, as I asked them questions, they would say, "Shut up. We're sick of you. We're tired of you." And they became more rude. I began to get a little worried about [them]; who are these people and why are they so rude and lacking in simple information like where are we going and how come this is taking so long?

Eventually I realized that we were in darkness. It had gradually gotten dimmer and dimmer and now we were in darkness. They were hepherding me along and I said "I don't want to go any further." They said, "You will go further. You're almost there." And I stopped. They started to push and shove and I tried to resist physically. And they began to push and pull. I tried to get them off me. Then they started to scratch and bite and tear. I was screaming and yelling and trying to defend myself and hit back. There were more of them now, I don't know how many. Because of the level of noise that they were making, I know that there were a lot of them. Maybe hundreds or thousands—I don't know how many. Hundreds or thousands. Literally they wanted a piece of the action.

And then they were saying things and doing things to invade and violate me. I don't talk about this any more. It's too awful. I really can't go there emotionally. Now I am lying on the floor of that place and I'm pretty much ripped up. Some of my organs are lying on the ground next to me and stuff like that. I really can't assess the damage. But what I was feeling was more the emotional and psychological violation. The physical was bad enough, but the emotional was worse.

I heard what sounded like my own voice say to me, and this was audible, I could hear this, "Pray to God." And I thought "dumb idea. I don't pray." Then I heard the same thing, "Pray to God." And I thought, I don't know how to pray. I couldn't pray. I wanted to pray. A third time I heard, "Pray to God." When I was little I prayed, when I was a child I prayed. But I didn't remember how to pray. I was simply trying to think of what had I said when I was a child. I was trying to remember the prayers I had been taught as a child.

It was all getting mixed up with things that I had had to memorize as a child. So there were bits of the Pledge of Allegiance, Abraham Lincoln's Gettysburg Address, The National Anthem, Lord's Prayer, and 23rd Psalm. Just bits and pieces of this stuff all mixed up. I kept trying to compose something and I couldn't manage it. In my frustration I was muttering some of these things.

The people around responded violently to any accidental mention of God in my attempt to simply remember a prayer or compose a prayer. They were saying to me, accompanied with great obscenity which I won't repeat: There was no God; nobody could hear me except them; and for saying these things they were really going to hurt me like they hadn't hurt me before. This was going to be much much worse than what they had done. In their threatening me I was encouraged to try and make mention of God, because I finally found a weapon to use against them. And it became quite evident that not only were they not touching me anymore, but they were literally retreating back into the darkness away from me, because the mention of God was unbearable to them.

It occurred to me that part of the reason why they were in this place and why they were trying to bring me into this place was because these were people who hated God and denied the very existence of God. People ask me all the time, "Were they demons?" and my answer is, "No they were not demons. They were people just like me who had hated God for whatever reason."

Eventually I was trying to make my prayer by shouting things about God, crazy stuff. They retreated. I realize that I'm all alone. They've gone so far away, I don't know how far they've gone, I can't hear them or sense them any more. I stop. I'm thinking about my situation and in that place without time I had all the time in the world to think about my situation. In eternity I thought about what I had done with my life and how I had ended up.

And to sum it all up in a nutshell, I concluded that I had led a lousy life. I had failed as a man, as a husband, as a son, as a brother to my sisters, as a husband to my wife, as a father to my children, as a teacher to my students, as an artist, as a human being. Somehow I had flunked the course. And on my report card it was all "F"s. I don't need to go into detail why I came to this conclusion, but that's the conclusion. This was my own assessment of my life.

To say that I had regret…I can't begin to describe how I felt. I felt like such a failure

As a consequence of the kind of life that I had led, I had been flushed down the toilet of the Universe into the cesspool. And that's where I was: with all the other garbage lives, with all the rubbish lives, I was in the cesspool. What I concluded was that, although I was in a cesspool, I was still on the surface and what these people were doing was processing me to take me down deeper into it where it would get much worse, much more intense, which I can't imagine, don't want to imagine. I just knew it would get much worse the deeper I went into it and where I went was still very superficial somewhere in the processing department, the welcoming committee.

The horror of it was that I certainly didn't want to go any further and I didn't want to be part of these people. But I also thought, how could I possibly get out of this situation? There was no hope at all; the despair of being stuck with absolutely no hope and feeling like my life was just the most miserable waste. I recalled my childhood and a Sunday school classroom song: "Jesus loves me." There were both the words *Jesus loves me* going through my head, but also a very intense recollection of being a child and believing that there was this wonderful being of God, from God, who loved me and cared about me and would protect me and rescue me from harm.

When I was a child I had been taught that and I had believed that. And I started to wonder about that. And I thought "I don't have time or energy to go through that speculation any more." I had done enough of that in my life. I am going to try it, I am going to take a chance on it. And I called out into the darkness, "Jesus please save me." I didn't have any idea whether there was a Jesus, or if he was real, but I was sure hoping that it was true. All I had was hope, but no faith.

To my astonishment, in that darkness, a light appeared. And that light got very bright, very fast, and came upon me. And, out of that light, hands reached down to me lying on the ground and touched me. In that light I saw what a horror I truly was. And it was utterly repulsive seeing myself in that light. As the hands touched me, all the gore and filth kind of drifted away as if it was just dust, and I was restored to wholeness.

But much more importantly than any of that was, as I was being touched, I felt sensations of being loved that I had never experienced in my entire life and cannot possibly begin to describe because of its intensity. And the hands that touched me now reached under me and were touching my back and picked me up. I was lifted up very gently and then I was embraced, and being hugged and held up against a very strong man whom I knew at that time was Jesus. And later when we began to converse I knew that it was he. Anyway at this time, I was just crying. I wasn't thinking. I was just so happy that the only way I could express my joy and happiness was crying. And he was rubbing my back like a father with his son or a mother.

He was just gently stroking me. And I was crying and holding on and we just started drifting up. At first we started off slow and then we started going really fast. I knew we were moving. As we were moving in time I saw that we were moving towards a world of light.

And suddenly I was very ashamed, just overcome with shame for who [I was] and what I had done with my life. I knew that God was in that light that we were headed toward.

We were going towards God and I had spent much of my adult life ridiculing and blaspheming God. I just thought in my head: you've made a terrible mistake. I'm garbage and you should put me back. [Then] we stopped moving towards God, towards the light. And Jesus said to me, this is the first time he spoke to me, telepathically into my head. In his voice he said to me, "We don't mistakes. You belong here." And I was stunned because we hadn't spoken before. But, of course, more stunned by the fact that I wasn't going to be rejected. I just said throw me back. And he said no. So that was a good thing.

We began to converse. I quickly found out that he had a tremendous sense of humor, he was not interested in condemning me, that he liked me. Not only did he convey his love for me, but he conveyed the fact that he liked me and he thought I was interesting, amusing to be with, and we were conversing.

He said he had some friends he wanted me to meet, and so he called out in musical tones and some other beings of light came and surrounded us. I was aware that they were angels who had been part of my life and knew about my life, and as they began to try and put me at ease, build a relationship with me, they said that they wanted to show me my life.

So they proceeded to unfold my life before us in what I would describe as holographic images beginning with my birth and my earliest infancy which, of course, I had no recollection of. So this was all for me a new thing, because I didn't remember any of it, although it seemed quite familiar, because they were mostly images of my mom and dad and our kitchen and my sisters and stuff like that. It all looked very familiar, although I didn't remember my earliest infancy, saw all the happiness and things like that. And then in time watched my life unfold and how things turned out the way that they did. As I grew from my childhood into my early adulthood and stuff like that, it was very embarrassing what was going on with my life.

There was a lot of dysfunctional family stuff and just making a lot of really bad choices.

I would say to Jesus and the angels "you skipped something very important. I got an award you know, I won a prize, I got an honor." And they would say, "well, we're not interested in those things. What we want you to see is this." And then they would show me how I had talked to my mother or how I had had a fight with my father or how I had shown some real compassion towards my sister, how I had failed to show any compassion towards a student of mine, and so on.

All that they were interested in was how I had interacted with other people. They had absolutely no interest whatsoever in any of my accomplishments. I was very disappointed because I had lived my whole life to achieve things, and I always felt that my interactions were sort of a means to an end. What they were showing me was quite the opposite, that my relationships with people was my life and that my accomplishments were of no consequence whatsoever.

It finally got to the point that I said, "okay, I've seen enough, I I don't want to see any more." They said, "no, no, you need to see more" and they insisted on showing me more and more of my life. It was very very difficult and I was terribly ashamed at how my life was turning out especially with them allowing me to know how they felt about what we were saying.

Because here I am with my new-found friends who had rescued me from this horrible place that I had been in. I had spent my adult life stabbing them in the heart saying that they were ridiculous, that they didn't exist and I didn't believe in them. And that was awful. That's not going to happen again.

I was so glad when it was over. And when it was finally over, my life review, they said, "do you have any questions?" I said, "I've got a million questions." They said, "ask anything you like." So I proceeded to ask them everything I could think about asking them from the most exquisite philosophical questions to the most ridiculous personal questions. And everything I asked they answered carefully, calmly, patiently, simply. And if I didn't understand the answer, they would restate it in a more simple fashion so that I could understand it. One of the things that I was very impressed with was them as teachers, because I was a teacher and I was interested in their teaching methods; it was like they didn't have anything that they had to prove. They were quite confident in knowing what they were. They weren't impatient with my inability to understand, they weren't impatient with my ignorance. They simply wanted me to understand to the best of my ability, at the level that I was at, which, if I were to compare my level of intelligence and understanding to theirs, I would be like a little bitty child and they would be very wise ancient people. There was a gap between their understanding and knowledge and wisdom and mine.

But they were anxious to bring me up to speed according to where I was in my ability.

And it was delightful to have all of their attention, it was delightful to have their interest and their love. It was just great being with them and all the things that they would explain to me. Eventually I got to the point where I simply couldn't think of anything more to ask about.

One of the things I asked about was Heaven. What do you do in Heaven? What is Heaven like? They would explain to me and they would show me images, although we had not gotten there. Was Heaven boring? It's just the opposite. Heaven is the most interesting place there is. Everything good and everything that ever was, is and will be is there. And the centerpiece of Heaven is God, who is the source of everything. Anything you ever wanted to know, do, think, or not do. You can go to Heaven and just relax.

I said I was ready to go to Heaven, I want to go to Heaven. That would be the obvious thing anybody would want. They gave me the first bad news during this whole process of question-answer. "You're not going to Heaven. You're going back to the world." What then took place was a huge argument. And the argument was me arguing for me going to Heaven and them trying to prove to me why it was inappropriate at this time. They won the argument. It was not my time to go to Heaven.

I was actually being given the privilege of having another opportunity in the world to live in the way God had created me to live in the first place. And when I ultimately accepted that and agreed to that, they sent me back to this world.

When I came back, I was right back in the pain that I had left. Only I was back in consciousness. It was very difficult for me even to speak, because going from the bliss to the pain was such a rude shock. They told me that was going to happen. I knew it was going to happen. But it is really hard to accept it when it happens. But I was gasping for my breath because I wanted to tell my wife what had happened to me. The nurse accompanied with several hospital personnel came into the room and said a doctor had arrived at the hospital and they were going to perform the surgery. And this was only a few minutes after I had gone unconscious. They physically removed my wife from the room. They prepped me for surgery and I was taken on a gurney and passed my wife in the hallway.

On the way past her I said, "everything's going to be fine now." She, of course, looked at me in total disbelief. She didn't know what had happened and I hadn't had an opportunity to tell her. I had the surgery. And on the next day, which was Sunday morning, when I saw her for the first time, I said to her, "guess what: It's all love, just love. And you don't have to do anything but just accept it and become part of it. There's more love than you will ever know." And she looked at me and she said, "Do you need to rest more?" I said, "No this isn't crazy, I said I've got so much to tell you." She said, "You must be so tired. Do you want to go back to sleep?" I said, "No, I don't want to sleep. I want to tell you about Jesus." She's looking at me like "He's lost his mind. He's crazy as a loon." I could feel her complete total disbelief in what I was saying. I was trying to tell her I just won the lottery of life, I just won the prize. I'm now the richest man in the world. Not materially. I got it. I finally got it. I understand. She says, "He needs to go back to sleep. He's dreaming." So from that day on I tried to tell my wife what had happened to me. But she never really accepted and one of the first questions in my mind was, although I knew what had happened to me had happened, there was no way I could rationally explain how it had happened, although I knew what had truly happened.

Gloria Polo

Gloria Polo is a Colombian dentist who now speaks around the world about her encounter with eternity. This is an abbreviated version of her story.

This was at the National University of Colombia in Bogotá. I was attending graduate school, along with my nephew, who was also a dentist. My husband was with us that day. We had to pick up some books at the School of Dentistry on a Friday afternoon. It was raining very hard and my nephew and I were sharing a small umbrella. My husband was wearing his raincoat and he approached the outside wall of the General Library. Meanwhile, my nephew and I approached the trees without noticing, while skipping puddles. As we were about to skip to avoid a huge puddle, we were struck by lightning. We were charred. My nephew died there.

In my case lightning came in this way and burned my body in a horrifying way, on the inside and outside. This body you see here, this reconstructed body, is through the mercy of our Lord. Lightning charred me, left me without breasts, practically made my whole flesh and ribs vanish. My stomach, my legs; lightning went out my right foot, my liver was charred, my kidneys were burned, just like my lungs.

The most beautiful part is that while my flesh was there charred, at that instant I found myself inside a beautiful white tunnel full of joy and peace, a happiness for which there are no human words that can describe the grandeur of the moment. The climax of the moment was immense. I was happy and joyful, nothing weighed me down inside that tunnel. At the bottom of that tunnel I saw like a sun, a most beautiful light. I call it white to name a color, because no color on earth is comparable with that most beautiful light. I felt the source of all that love, all that peace.

As I was going up I realized I had died. At that instant I thought about my kids and I said "Oh, my God, my kids! What will they say? This very busy mom never had time for them!" That's when I saw my life truthfully and I became sad. I left home to transform the world, and I couldn't handle my kids and my home.

And in that instant of emptiness for my children, I looked and saw something beautiful: my flesh was not in this time or space. I saw everybody in a single instant, at the same time, both the living and the dead. I embraced my great-grandparents and my parents, who had passed away. I hugged everyone; it was a full and beautiful moment.... I didn't see in the same way I did before, where I only noticed who was fat, thin, dark-skinned, or ugly, always with prejudice. Now, out of my flesh, I would see people on the inside. How beautiful it is to see people on the inside. I would see their thoughts, their feelings. I embraced them in an instant and, still, I kept rising and rising, full of joy. At that point I felt that I was going to enjoy a beautiful sight, an extraordinarily beautiful lake. At that moment, I heard my husband's voice. My husband was crying and with a deep cry, with deep feeling, he called out to me and said "Gloria, please don't go! Gloria, come back! The kids, Gloria, don't give up!" In that instant I took a big glance and I saw not only him, but I saw him crying in deep pain. And the Lord allowed me to come back, although I didn't want to. What a joy, how much peace, how much happiness! Then, I started descending slowly to find my body, where I found myself lifeless. My body was on a gurney at the medical center on campus. I saw how the doctors gave me electric shocks to pull me out of cardiac arrest. We lay there for two and a half hours. They couldn't pick us up because our bodies were still conducting electricity. When that finally stopped they were able to assist us and they started resuscitation. I set my feet here, on this part of my head, and I felt a spark that pulled me in violently. I went back into my body. It was very painful to go back because sparks came out everywhere. And I saw me fit into such a "small thing." My flesh hurt, it was burned. It hurt a lot. Smoke and vapor came out of it. And the most horrible pain was that of my vanity.

When I was under anesthesia, I came out of my body again. I saw what the surgeons were doing to my body. I was worried for my legs.

All of a sudden I went through a moment of horror...I saw demons coming for me and I was their prey. At that moment I saw many people coming out of the walls of the operating room. At first sight they looked normal, but with a look of hatred on their faces, a horrible look. At that point through some special insight given to me, I realized I owed each one of them. I realized sin was not for free and that the main infamy and lie of the devil was to state that he didn't exist. I saw how they were coming for me. You can imagine how scared I was. This scientific and intellectual mind was of no avail to me. I bounced off the floor, into my body, trying to come into it again, but my body wouldn't let me in. I ran away and I'm not sure when I went through the wall in the operating room. I was hoping to hide in some hallway in the hospital, but I ended up jumping into thin air.

I went into some tunnels heading downward. At first, they had light and looked like bee hives. There were lots of people. But I started descending and light became scarce and I started roaming some tunnels in pitch darkness. That darkness has no comparison. The darkest darkness on earth is like noontime sunlight compared to it. That darkness causes pain, horror, and shame. And it smells very bad. I finished descending down those tunnels and landed desperately on a flat spot. I used to claim I had an iron will, that nothing was too much for me. But that was useless now, because I wanted to climb up and I couldn't. At that point I saw a huge mouth opening up on the floor and I felt immense emptiness in my body, a bottomless abyss. The most horrifying thing about that hole was that not even a bit of God's love was felt in it, not a drop of hope. The hole sucked me in and I felt terrified.

I knew that if I went in there, my soul would die. In the midst of that horror, as I was being pulled in, I was grabbed by my feet. My body was inside that hole, but my feet were being pulled from the top. It was a very painful and horrifying moment. My atheism fell to the wayside. I started clamoring for the souls in purgatory to help me out of there. As I was shouting I felt intense pain because I realized that thousands and thousands of people are there, mostly young people. Very painfully, I heard the gnashing of teeth, horrible screams and moans that shook me to the core. It took me several years to assimilate this, because I would cry every time that I remembered their suffering. I realized that's where people who commit suicide in an instant of desperation end, finding themselves surrounded by those horrors. But the most terrible torment there is the absence of God. God couldn't be felt there....

After a test on the Ten Commandments they showed me the Book of Life. I wish I had words to describe it. My book of life started at conception, when my parents' cells united. Almost immediately there was a spark, a beautiful explosion and a soul was formed, my soul, grabbed by the hand by God my Father, such a beautiful God. So marvelous! Looking for me 24 hours a day. What I saw as punishment was nothing but His love, because He didn't look at my flesh, but rather at my soul, and He would see how I was straying away from salvation.

Before I finish I have to give you an example of how beautiful the Book of Life is. I was very hypocritical. I would tell someone "you look beautiful in that dress, it looks great on you," but inside of me I would think "What a disgusting outfit and she thinks herself the queen!" On the Book of Life, it would show up exactly as I had thought about it, even though my words also appeared, as well as the inside of my soul.

Do you want to know what the Lord kept on asking me? About lack of love and charity. That's when He told me about my spiritual death. I was alive, but dead. If you could have seen what "spiritual death" is it's like a soul that hates. Like a terribly sour and fastidious soul that injures everyone, full of sin. I could see my soul on the outside, smelling well, with good clothes on, but my stench on the inside, living deep in the abyss. No wonder I was so depressed and sour! And he told me: "Your spiritual death began when you stopped hurting for your brothers!" I was warning you by showing you their plight everywhere. When you saw media coverage on murders, abductions, refugee situations, and with your tongue you said, on the outside, 'poor people, how sad,' but you didn't really hurt for them. You felt nothing in your heart. Sin made your heart into a heart of stone."

You can imagine my deep sorrow when my book closed. I had deep sorrow with God my Father for having behaved like that because, despite all my sins, despite all my filth and all my indifference and all my horrible feelings, the Lord always, up until the last instant, searched for me. He would always send me instruments, people. He would talk to me, He would yell at me, He would take things away from me to seek me. He looked for me up until the very end. God is always "begging" each one of us to convert.

I couldn't accuse Him of condemning me! Of course not. Out of my free will, I chose my father, and my father was not God. I chose Satan, he was my father. When that book closed I noticed I was heading down into a pit with a door at its bottom.

I thought everyone back on earth was probably thinking I had died a Saint, perhaps even waiting eagerly to ask for my intercession. And look! Where was I headed? I lifted my eyes and they met the eyes of my mom. With intense pain I cried out to her "Mommy, how ashamed I am! I was condemned, Mommy! Where I'm going I'll never get to see you again! At that moment, they granted her a beautiful grace. She was still but her fingers moved and pointed upward. A couple of very painful scales fell from my eyes, that spiritual blindness. With that immense shame and pain I started to cry: "Jesus Christ, Lord, have compassion on me! Forgive me, Lord, give me a second chance! And that was the most beautiful moment. I have no words to describe that moment. He came and pulled me out of that pit. When He picked me up, all those creatures threw themselves on the ground. He picked me up and he pulled me onto that flat part and told me with all His love: "You will go back, you will have a second chance," but He told me it wasn't because of my family's prayer. "It's normal for them to pray and cry out for you. It's because of the intercession of all those foreign to your body and blood who have cried, have prayed, and have raised their heart with immense love for you." I began to see many little lights lighting up, as little flames of love. I saw the people who were praying for me. But there was a big flame, it was the one that gave out the most light. It was the one that gave out the most love. I tried to see who that person was. The Lord told me: "That person you see right there loves you so much that he doesn't even know you." He showed me how this man had seen an old newspaper clipping from the previous day. He was a poor peasant who lived in the foothills of the "Sierra Nevada de Santa Marta" (in northeastern Colombia). That poor man went into town and bought some processed sugar cane. They wrapped it for him in an old newspaper from the previous day. My picture was there, all burned. When that man saw the news, without even reading it in full, he fell to the ground and started crying with the deepest love. And he said, "Father, Lord, have compassion on my little sister. Lord, save her. Look, Lord, if you save my little sister, I promise you I will go on pilgrimage to the Shrine of Our Lord in Buga (in southwestern Colombia), but please save her." Imagine a very poor man, he wasn't complaining or cursing because he was hungry, but instead he had this capacity to love that he could offer to cross an entire country for someone he didn't even know. And the Lord told me: "That is love for your fellow man." And then He told me: "You will go back."

When each one of you gets his Book of Life opened in front of you, when each one of you dies, you will see that moment just as I saw it. And we will see each other just as we are…the only difference being we will see our thoughts in the presence of God.[6]

Part 2

*The Evidence of Experience—
The Pre-Death Awareness
of Consciousness, Thought,
and the Self*

Chapter 6

Science and the Soul

Wat can science tell us about a life after death? In a word, nothing. To reiterate a previous theme, science can only deal with the quantitatively measurable, and so it cannot demonstrate the existence or non-existence of realities that transcend the physical. It cannot even speak about such realities.

Science, however, can play a useful role in our quest. Scientific research can help us recognize more clearly today than ever that (a) the human self transcends the physical and (b) conceptual thought by its very nature is intrinsically immaterial. To be sure, neuroscience has advanced our knowledge of the brain and its operations beyond anything conceivable in previous decades. But the kinds of information that the scientists continue to unveil is necessarily quantitative. It will always be restricted to the observable and the tangible. Anything else would not be scientific!

Nonetheless, several neuroscientists and cognitive psychologists have announced that their research has now uncovered the self and shown it to be purely physical in nature. In so doing, they assume without argument that the transphysical, by which we mean a non-physical reality that interacts with the physical, just does not exist. It would, therefore, be useful for our inquiry to clarify what can be known about the physical and the transphysical, and where misconceptions and (to be blunt about it) mistakes creep in.

The evidence available to us here are the data of our immediate experience. We might call this the "pre-death" experience of the soul. The evidence of our experience complements, confirms, and "completes" the evidence available from NDEs, the universal testimony of humanity and after-life visitations.

10 Hard Transphysical Facts

Before considering errors and fallacies, we will review 10 hard facts that point to the transphysical nature of the human soul and that cannot be denied by any sane person.

1. We are conscious, and conscious that we are conscious. Our conscious experience includes sensations, memories, images, concepts, intentions, and choices.

2. In terms of how we experience them, conscious phenomena are qualitatively distinct from anything physical, anything that can be physically observed or described. Sensations and perceptions have no size or shape, no physical characteristics whatsoever.

3. In terms of scientific investigation, it is clear that there is nothing in the brain that has any property of consciousness. Consciousness cannot even be described in scientific terms.

4. We are capable of discerning meaning as demonstrated most clearly in our use of language whereby we process symbols and use syntactical rules effortlessly.

5. We instinctively create and grasp concepts. Our senses make us aware of the physical world. We then process what we thus perceive, the percepts if you will, to produce a concept, something which does not refer to a specific physical thing or being (from dogs we encounter, we can understand the concept of a dog, something which does not refer to a specific animal). We are exercised by ideals of liberty and justice, which have no physical counterpart. While sensations and perceptions are triggered by physical objects, conceptual thought is not driven by the physical (although we can use physical media like writing and speaking).

6. We see things from a first-person perspective (I, me, my, mine). The "first-person" is not something that can be included in any physical or scientific description of the world.

7. We have a center of our consciousness and unifier of our experiences.

8. We maintain our continued self-identity over the course of our lives, although the molecules in our neurons change thousands of times across a lifetime.

9. We are capable of intending and choosing and executing our intentions and choices, and most of our actions can only be understood as the result of intentions and choices.

10. Our thoughts and intentions have a "life" of their own and our processes of reasoning or deciding proceed on their own dynamic. These thoughts and intentions are accompanied by neural activity, but there is no question that it is the thoughts and intentions that drive the transactions in the brain and not the other way round.

Given this snapshot of the transphysical in everyday experience, it is, if nothing else, puzzling to see certain scientists and journalists falling all over themselves to proclaim that we are, sorry to say, just physical.

Their proclamations almost seem to be part of a comedy routine. "After more than a century of looking for it, brain researchers have long since concluded that there is no conceivable place for such a self to be located in the physical brain, and that it simply doesn't exist," proclaims *Time*[1] "Science of the Soul? 'I Think, Therefore I Am' Is Losing Force" notes the *New York Times*.[2]

Crick's Hypothesis

The co-discoverer of DNA, Francis Crick, turned to the study of consciousness. In his book on the topic, he writes, "The Astonishing Hypothesis is that 'You,' your joys and your sorrows, your memories and your ambitions, your sense of personal identity and free will, are in fact no more than the behavior of a vast assembly of nerve cells and their associated molecules."[3]

Crick continues to attract disciples. Asked by the *Guardian* what would be the next revolution in science, Steven Pinker of Harvard responded that his choice was Crick's astonishing hypothesis—"the idea all our thoughts and feelings consist in physiological activity in tissues of the brain, rather than in an immaterial soul." Pinker compares thinking to neural computation and concludes that "humans are not special in having an essence that is separate from the material universe. It means no life after death. That, in turn, means no divine rewards or punishments in a world to come."[4]

According to the neuroscientist V.S. Ramachandran, "All the richness of our mental life—our religious sentiments and even what each of us regards as his own intimate private self—is simply the activity of these little specks of jelly in your head, in your brain. There is nothing else." In an interview, Ramachandran goes on to say that "the soul as it is usually spoken of, namely an immaterial spirit that occupies individual brains and that only evolved in humans—all that is complete nonsense." Belief in that kind of soul "is basically superstition," he said.[5]

Synopsis: The Self Is Synaptic

"My notion of personality is pretty simple," writes Joseph LeDoux in *The Synaptic Self: How Our Brains Become Who We Are*. "It's that your 'self,' the essence of who you are, reflects patterns of interconnections between neurons in your brain. Connections between neurons, known as synapses, are the main channels of information flow and storage in the brain. Given the importance of synaptic transmission in brain function, it's practically a truism to say that the self is synaptic. What else could it be?"[6]

"Whatever the specialness of the human brain, there is no need to invoke spiritual forces to account for its functions," wrote Gerald Edelman, winner of a Nobel Prize for his work on immunology who (like Crick) later turned to a study of consciousness.[7]

Comedy Routine

What makes this seem like a comedy routine is the stunning incongruity between *what* is being said and *that* it is being said: Speaking as one blob of jelly to another, let "me" assure "you" that "you" and "I" are simply blobs of jelly and that "my" argument itself is just the "behavior of a vast assembly of nerve cells and their associated molecules."

Truth be told, there is no truth. There are neurons and synapses, amygdalas and prefrontal cortexes. But no "you" or "me" in between or above or inside these—that would be to introduce the "ghost" of the dreaded Descartes or "a spiritual force" or the "superstition" of an "immaterial spirit."

"We" are not having this conversation. All that can be said is that two groups of neural networks and vocal cords are emitting vibes of various kinds: There can be no "understanding" because that would mean encoding and decoding symbols and discerning meaning and such activities would require an understander.

"You" and "I" cannot possibly exist or be conscious because there are no properties of self-hood and consciousness in the "vast assembly of nerve cells"; and since there is continuous change in the molecules making up these cells there is nothing there that can sustain identity or continuity: The neural activities simply drive themselves since there is no "one" to drive them. Bottom-line: there's nothing but molecules in motion.

It is paradoxical indeed that the very professionals who study our mental functions promote a view that (coming from any other source) would be classified as a mental disorder.

Behaviorism Is Simply Misbehavior

The old Behaviorism, concerned only with our physical behavior, simply denied the fact that we are conscious at all. It died (and none too soon) after the awkward task of keeping up the pretence became too onerous even for the most hard-headed. The new Behaviorism, which admits consciousness but explains it solely in terms of neural behavior is headed toward the same watery grave.

To be fair, the scientists quoted here, with the exception of the enfant terrible Crick, are far more nuanced when they get to the fine print.

Concerning Edelman, a magazine story reports that he seems to be of two minds concerning whether or not the biochemistry underlying consciousness can adequately explain such features of higher-order consciousness as the self and language: "We evolved structures that invented language,' he says. Yet once humans acquired syntax, Edelman adds, 'all bets are off.' Biology, he seems to suggest, can take us only so far in understanding the symbol-using mind. It's not totally reductive, he says."[8] In *A Universe of Consciousness* he observes that "studies of the brain proper cannot, in themselves, convey what it is like to be conscious."[9]

Not surprisingly, Crick, a funda-physicalist, was highly critical of Edelman. Edelman also emphatically rejects the brain-as-computer model, an approach that did not sit well with another old-school physicalist, Daniel Dennett. "Your brain has to be creative about how it integrates the signals coming into it. Computers don't do that. Our brain is capable of symbolic reference, not just syntax," says Edelman in another interview.[10]

Synaptic and Spiritual

Despite occasional ambiguity, in *The Synaptic Self*, Le Doux takes pains to show that his claims are relatively modest. "Many people will counter that the self is psychological, social, or spiritual, rather than neural, in nature. My assertion that synapses are the basis of personality does not assume that your personality is *determined* by synapses; it's the other way around. Synapses are simply the brain's way of receiving, storing, and retrieving our personalities, as determined by all the psychological, cultural, and genetic factors. So as we begin to understand ourselves in neural, especially synaptic, terms, we do not have to sacrifice the other ways of understanding existence."[11]

He goes even further in an interview with *Salon*. He strongly affirms that a "spiritual view" is compatible with "a synaptic view of the self." He notes, in fact, that "I wasn't using brain research to try to dismantle faith. I had something more inclusive in mind."

When asked whether he agrees that in the light of studies on animal emotion and cognition "Descartes' dictum, 'I think, therefore I am,' loses its force" (coincidentally the thesis of the *New York Times* article cited earlier), he emphatically says "No: I do agree that much of the human brain can be understood in terms of animal brains—very basic emotions like fear are a good example. But when it comes to higher cognition I believe the human brain stands out."[12]

Concerning the self, Le Doux says in another interview, "To the extent that we are a product of our genes and experiences, we are our synapses. This doesn't mean that the essence of who you are is encoded at a particular synapse. It means that your self is a very complex pattern of synaptic connectivity in your brain."[13] There can be no question that our genes and our interaction with our environment help form our personalities, beliefs, and dispositions, and the "forming" is done by the wiring of the synapses. But this has no bearing on the entirely different question of whether there is a transphysical reality somewhere in the mix. In her review of Le Doux's book, Susan Blackmore, a convinced physicalist, rightly points out that "The 'self' of the title is more like personality, or the sum of our brain's activities. But his stirring conclusion that 'You are your synapses' is less than convincing."[14]

Monkeys and Mirror Neurons

Even Ramachandran is more restrained when he gets to the nitty gritty. Although he says that self-awareness is a matter of using mirror neurons for 'looking at myself as if someone else is looking at me,' he emphatically adds that "I am not arguing that mirror neurons are sufficient for the emergence of self; only that they must have played a pivotal role. (Otherwise monkeys would have self-awareness and they don't.) Have we solved the problem of self? Obviously not—we have barely scratched the surface."[15] We might ask in response: What or who drives the activity of the mirror neurons? The firing of the mirror neurons, in some respects, takes place "after the fact": it is the effect of an intention and not the cause. Our inquiry is concerned with the latter while neuroscience tells us about the former.

Where Neuroscience Fits In

It should be clarified that these reflections in no way discount the magnitude of what has been achieved by modern neuroscience. Contemporary neuroscience has given us extraordinary new insights into the workings of the brain.

The human brain has 100 billion neurons and each of these has about 7,000 synaptic connections that link it to other neurons. Neurons send and receive information with electro-chemical pulses called action potentials or "spikes"; these short-voltage pulses are transmitted across synapses from one neuron to another with signaling molecules called neurotransmitters. The encoding and decoding of information in such transmissions is called the neuron code. The sequence of spikes contains the information that is transmitted, but the exact nature of this code, the precise information represented, communicated and processed by a pattern of pulses, still has not been "cracked"; current investigations center on spike count, spike density, and the concerted firing of groups of neurons.

How Does the Neuron Code Convey Information?

What is the nature of the neuron code and how does it convey information? On this there are different views as reported recently in a *Scientific American* article titled "Jacking into the Brain:" "Theorists have advanced many differing ideas to explain how the billions of neurons and trillions of synapses that connect them can ping meaningful messages to one another." These range from the rate of firing of the neuron's voltage spikes to the timing between spikes and the changing patterns of neurons firing together.[16]

But reading voltage spikes is not going to tell us about the nature of the neuron code. "Just getting a lot of signals and trying to understand what these signals mean and correlating them with particular behavior is not going to solve it," notes Henry Markram, director of neuroscience and technology at the Swiss Federal Institute of Technology in Lausanne. This is because any input into a neuron can produce a specific output through many different pathways. "As long as there are lots of different ways to do it, you're not even close," says Markram who is head of the Blue Brain project.

Replication of how the brain processes complex information is currently entirely out of reach. The connections required in forming memories bear no resemblance to bits being magnetized on a hard disk. "Complex information like the contents of a book would require the interactions of a very large number of brain cells over a very large area of the nervous system," observes neuroscientist John P. Donoghue of Brown University. "Therefore, you couldn't address all of them, getting them to store in their connections the correct kind of information. So I would say based on current knowledge, it's not possible."[17]

Correlating Brain Regions to Mental Functions

Various regions of the brain have been correlated with various mental functions: the cerebral hemispheres with perception, cognition, emotion, and memory, for instance. Both hemispheres are believed to be required for consciousness, although some say the right hemisphere plays a dominant role. Brain imaging techniques such as functional magnetic resonance imaging show the changes that take place in the brain during specific mental activities, such as processing sensory information or thinking. For instance, there is an increase in blood flow in the motor cortex when reading verbs referring to a face or limb action. Again, individual neurons have been recorded in the act of summoning memories (although memory retrieval is a much more complex process than such an act).

Cognitive psychologist Bernard J. Baars, editor of the journal *Consciousness and Cognition*, believes that the data from brain imaging indicates that consciousness will be explainable in terms of neurons and synapses.[18] But even fellow materialists such as Roger Penrose find this implausible. Ian Tattersall, curator of anthropology at the American Museum of Natural History, notes, "While we know a lot about brain structure and about which brain components are active during the performance of particular functions, we have no idea at all about how the brain converts a mass of electrical and chemical signals into what we are individually familiar with as consciousness and thought patterns."[19]

Selfs and Circuits

Often enough, popular articles on the implications of neuroscience tend to err on the side of sensation. In an article titled "Flesh Made Soul," Sandra Blakeslee writes that certain brain regions, the medial prefrontal cortex, precuneu, and posterior cingulate cortex, "light up in imaging studies when subjects think about themselves, their hopes, and aspirations and retrieve episodic memories related to their lives. The sense of being—me, myself, and I—is located in this circuit, according Dr. Marco Iacoboni, a neuroscientist at the University of California, Los Angeles."[20]

But some contemporary studies militate against the idea that self-awareness springs from the right hemisphere. But, be that as it may, what is even more surprising here is Iacoboni's confident pronouncement that the self "is located in this circuit." This pronouncement to a journalist should be contrasted with his more measured statement in a journal article, "Self-recognition has been demonstrated by a select number of primate species and is often used as an index of self-awareness. Whether a specialized neural mechanism for self-face recognition in humans exists remains unclear." [21] And, of course, the thought processes associated with the recognition of oneself in a picture or mirror is by no means what we mean by the self.

Drawing Conclusions From Brain Imaging Data

Iacobini's tendency to readily identify neural activity with specific mental processes touched off a firestorm of controversy after his op-ed article in *The New York Times* titled "This is Your Brain on Politics." This article, which sought to determine subjects' political preferences using brain imaging data, elicited a strong counter-response from 15 of the world's leading neuroscientists. The scientists said emphatically that it is not possible to read the minds of potential voters by studying their brain activity. After pointing out that they are cognitive neuroscientists who use the same brain imaging technology, they said, "We know that it is not possible to definitively determine whether a person is anxious or feeling connected simply by looking at activity in a particular brain region. This is so because brain regions are typically engaged by many mental states, and thus a one-to-one mapping between a brain region and a mental state is not possible."[22]

No Mental Modules

Patricia Churchland, author of *Brainwise: Studies in Neurophilosophy* and *Neurophilosophy: Toward a Unified Science of the Mind*, notes that "Mental modules are complete nonsense. There are no modules that are encapsulated and just send information into a central processor. There are areas of specialization, yes, and networks maybe, but these are not always dedicated to a particular task."[23]

If nothing else, the Iacobini controversy was a useful reminder of the limitations of what brain imaging and scanning can tell us about consciousness, thought, and the self.

Neurons—What Matters Is Quantity!

One puzzling fact has emerged in recent studies. The differences in brain-based activities among species are driven by the quantity of neurons rather than by specific differences in the kinds of neurons they have. The neurobiologist Robert Sapolsky has said that the neurons from a sea slug and a human brain look essentially the same; they have the same number of neurotransmitters and function as the same building block. The difference between the two lies in the fact that the human brain has 100 million times more neurons than the brain of the sea slug. The difference between the chimpanzee and human brain is similarly one of the numbers of "off-the-rack" neurons they have. Neural development in each species is driven in the genes that regulate cell division.[24]

In "How Do Neurons Know?," Patricia Churchland comments on the commonality of structure, developmental organization, and basic cellular functions across all vertebrate animals. "All nervous systems use essentially the same neurochemicals, and their neurons work in essentially the same way, the variations being vastly outweighed by the similarities. Our brains and those of other primates have the same organization, the same gross structures in roughly the same proportions, the same neuron types."[25]

Physicalist Fancies

Given what we know from neuroscience, we can now consider the stances taken by today's physicalists. Chief among them are Daniel Dennett and Paul and Patricia Churchland.

Dennett does not see anything special about the cells that make up the brain: these neurons are cells just like the germs that cause infections or yeast cells. Billions of years of evolution has created the huge neural network that is the brain. "We are descended from robots and composed of robots," he says.[26] What about our minds? "Conscious minds are more or less serial virtual machines implemented—inefficiently—on the parallel hardware that evolution has provided for us."[27] "There is no "central conceptualizer and meaner." As for conscious experiences, he says, "These are *all* 'merely' the 'performance of functions' or the manifestation of various complex dispositions to perform functions. In the course of making an introspective catalogue of evidence, I wouldn't know what I was thinking about if I couldn't identify them for myself by these functional differentia. Subtract them away, and nothing is left beyond a weird conviction (in some people) that there is some ineffable residue of 'qualitative content' bereft of all powers to move us, delight us, annoy us, remind us of anything."[28] He is clear in stating that his aversion to transphysical phenomena is dogmatic: "In this book, I adopt the apparently dogmatic rule that dualism is to be avoided at all costs."[29]

In *The Engine of Reason, the Seat of the Soul*, Paul Churchland writes, "You came to this book assuming that the basic units of human cognition are states such as thoughts, beliefs, perceptions, desires, and preferences.... Their universality notwithstanding, these bedrock assumptions are probably mistaken."[30] And in *On the Contrary*, the Churchlands note, "Our sensory, cognitive, and motor activities, to the extent that we understand them, are just a further mix of chemical, electrical, and mechanical goings on."[31]

Patricia Churchland is far more restrained and nuanced than Dennett. Although she pointedly denies the existence of a nonphysical soul, she acknowledges the challenges facing the physicalist: "Conscious phenomena are under study at many different levels of brain organization, using many different levels of attack. So far, however, no explanatorily competent theory has yet emerged."[32]

Higher Cognition Still Out of Reach

As noted in "Jacking into the Brain," the brain chemistry accompanying higher-level cognition lies beyond our reach. The article notes that the hype over the idea of thought-controlled prostheses "obscures the lack of knowledge of the underlying mechanisms of neural functioning needed to feed information into the brain to recreate a real-life cyberpunk experience." Richard A. Andersen, a Caltech neuroscientist observes that, "We know very little about brain circuits for higher cognition."[33]

The Gulf Between Humans and Other Animals

The unbridgeable gulf separating the human person from other animals was highlighted in a September 2009 *Scientific American* article titled "The Origin of the Mind" by Harvard biologist Marc Hauser. Hauser notes that Darwin's idea of a continuity of mind between humans and other species is now passé, and it is now understood that there is "a profound gap" between the human intellect and that of other animals. He identifies four uniquely human mental traits (what he calls humaniqueness):

1. "Generative computation," which is the ability "to create a virtually limitless variety of 'expressions.'" These include "arrangements of words, sequences of notes, combinations of actions, or strings of mathematical symbols."

2. The mind's capacity for promiscuously combining ideas.

3. The ability to use mental symbols whereby humans spontaneously convert sensory experiences into symbols.

4. "Only humans engage in abstract thought." Animal mental life, however, is "largely anchored in sensory and perceptual experiences."

Remarkably, he concludes that "our mind is very different from that of even our closest primate relatives and that we do not know much about how that difference came to be."[34]

The Father of Cognitive Neuroscience—Physicalists as Second Year Graduate Students in Neuropsychology

Michael Gazzaniga, described as the father of cognitive neuroscience, gives us an interesting perspective on some of today's well-known physicalists in an interview with Tom Wolfe. He cites the neuroscientist Jose Delgado as saying that the human brain is complex beyond anything anybody can imagine. According to Delgado, as far as brain research is concerned, "We are not a few miles down a long road; we are a few inches down the long road." And "All the rest is literature." Gazzaniga notes that theorists like E. O. Wilson, Richard Dawkins, and Daniel Dennett "know about as much on the human brain as a second-year graduate student in neuropsychology." He notes that this area is simply not their field. He acknowledges that Wilson is a great zoologist and then adds, "Dawkins, I'm afraid, is now just a PR man for evolution. He's kind of like John the Baptist—he goes around announcing the imminent arrival. Dennett, of course, is a philosopher and doesn't pretend to know anything about the brain. I think it has distorted the whole discussion."[35]

The Fallacy of Physicalism

The fundamental fallacy of many of the physicalists when it comes to the human self is this: They assume that a correlation between certain neural activities and certain conscious experiences shows that each activity and the corresponding experience are one and the same. This is a fallacy for three reasons:

1. The fact that a given conscious experience is accompanied by a specific neural action does not prove anything. As Neal Grossman points out, "William James (1898) showed, more than a hundred years ago, that (1) the most that the facts of neurology can establish is a correlation between mental states and brain states and (2)

correlation is not causation. The data of neuroscience will always be neutral with respect to the hypotheses of (1) causation or materialism and (2) what James called "transmission," the hypothesis that the brain merely transmits an already existing consciousness into the particular form that is us. Neuroscience cannot in principle distinguish between these two hypotheses."[36]

2. More importantly, there is the problem of putting the cart before the horse: my thoughts drive my neurons and not the other way round. Let's say that I'm thinking of the different forms of transportation devised by humankind. We ask: "Are my neurons causing and driving my thoughts on transportation or are my thoughts moving forward on their own momentum?" The obvious answer is the second one. The real question is: how do intentions and trains of thought drive neural activity?

3. Things get even worse when we ponder the question of what or who is doing the intending and thinking. Where is this "agent" located? In the right hemisphere? How can it stay the same when the molecules in your neurons are changing thousands of times?

It is critical for us to recognize the priority of thought and intention. These come first and the neural activity follows in their tracks, so to speak. Where do they come from? As he does so often, the neuroscientist Gazzaniga hits the nail on the head in the book *Human*: "How the brain drives our thoughts and actions has remained elusive. Among the many unknowns is the great mystery of how a thought moves from the depths of the unconscious to become conscious."[37]

The Nobel Prize-winning neuroscientist Roger Sperry led the rebellion against Behaviorism with this question of which came first, the conscious intention or the resultant neural events. Sperry's "mentalist" view that consciousness controls physical events finally received scientific status in the 1970s with the eclipse of behaviorism. This "consciousness/cognitive revolution," noted Sperry, legitimized "consciousness and the subjective for science."[38]

Some scientists justify their physicalism by pointing to studies that show our brains reacting in predictable ways to certain physical stimuli—colors and smells, face in the mirror, hallucinogens, electrodes, and implants. There is no question that physical stimuli do cause sensory reactions. Our emotions, feelings, desires, and perceptions can be manipulated by these stimuli. We are physical beings and physical stimuli have an effect on us. But this has no bearing at all on whether or not there is a transphysical dimension to our being. We are conscious of a rock striking us in a way that a mountain or a pond cannot be. Where does this property of being aware of our environment come from? True, we would not be aware without the neurons, but the neurons themselves have no property of consciousness. And also the neurons are made of the same "stuff" as the mountain and the pond.

Another strategy adopted by physicalists is to argue that introduction of a transphysical soul violates the laws of physics. In "The Rise of Physicalism," today's leading philosophical physicalist, David Papineau, notes that physicalism is not the claim that everything is physical. Rather it is "the significantly weaker claim that everything which interacts causally with the physical world is physical." He acknowledges that, as with other empirical matters, there is nothing certain with regard to this claim. "There is no knock-down argument for the completeness of physics," he writes. "You could in principle accept the rest of modern physical theory, and yet continue to insist on special mental forces, which operate in as yet undetected ways in the interstices of intelligent brains."[39]

In *Thinking About Consciousness*, Papineau confesses that "something stops us really believing the materialist identification of mind with brain, even those of us who officially profess materialism." The only effective remedy for this, he writes, is not an improved theory but philosophical "therapy."[40]

Physicalists Avoid the Problem of Conscious Experience

What is remarkable about these kinds of physicalist critiques is that they neither deny nor address conscious experience. They simply adduce extraneous reasons for rejecting it as a reality in its own right. Papineau is worried about its infringing on the completeness of physics. Dennett is concerned that the slightest concession will bring back the dreaded specter of Cartesianism (the philosopher Descartes is credited with popularizing dualism, the notion that body and mind are two separate substances). Once again we sense the same refrain: We've made up our minds (or brains!) and don't want to be bothered with the facts.

Functionalism, Dennett's "explanation" for consciousness, says we should not be concerned with what makes up so-called mental phenomena. Rather we should be investigating the functions performed by these phenomena. A pain is something that creates an avoidance reaction, a thought is an exercise in problem-solving. Neither are to be thought of as private events taking place in some private place. Ditto with all other supposedly mental phenomena. Being conscious means performing these functions. Because these functions can be replicated by non-living systems (a computer solves problems, for instance), there is nothing mysterious about "consciousness." And certainly there's no reason to go beyond the physical.

But what this account leaves out is the fact that all mental actions are accompanied by conscious states, states in which we are aware of what we are doing. In no way does functionalism explain (or claim to explain) the state of being conscious, of being aware, of knowing what we are thinking about (computers don't "know" what they are doing). Still less does it tell us who it is that is conscious, aware, and thinking. Dennett, amusingly, says that the foundation of his philosophy is "third-person absolutism," which leaves him in the position of affirming that "I don't believe in 'I.'" Amusingly, some of the strongest critics of functionalism are themselves physicalists. Searle is especially sharp: "If you are tempted to functionalism, I believe you do not need refutation, you need help."[41]

Physical Laws and the Transphysical Dimension

Papineau's strategy is to simply argue that modern science holds that all physical events are completely explained by physical factors. To introduce anything transphysical is to violate this principle of the completeness of physical explanation. To say that an immaterial intellect can "cause" physical events to take place, according to this argument, is to defy the principle of the conservation of energy. In response, we should first point out that the argument that physical explanations are complete is derived from a transphysical concept (the idea of conservation) applied by a transphysical self (Papineau). Then we ask, who is doing the arguing? Is the argument simply a matter of neurons firing or is it a collation of certain reasons arranged in a certain pattern to convince us of it truth? If reasons are involved, does this violate the conservation principle? *More important, we should note that transphysical mental acts do not violate the principle of the conservation of energy because the action of the soul applies to the distribution of energy and not to its quantity.*

Beyond that, we should point out that we don't even know why one physical event causes another (as has been highlighted by David Chalmers among others). So it is presumptuous to suppose that we should be able to give an account of how the soul affects matter. We do, however, know this: The transphysical experience (the thought) comes first and thereby causes certain physical events. It's not neural firings that cause a thought: the thought drags the neural cart behind it. But where did it come from and how? What causes the mental events that cause the brain events? Other brain events? Then, is the thought "our solar system has nine planets" simply a set of brain events caused entirely by other physical transactions in the brain? Clearly it is the soul acting on the brain that is the source of all our experience. There is no chicken or egg question here. The thought comes first and, as a result, causes certain brain events.

In sum, the ability to be conscious—to be in pain, to see—is something entirely different from the physical. Of course sensations come through the senses and are transmitted through the nervous system. But the sensing and the feeling, the experiencing, is an entirely new plane of being. When a photon acts on the rhodopsin protein in a rod cell it sets off enzymatic activities that transmit information through the optic nerve to the brain. Electromagnetic waves are translated into electrical signals that end up as subjective visual images. You see, you become aware of something "outside." What does it mean to be aware? Visual awareness cannot be described in physical terms. Nor do any of the physical components that make it possible have any of the properties of aware-ness or consciousness. Dependent though it is on physical media, consciousness is nonetheless self-evidently a certain kind of transphysical reality. When we say that a certain collection of particles becomes visually aware of another such collection, we are making a statement that is simply incomprehensible in terms of physics and biology. It is nevertheless precisely what happens every time we open our eyes.

If the ability of being conscious of our physical environment has no physical explanation, the situation gets even more desperate when we get to the realm of thought. And here language is a key marker.

Understanding Understanding

What is central to language and thought is the ability to grasp the meaning of something and this, by its very nature, includes the abilities of using concepts and reasoning. Let's look at these three processes carefully: grasping meaning, thinking in concepts, and reasoning.

Let's say I tell you that this is a good day for golf and you nod in agreement. What happens here is that you are thinking of this game called golf, not a par-ticular game with particular players, but the idea of a game of golf. You notice also that this is a cool day and infer that it is the kind of day that lends itself to a pleasurable outdoor sport like golf. Hence you understand what I'm talking about and signal your assent. To understand here is to grasp the meaning of my message, and this entails decoding the concept of golf and deciphering its connection to the weather.

It would be obviously false to suggest that this brief interchange is simply a matter of neurons firing in one brain and then in another. Neurons do fire, but the fundamental dynamic here is that of conceptual and logical processing that results in meaning transmission. The neuronal firing is strictly a by-product—not the driver of what takes place. Once you understand *this* you will see why it is incorrigibly incoherent to suppose that thoughts are nothing more than brain waves in motion.

Thought, in essence, is understanding. To understand understanding better, it might be helpful at this point to distinguish thought from the operations of a computer.

There Is No Such Thing as a Computer

Instinctively, people tend to personalize computers thinking of them as entities that process information and spit out conclusions and answers. What is forgotten is the following: There is no such thing as a computer. There are nuts and bolts, silicon chips and sub-routines, transistors and data buses, clock cycles and electrical pulses. These are made to interact in such a way as to perform useful functions. But no matter how sophisticated it might be, this body of components does not know what it's doing. There is in fact no "it" and no "knowing" in the sense of conscious awareness by an agent. To suggest that the computer "understands" what it is doing is like saying that a power line can meditate on the question of freewill and determinism, or that the chemicals in a test tube can apply the principle of non-contradiction in solving a problem, or that a DVD player understands and enjoys the movies it plays.

The problem posed by language has been acknowledged by physicalists ranging from Richard Dawkins to Gerald Edelman, and in the next chapter we will be considering it in relation to the question of the soul's independence from matter.

But for the present we will turn to an equally fundamental question: Who does the understanding and the thinking? Who or what is the understander?

I Am, Therefore I Think

This is the question of the self, the "I." We start with another priceless gem from Gazzaniga. Gazzaniga points out that in our interactions with others we do not think that it is a matter of our brains talking with other brains. He thinks that it is he, Mike Gazzaniga, talking to Tom Wolfe, who is listening to him. "We instantly convert to that." In essence, "I put you at the level of a person with mental states and all the rest of it." This mechanism, he says, "is the deep mystery of neuroscience, and no one has touched it yet. No one knows how that works."[42]

The self is not some mysterious esoteric entity that can only be discovered through metaphysics or meditation. In essence:

1. It is the center of our consciousness and unifier of our experiences.
2. It maintains our continued self-identity over the course of our lives (individual brain cells are just as incapable as the chips in a computer to serve as a self).
3. It is the basis on which we act as self-conscious free agents. Moreover, the sense of responsibility that all human persons have can only be explained in terms of a self and not in Darwinian or Pavlovian terms.

Aware That I Am Aware, Conscious That I Am Conscious, Cognizant of My Cognition

How do I know the self exists? Well, first I have to become aware that I am aware, conscious that I am conscious, and cognizant of my cognition. What is most obvious in my everyday experience is the fact that I do experience things—and that this "I," which does the experiencing, exists, and that its experiences are "my" experiences. I am directly aware of myself, writes Geoffrey Madell, a modern defender of the self, and there is no other way to know the "I" than through such direct awareness. We do not become aware of the self as something separate from its acts of thinking and willing. Rather, as H.P. Owen put it, it "underlies, pervades and unifies" all its acts.

Some philosophers have said that the "I" is simply a series of brain-states. Yet others have pointed out that there is no continuing "I," just a series of "person-phases" or "I-thoughts." The first group claims that whatever we think of when we say "I" is simply constituted by the continuity of my physical body.

The second group adopts a different approach and says that the "I" is simply the continuity of certain psychological features such as memories or desires. Another group claims that the "I" is simply a grammatical mistake. Finally there are the thought-experimenters who lay out imaginary scenarios (split-brains is the favorite) to show that the "I" is incoherent.

About the "bodily continuity" claim, it must be said that any attempt to show that the "I" is purely the body ends up being circular. To show that the body is the "I," points out Madell, you have to not only assume the existence of an "I" but also that you can already identify and be aware of the "I," There is no way to verify an experience as mine without independently knowing the "I" and knowing the experience as mine. Our experience of the first-person shows that persons cannot be seen as being like any other objects in the physical world. Moreover, continues Madell, whereas physical objects exist in two dimensions, time and space, our experiences exist in three: time, space, and subjectivity. The physicalist has no place either for the subject of experience or the first-person perspective.

Concerning the psychological continuity argument, the idea that "person" is simply a word used to describe various moments of consciousness is, on the face of it, absurd. There is an obvious continuity and unity to all our experiences. Just completing this sentence shows that we are not a series of selves performing individual acts of thought, but one consciousness unifying a succession of acts.

What about the idea that the "I" is simply a grammatical mistake? Gilbert Ryle, in his *The Concept of Mind* dismissed what he called "the systematic elusiveness of the I" as a grammatical feature and said "I" is no different than "here" and "this" in being unanalyzable. None of these words actually refer to anything. But, as Madell and other thinkers have shown, "here" and "this" are defined in the context of an "I," and are in fact parasitic on "I." "Here" and "this" are understood relative to "I." It is only "I" that is unanalyzable while referring to something definite.

Thought-Experiments

So lethal is the self for physicalism that an entire library of works has sprung up in modern philosophy for the express purpose of extinguishing all traces of the "I." The standard practice has been to construct various improbable thought-experiments that throw into question the idea of a unitary self. Apart from the fact that these thought-experiments pointedly ignore the transphysical nature of the self, it is now evident that the scientific presuppositions behind some of these experiments are demonstrably wrong.

The Oxford philosopher Derek Parfit has pioneered the art of using thought-experiments to resolve the issue. Parfit's ploy is to talk of instances where different parts of the brain are placed in different bodies. One person is thus split into two. Now if a person can be split into two then it is simply not possible to say that we are both of those persons. We can only be one of them. But each possesses the same characteristics and there is nothing to differentiate them. So the original person survives in both. This shows that the "I" is not something fundamental, and personal identity is simply a collection of experiences.

But if such experiments were in fact possible, they still do not address the question of the first-person perspective. Neither do they consider the unsplittability and simplicity of consciousness. But the real Achilles Heel of these thought-experiments is the question of whether or not they are in fact viable. Another Oxford philosopher, Kathleen Wilkes, has shown decisively that the thought-experiments proposed by Parfit and others are in fact not scientifically plausible (some are even theoretically impossible) and therefore irrelevant to the discussion. "We are completely ignorant about what would happen if the detachable parts of two half-brains from one head were sewn on to the undetachable parts of the two different brains (death is certainly the most likely outcome), and thus no conclusions relevant to personal identity could be drawn," writes Wilkes. "Thought-experiments that are the product of ignorance simply mislead." She concludes that, "We cannot extract philosophically interesting conclusions from fantastical thought-experiments."[43]

"Capturing" the Self Scientifically Is Simply Science Fantasy

"Jacking into the Brain" points out that the idea of "capturing" the self with digital tools is simply science fantasy. "The wholesale transfer of self…is still nothing more than a prop for fiction writers."[44]

In a review of books by two key thinkers on consciousness, Andrew Ross points to the uniqueness of the I: "The uniquely vivid quality of *my* experience remains unexplained." This is "devastating to any theory of consciousness that fits within science as we now know it, because that science is built from a third-person perspective." What we need is "a logicophysical frame that can accommodate the asymmetry between the first-person and third-person perspectives."[45]

Lund's *The Conscious Self*

In his magisterial work, *The Conscious Self*, David Lund comments on what science can show about brain states, consciousness, and the self:

- ✧ "Science shows that brain states are connected to states of consciousness, but not that the connection is one of identity. Nor does it show that experience is subjectless or, conversely, that an experiencing subject is intrinsic to consciousness."

- ✧ "What is only rarely acknowledged is that some of the problems facing the materialist appear to be nothing less than insuperable. It seems clear that there can be no satisfactory materialist treatment of either the qualitative phenomenality of experience or the intentionality of consciousness."

The subjective nature of experiences results from the fact that they are experiences of a subject. You are a subject of consciousness because of certain intrinsic properties, not extrinsic properties, like dependence on the brain. Moreover, "in first-person terms, there can be no answer to the question as to what it is for some item in the centerless material order to be *me*." No physicalist account can explain a subject of conscious experiences, the self. Also, consciousness is a fundamental reality that cannot be reduced to or seen as emerging from "any assembly of nonconscious physical things."

Experiences by their nature call for the existence of the self. The idea of an individual experience without a subject who experiences it is unintelligible, says Lund. Moreover, the unified nature of consciousness can only be explained if it is the consciousness of a single subject."[46]

The self is subject and agent. "The self is a continuous intellective and creative activity which proceeds by concentration into successive particular acts," writes Austin Farrer in his *Finite and Infinite*. Also, "The unitary being of the self is not an aspect of the self, but the self expressed in all its aspects."[47]

Yet another objection comes from those who point to seemingly intelligent computers. In *Infinite Minds*, John Leslie points out that a computer that exactly duplicates the information processing found in the brain would still not be a conscious self. Its components are obviously distributed over different locations, and do not and cannot have the particular kind of unity characteristic of our conscious experience.

Moreover, there is no part of the brain where the self is located. Some physicalists have said that there is no royal "I," just a number of agents in the brain that direct different activities. In *How the Mind Works*, Steven Pinker (himself a physicalist) retorts that this doesn't make sense, because we have only one body and multiple agents would make it impossible for us to function at all, since there is no unifier. Certain parts of the brain, for instance, the frontal lobes, may be essential in the decision-making processes but, as Pinker says succinctly, "The 'I' is not a combination of body parts or brain states or bits of information, but a unity of selfness over time, a single locus that is nowhere in particular."[48] At the end of the day, no arguments against the self will ever work because of what they say. They present a world without experiencers—just experiences that aren't even experienced.

How Does the Self Retain Its Identity?

The Canadian neuroscientist Mario Beauregard asks how the self is able to retain its identity despite the constant flux at the neuronal level: "The average neuron, consisting of about 100,000 molecules, is about 80 percent water. The brain is home to about 100 billion such cells and thus about 10^{15} molecules. Each neuron gets 10,000 or so connections from other cells in the brain. Within each neuron, the molecules are replaced approximately 10,000 times in an average life span. Yet humans have a continuous sense of self that is stable over time."[49]

The Human Person Is Body and Soul

It should be stressed at this point that I am not suggesting that the human person is essentially a transphysical soul. The primary methodology underlying this book is that of being true to our experience. And it cannot be denied that we experience ourselves as both physical and transphysical. The human person is body and soul. Soul here is used in Aristotle's sense of being the principle of life of the body. Body and soul are not two substances that are conjoined in this life. Rather there is one substance, the human person, that has two dimensions. The soul forms the body just as the body "forms" the soul. For it is the soul that makes the body a body (as opposed to any mass of matter), and it is the body that makes the soul. Human nature is the unity of body and soul and the "center" of this unified reality is the person or self. Thus, the self is both ensouled and embodied. Our position here is not dualism, but holism. We are neither machines nor ghosts trapped in machines. We are, as Aristotle put it, rational animals: we can conceive just as easily as we can perceive.

Given the union of body and soul, it should come as no surprise that the body affects the operations of the soul just as the soul exerts its influence on the body.

If the body malfunctions, you malfunction. If your brain is damaged or you lose your hand, this has an effect on the functions that you can perform as a person. The self is dependent on the body for its normal functioning in this world. It is, after all, an embodied self.

In considering the unity of body and soul in the self, we should consider two phenomena that have sometimes been used as arguments against the existence of a unitary self, the functional distinctions between the right and left hemispheres of the brain, and the phenomenon of Multiple Personality Disorder. Daniel Dennett, in fact, has used the latter as an argument against the reality of a self. Space does not permit a detailed treatment, but a quick overview of the issues will be helpful.

Take split brains. Lund rightly points out that "the disunity exhibited by commissurotomized persons [that is, those whose left and right brain hemispheres have been surgically divided] is not a disunity in consciousness but a phenomenon brought about by the parallel processing of information. Information may be simultaneously processed at multiple sites in the brain, but such activity comes to be associated with only a single center or stream of consciousness."[50]

In Multiple Personality Disorder (today called Dissociative Identity Disorder), certain people manifest various personalities that might be called selves. As noted, Dennett seems to have built his whole argument against the self around the existence of this condition. But a lot has happened in the study of this disorder since Dennett first floated the argument. The existence of so-called "alter" personalities is no longer blindly accepted by specialists as it was by Dennett. More important, a study of the phenomenon shows that it cannot be considered an instance of different selves in the same body, but of a single self in turmoil. The very fact that the condition can be "cured" and that all the alleged personalities can be "integrated" shows that we are not talking of different selves, but of one.

Harold Merskey, an authority on MPDs, writes that there has been an enormous proliferation in the diagnosis of MPD. Concerned that this proliferation may have nothing to do with actual MPDs, he reviewed all the major historical cases. He found that "to my surprise, there was not a single case which allowed a valid diagnosis of MPD, free either from a misunderstanding or from the effects of suggestion. Several early cases were misdiagnosed examples of rapid cycling bipolar affective disorder. Later cases all showed the influence of suggestion—often frankly acknowledged."[51] A important recent work on MPDs and DIDs is *First Person Plural: Multiple Personality and the Philosophy of Mind* by Stephen Braude.

Mental disorders are the result of malfunctions of the brain caused by chemical imbalances or synaptic changes or injuries. But even in disorders ranging from amnesia to insanity, it can hardly be denied that the human person retains a first-person perspective. Even in these abnormal conditions, the self is known in every implicit or explicit first-person act whether in understanding and reasoning or in various conscious states or in a whole range of intentional activities. Neurologist Todd Feinberg has made an invaluable study of the relation of the self to various brain disorders in *Altered Egos: How the Brain Creates the Self.*

An Idea With Consequences

Our review of physicalist arguments indicates that the reality of the conscious, rational self cannot be evaded or explained away no matter what our ideology. The problem with physicalism is that it is an idea with consequences; it actually hinders the progress of science and technology. If indeed we do have a transphysical soul that intends, chooses, and thinks, then assimilation of this truth is important at many levels including the development of therapies and treatments.

This has been highlighted most graphically in the work of UCLA neuropsychiatrist. Jeffrey Schwartz, who has revolutionized the treatment of Obsessive Compulsive Disorder. Schwartz has authored more than a hundred scientific papers in neuroscience and psychiatry. In his work on OCD he noted that efficacious treatment of his patients required the assumption that they have a freewill and a mind separate from the brain that can control the brain's chemistry.

Although OCD itself can be explained by biochemical processes (repetitive firing of the error detector in the frontal cortex and anterior cingular), Schwartz has shown that it can be effectively treated only if the mind (so to speak) reprograms the brain. Schwartz highlights the implications of this approach: "The primary philosophical implication of the scientific work concerns the need to interpret neurobiological data with respect to active volitional processes as opposed to viewing all aspects of human experience as being simply the result of material brain-related phenomena."[52] In *The Mind and the Brain: Neuroplasticity and the Power of Mental Force*, Schwartz writes, "The time has come for science to confront the serious implications of the fact that directed, willed mental activity can clearly and systematically alter brain function."[53]

In his own extensive research, Mario Beauregard has also shown how recognition of a transphysical reality will enable effective therapy. He points out that neuroimaging studies show that the subjective nature and the intention-centered content ("what they are 'about' from a first-person perspective") of mental processes "significantly influence the various levels of brain functioning (for example, molecular, cellular, neural circuit) and brain plasticity. Furthermore, these findings indicate that mentalistic variables have to be seriously taken into account to reach a correct understanding of the neural bases of behavior in humans."[54]

Nobelist Neuroscientists on the Transphysical

It should be stressed that there is nothing anti-scientific about the idea of a transphysical dimension of our being. In fact prominent scientists, including at least three Nobel Prize-winning neuroscientists, have emphasized the undeniable reality of the transphysical.

Physicists on Physicalism

Let's consider first what two of the progenitors of quantum theory—experts on the nature of matter—had to say. When asked by *The Observer*, "Do you think that consciousness can be explained in terms of matter?" the pioneer of quantum theory Max Planck replied: "No, I regard consciousness as fundamental. I regard matter as derivative from consciousness. We cannot get behind consciousness. Everything that we talk about, everything that we regard as existing, postulates consciousness."[55]

Erwin Schroedinger, another prominent quantum theorist, said: "Consciousness cannot be accounted for in physical terms. For consciousness is absolutely fundamental. It cannot be accounted for in terms of anything else."[56]

Four of the greatest neuroscientists of the 20th century, three of them Nobel Prize winners, strongly affirmed the reality of the transphysical.

Sherrington

Charles Scott Sherrington, winner of the 1932 Nobel Prize for Medicine and Physiology, said in his Gifford Lectures: "If as you say thoughts are an outcome of the brain we as students using the energy-concept know nothing of it; as followers of natural science we know nothing of any relation between thoughts and the brain, except as a gross correlation in time and space. In some ways this is embarrassing for biology.... We have to regard the relation of mind to brain as not merely unresolved but still devoid of a basis for its very beginning."[57]

Eccles

Sir John Eccles, winner of the 1963 Nobel Prize for Medicine and Physiology, wrote extensively on the mind and brain. Here are a few of his many comments on the topic.

- ⚭ "I regard this theory [promissory materialism] as being without foundation. The more we discover scientifically about the brain the more clearly do we distinguish between the brain events and the mental phenomena and the more wonderful do the mental phenomena become. Promissory materialism is simply a superstition held by dogmatic materialists. It has all the features of a Messianic prophecy, with the promise of a future freed of all problems—a kind of Nirvana for our unfortunate successors."[58]

- ⚭ "I maintain that the human mystery is incredibly demeaned by scientific reductionism, with its claim in promissory materialism to account eventually for all of the spiritual world in terms of patterns of neuronal activity. This belief must be classed as a superstition."[59]

- ⚭ "We have to recognize that we are spiritual beings with souls existing in a spiritual world as well as material beings with bodies and brains existing in a material world."[60]

Sperry

As we have seen, Roger W. Sperry, winner of the 1981 Nobel Prize for Medicine and Physiology, was a leader in the battle against Behaviorism. In a paper titled "Turnabout on Consciousness," he observed that an objective understanding of mental activity requires us to take subjective qualities seriously. In this context, he warns that to think of these as "nothing but" or "identical to" the neural events themselves is to be misled. "A neural event, or, preferably, a brain event or brain process," he wrote, "is many things: it includes the physiology of nerve-impulse traffic, the underlying chemistry, plus all sorts of subatomic low- and high-energy physical phenomena. While these may be the stuff of neural events, they are not, as I see it, the conscious phenomena."[61]

Penfield

Finally, we cite Wilder Penfield, one of the pioneering neuroscientists of the last century. Penfield (1891–1976) said:

> For my own part, after years of striving to explain the mind on the basis of brain-action alone, I have come to the conclusion that it is simpler (and far easier to be logical) if one adopts the hypothesis that our being does consist of two fundamental elements. Because it seems to me certain that it will always be quite impossible to explain the mind on the basis of neuronal action within the brain, and because it seems to me that the mind develops and matures independently throughout an individual's life as though it were a continuing element, and because a computer (which the brain is) must be programmed and operated by an agency capable of independent understanding, I am forced to choose the proposition that our being is to be understood on the basis of two elements. This, to my mind, offers the greatest likelihood of leading us to the final understanding [for] which so many stalwart scientists strive."[62]

Considering the present-day popularity of physicalism, it is astonishing that four of the greatest brain scientists of all time were led by their work to affirm the reality of the transphysical.

Scientists on Life After Death

What about life after death? Astonishingly, an amazing 40 percent of American scientists believe in a life after death according to a major recent survey: "One number rings down through more than eight decades: 40 percent. Four in 10 of Leuba's scientists believed in God as defined in his survey. The same is true today. Somewhat more, about 50 percent, held to an after-life in Leuba's day, but now that figure is also 40 percent."[63]

The neuroscientist Wilder Penfield laid out his rationale for a life beyond death.

"The physical basis of the mind is the brain action in each individual; it accompanies the activity of his spirit, but the spirit is free; it is capable of some degree of initiative ... The spirit *is* the man one knows. He must have continuity through periods of sleep and coma. I assume, then, that this spirit must live on somehow after death. I cannot doubt that many make contact with God and have guidance from a greater spirit. But these are personal beliefs that every man must adopt for himself."[64]

Sir John Eccles was also a defender of the idea of life after death. He said, for instance, "I do believe that we are the product of the creativity of what we call God. I hope that this life will lead to some future existence where my self or soul will have another existence, with another brain, or computer if you like. I don't know how I got this one, it's a pretty good one, and I'm grateful for it, but I do know as a realist that it will disappear. But I think my conscious self or soul will come through."[65]

An Interview With Sir John Eccles

I was fortunate to be able to interview Sir John on the soul and life after death. Below is a transcript of our discussion on this topic.[66]

Do you accept the existance of a non-physical soul and how did it come to be?

The only certainty we have is that we exist as unique self-conscious beings, each unique, never to be repeated. This I regard as outside the evolutionary process. The conscious self is not in the Darwinist evolutionary process at all. I think it is a divine creation.

Do you see the soul as surviving death?

Yes. Although the theater is gone, the programmer can survive. It's all in God's mercy as to what further opportunities we have. After all we came from nothing. We have to trust God that the great adventure of being that he gave us is not finishing here on earth, but in a transcendent manner going on to another existence. That's the way I look at it—just to trust God in the future after death.

How would you respond to the materialist who denies a spiritual soul?

I would say that, when he is saying that, the materialist is making the statement that those statements are simply the brain generating lots of complicated impulses in the neurosystem and the sounds that make these words. This is entirely a material creation. You can ask, "did you think it out first in thoughts and did your thoughts have anything to do with what you say?" He will reply, "No, what I say is simply what the brain does and I listen to it." In other words, somebody says that I don't know what I think until I listen to what I say! I think if people believe that the brain is the creator of all their linguistic expressions and that they are merely passive recipients of the creations of their brain in language, then I don't argue with them. I don't argue with robots. I only argue with people who have a conscious, critical ability to think and to judge and to create and to recognize logic and to be defeated in argument. These are the qualities, I would say, of a human conscious person. Then you can have a dialogue, and the dialogue would be meaningful. But dialogue is not meaningful with a robot.

Chapter 7

To Be and Not to Be—What Does It Mean to "Survive" Death?

O ur review of the scientific data shows that science erects no barrier to the affirmation of the soul. But, in the light of modern science, is it possible for us to affirm the reality of a life after death? And is this a question for the philosophers? To start with, let me say that it is senseless to ask a certain class of philosophers if there is a life after death. This is because, as we have seen in the previous chapter, they do not admit there is a life before death (in the sense of continuous subsistence as a person)! Not only do they not believe in the existence of God, but they don't believe in their own existence!

Now any study of the possibility of an after-life must include an intelligible account of our life-before-death. An obvious starting-point is the "stuff" of which we are made. We know that there is a transphysical dimension to our nature. But is it entirely dependent on the physical and consequently doomed to perish with the body? And what is the nature of the human person?

Here we move beyond the tangible and the scientific since understanding, willing, and the self cannot even be physically described. Nevertheless we know that our acting in the world, our identity as persons cannot be understood without the physical. We are unified in thought and intention, sensation and action, to such an extent that it simply does not sound plausible to talk of a "mind" instructing a "body." Just as clearly we cannot (like the physicalists) talk of the brain instructing the body. The "I" is a unity that neither dualism nor physicalism can separate. So what is this "I"? Above all, can we give any sense to the idea of the posthumous existence of the human person?

In this book, we are exploring what we have called a cumulative case for the existence of an after-life. On the one hand, we consider the kind of information that comes to us from "external" data sources be they near-death experiences, primordial universal beliefs, or after-life visitations. On the other, we review what everyday experience and (if relevant) empirical science tell us about the nature of the human person. Our focus in this final chapter is on what we know about "survival" just from knowing ourselves.

Four Approaches to the After-life

Historically, there have been four basic kinds of answers given to the question of whether there is a life after death.

1. *There is no after-life.* We are simply physical through and through, and death is the permanent dissolution of the human person: it is literally annihilation. This is the view taken by materialists and physicalists. There are some non-physicalists who admit that there may be a non-physical dimension to human nature, but then assert that this dimension ceases to exist at death.

2. *Immortality of the soul.* We are made up of two entities, a body, and a soul or mind. The soul or mind is the real "me," while the body is a temporary add-on. When the body dies, the soul persists in some otherworldly realm doing we know not what.

3. *Reincarnation.* As with the immortality of the soul, it is believed that we are made up of two entities, a body and a soul, with the added proviso that the same soul can inhabit different bodies. When the present body dies, the soul enters another body.

4. *Resurrection.* The human person is a unified subject that has material and immaterial dimensions, an indivisible whole that is not a mixture of parts. You still use the language of soul and body, but here the soul is the principle of life of the body; the soul is "formed" by the body just as the body is "formed" by the soul. The person is not soul or body, but a unique union of both. Death is the cessation of the person's ability to perform physical operations, but his or her soul continues to survive in an incomplete, unnatural state. At some point the soul, while retaining the identity

it received as the "life" of a particular body, could again become the animating principle of a new set of physical processes and systems (which therefore constitute its body), and this would be described as a resurrection. Notice that the identity of the person remains the same at all times even with the changes in the matter of the body.

A Preliminary Verdict on the Four Options

We will consider these views briefly, but study them in more detail as we proceed.

1. *No after-life*. This view largely depends on whether or not physicalism or materialism are true. But, as we will be seeing, there is a dimension of our being that is clearly non-physical or immaterial. So this means that physicalism and materialism are false. Admittedly, the falsity of physicalism does not thereby show that there is a life after death, but it certainly opens the door to its possibility.

2. *Immortality*. The immortality of a soul that is a distinct substance from the body was popular among some Greeks thinkers, as well as philosophers like Descartes. But it has rightly been pointed out that such views cast doubt on the self-evident unity of the human person: we are one not two. It is the same subject that performs physical and non-physical acts. We should be talking of a unified subject instead of minds and bodies.

3. *Reincarnation*. This view was popular among certain Greek thinkers and is held by most of today's Hindus and Buddhists (the latter call it rebirth) and many modern Europeans and Americans. This was not the view taken by the Vedic Hindus, and even in post-Vedic Hinduism reincarnation is considered a "fallen" state. Moreover, it is a view that flies in the face of the self-evident unity of the human person, as well as the self-evident awareness of the immediacy and ultimacy of our personal identity. A belief in reincarnation is often tied to a prior belief in monism or pantheism. In monism it is assumed that each soul successively "occupies" various bodies in the process of liberating itself from the phenomenal

world as it realizes its identity with Brahman, the Absolute. The Buddhist theory of rebirth is different from Hindu theories of reincarnation, because Buddhists do not recognize the continued existence of a substantial self. Rebirths in Buddhism affirm the transmission of dispositional traits not of a single soul. For the monist the culmination of the soul's journey of liberation from ignorance to enlightenment is its dissolution in the Absolute. The notion of dissolution in the Absolute has been criticized by Eastern and Western philosophers for not taking our experience of self-consciousness and personal identity seriously.

4. *Resurrection.* This view, held by Zoroastrianism, Judaism, Christianity, and Islam, is consistent with what we know about the unity of the human person and our experience of the non-physical. Clearly, belief in the ultimate resurrection of human beings is usually based on acceptance of a claim of divine revelation. Nevertheless, such a prior belief in revelation is not necessarily required. On a natural level, we can, at the very least, come to see that some kind of life after death is to be expected given that we perform intrinsically non-physical operations (such as understanding the content of this sentence). These operations could not be performed without a non-physical soul. But when you add to this data-point the kinds of data brought to bear in this book (NDEs and After-Life Visitations, for instance), we are led to a plausible visualization of "risen" bodies. These encounters in themselves are not "religious" revelations. Thus, the idea of the resurrection of the body can suggest itself from sources other than revelation.

Claims of divine revelation, in any case, do not simply concern the resurrection of the body. Just as important is the proclamation that there are one of two final states that will be chosen by every human person: a state of unending happiness or one of endless suffering. Heaven or Hell. This is an idea that goes beyond Judaism or Christianity, and is implicitly or explicitly taught in all the ancient religions. It is interestingly also a feature of today's after-life experiences.

Soul-Searching

Any coherent idea of an after-life requires us to speak of the soul surviving the death of the body. But what exactly do we mean by soul? And how do we know that it not only exists, but continues in existence after the death of the body?

There are three ways in which we can answer the question:

1. The *dualists* say that the soul and body are two separate entities or substances. It is the soul that is the real "you." It just happens to occupy a body for a given time and upon death continues in existence either on its own or in another body as a new "you."

2. The *physicalists* say that there is no soul and all our mental activity is simply a matter of neurons in motion.

3. The *holists* hold that the soul, the body, and the human person come to be in a simultaneous action. Here the soul is that which animates, organizes, and unifies a conglomerate of matter, so that it is now a body and it is the ensouled body that constitutes the person.

How Holists Talk of Surviving Death

Let us explore the holist answer further. Without the principle of life that is the soul there is no body. But without the body there is no soul, because the human soul (as opposed to a pure spirit) is intrinsically oriented to a body. Nevertheless, it is the soul that brings a body into being: it has its own act of existing into which it brings the body. The human soul does perform certain fundamental operations, such as understanding and willing that are intrinsically non-physical. Therefore, its act of existing is not only non-physical, but one which does not depend on the body for continued subsistence. But such an existence without a body is unnatural, because a human person is essentially embodied and ensouled. It is not you in your fullness and integrity who continue in being, but your soul.

Hence, at the very same time, we can "be" after death, but "not be" in the fullness of our nature.

Why Holism Is True to Experience

This might seem to be a distinction without a difference, but it goes to the heart of how we go about our inquiry. Do we want to be true to our experience? If so, as previously shown, we have to admit the existence of the transphysical. And this means physicalism is a non-starter. But it also means that hard-core dualism doesn't do the job (although it is far superior to physicalism). We are not two entities. Every one of my actions is the action of the embodied person that I am, and these actions are almost always simultaneously physical and transphysical. I say "almost" because intellectual acts such as your understanding of the arguments I am laying out here have no physical correlate or structure:

it is purely a transphysical act; it is an act of the transphysical soul. Nevertheless it is "your" act: it is you the person who thinks through the arguments using your soul just as it is you who go for a walk using your body. Thus, to be true to our experience is to see things holistically.

This was recognized by Aristotle and Thomas Aquinas, his most influential successor, as also by the modern phenomenologists and (to some extent) such thinkers as Ludwig Wittgenstein and Gilbert Ryle. "Aquinas contends that the capacities of a human being must be attributed to the human being itself," writes David Braine. "And not to any of his parts. A human being's soul is the source of his capacities; a human being's body is the material support for such capacities. However a human being is that which has the capacities."[1]

The Greeks on Dualism, Physicalism, and Holism

The three options cited here, dualism, physicalism, and holism, were articulated by the Greeks. Epicurus represented physicalism, Plato dualism, and Aristotle holism. These were the three fundamental views of personhood—the human person as physical, as non-physical, and as a unique composite of animal and spirit. It can be argued that the major religious traditions have opted for an Aristotelian approach. Thus Zoroastrianism, Judaism, Christianity, and Islam proclaimed a life after death that revolved around the resurrection of the body.

Hinduism and Resurrection

Paradoxically the post-Vedic Hindu view of reincarnation is, in its own way, an affirmation of the resurrection of the body. Intuitively, the reincarnationists recognize that the human person is somehow incomplete without a body. I shall be arguing that the doctrine of reincarnation is incoherent for various reasons, but primarily because it flies in the face of immediate experience (the enduring identity of this particular "I," for instance); furthermore, it is not to be found in primordial Hinduism. But, curiously, its popularity highlights the human mind's inability to rest in the idea of a disembodied soul. A soul needs a body to be a complete person. Thus, in the reincarnationist scenario, it has to move from body to body—when it stops reincarnating it "dissolves." To be a human being you need body and soul.

Immortality of the Soul

The immortality of the soul, in short, is not one of those ideas that can be universally embraced with religious fervor. It is a philosopher's dream. This is not because the idea of a pure spirit is foreign to the human mind. As a matter of fact, most of the major religions do believe in pure spirits who are active in the world, spirits good and bad. But the same religions recognize that a human being is different from an angel.

The holist view is the one that accords best with our immediate experience, because it does not try to explain away the physical and transphysical dimensions that are fundamental to our being. A study of the holist approach is simultaneously a review of the competing physicalist and dualist positions.

A lot more needs to be said, of course. The first priority is reaching a resolution on the nature of the human person. From there we move on to the grounds from immediate experience for believing that humans survive physical death. Finally, we address the questions of reincarnation, resurrection, and separated souls.

The Human Person— A Psychophysical Organism Capable of Thinking and Willing

It has often been said that English is a language divided by two countries. We might well say that "soul" is an idea divided by two philosophies. What Plato and Descartes meant by soul was entirely different from what Aristotle and Aquinas had in mind.

Plato thought of the soul as the essence of the person. It is made up of mind, emotion, and desire. It "uses" the body temporarily, but the body is regarded as a prison or tomb from which the soul needs to be liberated.

Aristotle held that all life-forms had souls, although the kind of soul varied with the kind of being we were speaking about. Essentially the Aristotelian soul is a principle of organization that gives matter a specific unity, identity, and agency whether as plant or animal. We do not have two substances but one reality, one being—matter that is "informed" or organized by a principle of life into a particular kind of being. We call it a particular life-form (tree or mammal) depending on the kind of "form" into which the living matter is organized. The idea of separating soul and body makes no sense, because without the soul there is no body, and without the body there is no soul.

A Living, Sensing, Moving, and Thinking Thing

"One way to understand the notion of a human soul, as a substantial form, in contemporary terms is to think of it as a principle of organization for material particles," writes Jason Eberle. "A human body is an organic construct. It has a variety of parts that operate both independently and collectively to support the existence and activity of a living, sensing, moving and thinking thing. Both the independent operation of one of a body's organs and its functional unity with the body's other organs, are governed by the formal unity of the organism itself."[2]

A Person—Not a Soul Plus a Body

Exploring the idea of the soul in relation to human life-forms we ask:

- ⮑ What makes me something that can act?
- ⮑ What makes the matter with which I act a body (my body!)?
- ⮑ What keeps everything about me organized, unified, and continuous?

It is this principle, this source and root of our life, unity, and actions that we call the soul.

We do not talk of soul plus body because the very nature of a soul is to be that which makes a body a body: the soul and the body come to simultaneously form a single being, the I or self. Starting with Boethius's definition of the human person, "an individual substance of a rational nature,"[3] Aquinas went on to describe the person as "a substance, complete, subsisting *per se*, existing apart from others."[4]

The person/I/self is agent—the source and center of all its actions. The person is subject—the observer with subjective consciousness. The kind of being I am is a body animated by a transphysical soul. But what happens to the I/self when the body ceases to function? My soul—the soul of any human— does not simply animate and organize the body. It also performs actions that are entirely non-physical.

- ⮑ Does this mean that it is independent of the physical, that it can operate independently of the body (as it does in acts of the intellect and will)?
- ⮑ Do I have any reason to believe that the soul will survive dissolution of the body?
- ⮑ Can I, the agent and subject, survive if only my soul survives?

The answers to all these questions is yes. The operations of the soul and the very nature of the self indicate that there is something here independent of matter. This something can survive separation from the physical albeit in an unnatural and impoverished state.

The Soul Creates the Body

Before turning to the matter-independent powers of the human soul, we should grasp something more fundamental. This is the fact that the soul, in a sense, creates the body.

As we shall see, a study of the operations of the human soul will show that it has capacities that are non-bodily in origin and nature. Important as this is for the question of survival, the relation of soul to body is even more fundamental. As Aquinas saw it, the most relevant issue is how the human being comes into existence: "Although the soul and the body of man have one and the same act of existing in common, nevertheless that act of existing is communicated to the body by the soul. Thus the human soul communicates to the body that very act of existing by which the soul itself subsists."[5]

In short, the human soul shares its act of existing with the body and this single act of existing is the human person. And if the soul's act of existing is intrinsically immaterial then the death of the body does not preclude the survival of the soul. Talk of the act of existing may sound somewhat esoteric, but it is germane to the question of survival and needs elucidation.

Existing Is an Act

To exist is an act. There is a distinction between the attributes of a being (humans or trees or unicorns), and its act of existing. It is the act of existing that makes that being real and actual. The existence of a being is the act of existing of its essence, of what it is. Now a human being, a composite of body and soul, has one act of existing. This act comes from the soul, which communicates it to the body thus bringing about a single person. Although your act of existing is yours alone, the attributes of your being are common to all humans. But each person is unique, because each is a person through a unique act of existing and a unique history.

It is the body that shares the soul's act of existing and not the other way around. In the case of other animals, the death of the body is also the cessation of the soul, because the soul's operations are entirely dependent on the physical. But cannot the same be said of the human soul given the vital role played by the brain? The answer here, for reasons given below, is no.

Thoughts on Thought

We know that the operation of sensory organs and networks are essential to our knowledge of the world. Of course these operations are dependent on the physical, although the resultant conscious states are transphysical. But are there any powers of the soul that establish it as independent of the physical? Previously we spoke of 10 hard facts that establish the reality of the transphysical. But just because something is transphysical there is no reason to believe that it can exist independently without some link with matter. Nevertheless, we have said that the human soul is not simply transphysical, but capable of independent existence. We will now consider the four hard facts that point to the physically independent reality of human thought. These facts have been highlighted by some of the most sophisticated logicians and thinkers of our time.

Four Hard Facts About the Physically Independent Nature of Thought

These facts are:

- ⬧ The nature of thinking is an activity that is both basic and not clockable in physical time.
- ⬧ Normal human thinking, if it were a physical process, would require the impossibility of an infinite number of physical states.
- ⬧ Understanding and thinking in the medium of language cannot be carried out by any physical organ or process.
- ⬧ Concepts and universals, which are an integral part of all our thinking, cannot be understood in terms of the physical.

It should be said that several of the physicalists we reviewed earlier, such as Stephen Pinker and Gerald Edelman, have marveled at the infinite reach of language. But it is the philosophers and logicians who have taken such observations to their logical conclusion.

Geach on Thinking as a Basic Activity

Peter Geach, a noted logician, holds that thinking is a basic activity in the sense that there is no activity underlying thinking that is more fundamental. Also, thinking is not something that can be correlated with the physical time-series. This is because it is not possible to correlate specific thoughts to specific periods. Consequently, physicalism cannot work because "the basic activities of any bodily part must be clockable in physical time in a way that thinking is not."[6]

Ross on Thinking as Involving a Capacity for an Infinity of States

Another prominent philosopher, James Ross, argues in a paper titled "Immaterial Aspects of Thought" that we cannot use logic or pure mathematics or thinking in general if our judgments are physical processes. "In principle," writes Ross, "truth-carrying thoughts cannot be wholly physical (though they might have a physical medium) because they have features that no physical thing or process can have at all." The human person can understand any arithmetical theorem or any well-formed utterance in any language given appropriate circumstances. But if understanding was a matter of brain-states this would not be possible because no physical object can be in an infinity of states.

Because our thinking occurs with an immaterial medium we have the selective infinite capacity that is required for our normal operations of theoretical and practical reason. Our brain is capable of being in a finite number of electrochemical states. But even if all of these states were realized, for instance 10^{140} different thoughts, we still could not *understand* "an infinity of mathematical theorems" because there would not be brain states or functions among brain states to realize these. Humans, however, "are able to be in an infinity of states of understanding, not successively but qualitatively. That is, we have the active ability to understand anything (accidents of presentation of intelligence quotient being ignored for now). Thus, there is no arithmetical theorem we cannot understand."[7]

Braine on Why Linguistic Understanding Has No Associated Bodily Activity

The magnum opus in this domain is clearly David Braine's *The Human Person—Animal and Spirit*. In a book of some 555 pages, Braine seeks to show that linguistic understanding is a complete act of its own that has no bodily organ and excludes any bodily activity from being internal to it. Understanding and thinking in the medium of words "are 'operations' of the human being which have no inner neural realization: they have a bodily expression in speech, and are typically directed towards bodily objects (bodily things as real or intentional objects), but are not operations of any bodily organ."[8]

Braine's major point is that thought expressed in language and the understanding of language "cannot have any physical process internal to them as physical processes are internal to perception, imagining, emotion, and intentional action." He gives four reasons for this position.

It is the person who speaks and understands	In thinking expressed in words whether in writing or speech, "it is the person or human who understands, speaks, hears, and thinks, and these are not operations of some inner part of him or her, but of the person him or herself."
The power of conceptual thinking	The use of general concepts cannot be emulated by any material process or state, because what is required is "a capacity or principle of operation making it possible for the human being to grasp the essence of the likeness" between different instances of the same concept, for example, knowing what are the features common to different humans. Physical structures in the brain or images of various humans will not do the job since we have to stand back from all humans and make a judgment on what is alike about them using our understanding.
Use of language involves indefinite number of ways of using words	Linguistic expression and understanding require us "to use words in an indefinite number of logically distinguishable types of use." This cannot be correlated with any physical organ or process, "because any supposed correlate would lack the flexibility, or extensibility in type of relation to different types of case, which is required." "The fact that understanding explains something, without there being a deterministic mechanical process involved, is shown by the impossibility of calculating rather than 'seeing' meaning."
Language requires a subject capable of self-reflection	The capacity for language or linguistic understanding or for thought in the medium of words requires "a judging subject and within it structures of self-reflection and of reflection on procedures of coming to judgements." This structure has to be unitary while incorporating these sub-systems. No mechanically operating system can emulate these structures. Also the ability to critically reflect cannot be tied to any physical process internal to it.[9]

In sum, writes Braine, "there can be no neural correlate or other inner physical embodiment of the understanding expressed in linguistic activities. This understanding has a public expression, physical in its way, but the understanding which underlies it, of which it is the expression and ergon, has no organ, no inner voice waiting to be inwardly heard. In brief, there are no mechanisms of any kind, non-physical or physical, digital or analog, internal to linguistic understanding and thinking in the medium of words."[10]

Conceptual Thinking Is Clearly Immaterial

The mystery of conceptual thinking is another testament to the soul's independence from the physical. Whatever we know about the world we know through concepts. We notice differences and similarities between things and generalize and universalize from this. Thomas Sullivan points out that all human thought revolves around our ability to effortlessly think of universal characteristics that can have local instances, for instance the ideas of hot and blue. This is clearly an immaterial activity because these ideas are not linked to something physical (for instance, we do not have think to of a blue object when we think of blueness). John Haldane has shown that concepts transcend material configurations in space-time because (a) here any property of a thing can be described in many non-equivalent ways of thinking; (b) this order of concepts is thus far more abstract than the natural order; (c) it's hard to see how the former then could spring from the latter.

How Does the Soul Think?

We might ask at this stage, what does it mean to think "by virtue of the soul"? The soul is not a "thing" or a "part" that exists in parallel with the body. It is a reality without question, but one which is not in any sense physical. It does not occupy space, but operates in space. Now conceptual thought is not something that takes place with a specific mechanism. It is an action performed by me, but an action that has no sub-systems. So what is the relationship between such thought and the brain? Quite clearly the brain and the body are inextricably involved with our feelings, perceptions, emotions, sensations, and imaginings. I am the subject of all such "operations," but all of these are embedded in matter, impossible without the physical. Moreover, they furnish the raw data for our concepts and thoughts.

But conceptual thought itself does not have any of the accoutrements of matter. There are no photons or quarks involved in my thoughts about energy as the product of mass multiplied by the square of the speed of light. There are no images of plus signs in my use of the conjunction "and." Conceptual thought is an activity that is entirely independent of the physical, although it is expressed through physical media (symbols and sounds).

And to the extent that "I" am not divided into several subjects, one for seeing, another for feeling, and a third for thinking, it is the same "I" who performs all these actions some through the joint action of soul and body and some entirely by means of the soul. The soul is the seat of intellect and will, but, at the same time, it is the "organizer" of the body. Consequently, the intellectual and volitional acts that I perform via the soul are affected by the state of the body it animates. If I suffer from Alzheimer's or some disorder of the nervous system, I, the composite of body and soul, am affected at all levels of my normal functioning.

But both benefits and barriers issuing from the unity of soul and body are eliminated when they separate. The soul's operations of intellect and will are not helped or hampered by the body in this new state. There will be no more sensory images or bodily sensations, but thinking and willing will continue without the limitations of matter.

Am I Willing?

The other dimension of the human soul that entirely transcends the physical is the will. What is it that impels us to intend, choose, and act that instills us with a sense of obligation and responsibility? It is the will, a reality that determinist and physicalist accounts sweep under the rug, but keeps popping up and pulling the rug from under them.

The "argument from the will" has been elegantly set out by John Coons. After reviewing Hume's vain efforts to "locate" his self by looking inward, Coons makes the point that our experience of responsibility is not just something we perceive, and its singular nature makes it a good candidate for the ground of the self.[11] Coons clarifies that by the experience of responsibility he means the awareness that everyone has of being called to follow a correct choice of conduct. This is verified universally—even among Humeans.

The content of our consciousness "caught" by Hume can be explained away as products of the senses and neural resources. Human responsibility, on the other hand, is experienced, "not because we 'catch' it, but—to the contrary—because it catches us." It is not an experience of perceiving something but of being perceived. This "experience cannot be explained descriptively as the product of mindless matter and neural energy."[12]

The drive of the will is not dependent on memory. Even in cases of amnesia where a man forgets his place in the world, what "he retains is the experience of responsibility; he knows that there is correct conduct to be sought, and that he has the capacity to commit to its search."[13]

The Will Initiates Acts and Executes What Is Conceived and Intended

The classic account of the will in modern times was laid out by Austin Farrer in his *Finite and Infinite*. In this work, he starts with himself self-disclosed as the subject of his acts. To exist is to be active and alive. The will is that which initiates acts and makes real what is conceived and intended. Its acts are unique and irreducible. Farrer notes that "in the nature of the case self and will must be indescribable, except by metaphors, which are always wrong." The structure of the self "can be described to some extent. We find that structure to be systematic and continuous, though not fixed; and it is filled and vivified by a will itself continuous, forming it and formed by it. This will, taken in its extension, we call the self; in its focused expression, the will."[14]

The Subsistence of the Soul

Can the soul subsist on its own upon the death of the body? Our accounts of the non-physical operations of the soul and its own act of existing give us good reason to affirm that it can survive the death of the body. But more needs to be said on this if only for clarity's sake.

Aquinas's Argument

Aquinas's key point is the nature of intellectual understanding. His argument for the subsistence of the human soul is laid out in question 75, article 2 of the *Prima Pars* (as pointed out by Denis Bradley):

1. Since only what subsists in itself apart from the body could operate apart from the body.
2. Since the rational soul in intellectual understanding does per se operate apart from any organ of the human body.
3. The human soul must be incorporeal, separable, and subsistent.[15]

Ross on How Understanding Shows Us Who We Are

James Ross and David Braine develop this argument further. "The subsistent being of the soul is required by the fact that it has an activity independent of the body, namely understanding which it performs constantly on account of what it is for; for, as Aquinas says, activity follows upon being," writes Ross. "The nature of understanding requires such action; such action requires such being."[16]

Braine on Why the Human Understander is Undivided and Indivisible

Braine considers another dimension: "Under the aspect under which the human being transcends the body as the subject of understanding and thinking, it is undivided and indivisible in a way in which no body is and many lower living things are not. Nonetheless, while it is essential to human nature that the subject of linguistic understanding and thought be also the subject of perception and imagination, it remains that distinction of bodily parts and bodily function are not internal to the operations of understanding and thought as they are internal to the operations of perceiving and imagining."[17]

The Intellectual Nature of the Soul Shows It to Be a Divine Creation

The intellectual nature of the human soul also indicates that the coming into being of each human soul can only be a direct divine creation: "Since intellective capacities surpass the limits of matter," writes Eberle, "No purely material process can be responsible for the generation of substantial forms with such capacities. All other substantial forms of material substances can be generated through purely material processes. Aquinas thus argues that a human soul must receive its being (*esse*) directly from God."[18]

The neuroscientist Sir John Eccles came to the same conclusion from a different direction:

> Since materialist solutions fail to account for our experienced uniqueness, I am constrained to attribute the uniqueness of the psyche or soul to a supernatural spiritual creation. To give the explanation in theological terms: each soul is a new Divine creation ... It is the certainty of the inner core of unique individuality that necessitates the 'Divine creation.' I submit that no other explanation is tenable; neither the genetic

uniqueness with its fantastically impossible lottery nor the environmental differentiations which do not determine one's uniqueness, but merely modify it. This conclusion is of inestimable theological significance. It strongly reinforces our belief in the human soul and in its miraculous origin in a Divine creation. There is recognition not only of the Transcendent God, the Creator of the Cosmos, the God in which Einstein believed, but also the loving God to whom we owe our being."[19]

The Contemporary Philosophical Case for Life After Death

The nature of the human soul as revealed in the immaterial and physically independent operations of knowing and willing points to its surviving the death of the body. Before further exploring these implications, we will consider what three contemporary philosophers and a prominent neuro-psychiatrist, taking entirely different routes, have said about life after death.

Stephen Braude

The first of these is Stephen Braude, the author of *Immortal Remains— The Evidence for Life After Death.*[20] Braude finds that a cumulative case approach to the evidence for a life after death is the most fruitful: "The totality of survival evidence has a kind of cumulative force, even if individual strands of evidence are less than convincing when considered on their own merits. Evidence taken collectively is stronger…because each of the kinds of evidence increases the antecedent probability of a survivalist interpretation of the others."[21]

Neal Grossman

Neal Grossman's trenchant analyses have served as a powerful wake-up call to skeptics lost in their dogmatic slumbers. His great achievement has been that of calling their bluff. Here is one of many memorable contributions:

If the fundamaterialist says that the hypothesis of an afterlife is so extraordinary that we should prefer any other hypothesis, so long that it is consistent with materialism and not self-contradictory, my reply is as follows: There is absolutely nothing extraordinary about the hypothesis of an afterlife. The overwhelming majority of people in the world believe it, and have always believed it. I grant, however, that there exists a rather peculiar subgroup of human beings for whom the survival hypothesis is extraordinary. This subgroup consists of people who have been university-educated into accepting materialist dogma on faith. We have been brainwashed by our university education into accepting that the hypothesis of an afterlife is extraordinary. It is perhaps time to acknowledge this, and to acknowledge that we are all suffering from what Gary Schwartz has called "post-educational stress disorder" (Schwartz and Simon, 2002, p. 224). Part of this "disorder" is that we have internalized the academy's materialist worldview, and we call anything that falls outside that worldview "extraordinary." But it is the materialists' worldview that is truly extraordinary, especially when one considers the ridiculous hypotheses that that worldview advances in order to save itself, such as...nonfunctioning brains still somehow producing conscious experience. Survival researchers are under no obligation to refute every, or even any, logically possible alternative hypothesis. Such "hypotheses" are nothing more than the imaginings of the fundamaterialists; the burden is on them to provide non-ideological empirical support for their hypotheses before scientists should take them seriously. In the absence of empirical support, such hypotheses merely reflect the fantasy life of the debunkers, and science is not obliged to take unsupported imaginings and fantasies seriously.[22]

David Lund

David Lund has emerged as one of the premier American thinkers on the self and consciousness. In *Death and Consciousness—The Case for Life After Death* he concluded, "On the basis of what we consider essential to our being persons, we found that survival of death is conceivable and that we can form a clear, detailed conception of a Next World in which we could continue to have experience in such a manner that personal identity is unambiguously preserved. Then we examined various kinds of phenomena which suggest that we do in fact survive death and found that many constitute impressive evidence for thinking that we survive."[23]

In his recent work, *The Conscious Self*, Lund gives an update on the state of the discussion. Although physicalism may be dominant in certain circles, it has not "succeeded in providing an adequate account of persons and their experiences." Nor is it a view that has commended itself to humanity in general. "The widespread acceptance among philosophers and other thinkers of a thoroughgoing materialist view of persons—the view that persons are entirely material beings—is a recent and rather remarkable phenomenon. This view has been rejected, at least implicitly, by the great majority of people through the ages. In nearly every society of which we have any record we find the idea of an afterlife and the belief that the soul or essence of a person survives the death of the body."[24]

Peter Fenwick

We have already referred to the work on NDEs done by the internationally known neuro-psychiatrist Peter Fenwick. Dr. Fenwick addresses the question of what follows death with Elizabeth Fenwick in *The Art of Dying*. "The evidence points to the fact that we are more than brain function, more than just a speck in creation, and that something, whether we regard it as soul or consciousness, will continue in some form or another, making its journey to 'Elsewhere.' It suggests that when we enter the light we are coming home, that we do indeed touch the inner reaches of a universe that is composed of universal love." [25]

Reincarnation

The main competitor for belief in the post-mortem continuation of our identity as the persons we are today is reincarnation, which literally means "to be made flesh again." The essential claim of the reincarnationists is that the soul will enter some other physical being, be it plant, animal, human, or extra-terrestrial. Reincarnation has also been termed metempsychosis and transmigration. Now not all theories of survival can survive the tests of experience, evidence, and coherence. Nowhere is this truer than in the case of reincarnation.

In my view, the doctrine of reincarnation is not viable for three reasons:

↬   It is not coherent in terms of what we know about human nature or modern biology.

↬   The evidence offered in support of it is always anecdotal, sometimes fraught with fraud and self-deception, and, for those who wish to accept the authenticity of certain past-life memories, better accounted for by other plausible paranormal explanations.

↬   The structure of reality that has to be hypothesized by the reincarnationist is implausible in the extreme (to mention two issues, how is the system of body selection monitored? How can the theory relate to such facts as the growth in world population?).

Our criterion thus far has been to stick with what is consistent with and evident from our everyday experience. The idea that there is a transphysical dimension to our being, that our thoughts are intrinsically immaterial is certainly evident in our experience. But so is the idea that our body is integral to who we are—as integral as its principle of life and organization—the soul. I am a unity of matter and spirit not an identity-less astral being who passes in and out of gross bodies.

Applying this approach to reincarnation, we ask:

- ↜ Is there anything in our everyday experience that supports the belief in question (much as intellect and will and physicality ground our conviction that we are a unique union of soul and body)?
- ↜ Does the claim of reincarnation fly in the face of everyday experience?
- ↜ Does it make sense in itself? Is it coherent?
- ↜ Can the purported evidence for reincarnation be explained in any other way?

In this investigation of reincarnation, I had the privilege of working with one of the leading scholars in the area, Dr. C.T. Krishnamachari, a devout Hindu who was inducted into the Indian Council of Philosophy by the Government of India. Chari (as he was popularly known) had occasion to interview many of the alleged recipients of past-life memories and also interacted extensively with the best-known Western proponent of reincarnation, Dr. Ian Stevenson. Chari's comprehensive case against the theory of reincarnation has yet to be addressed or answered (it should be remembered that Chari remained a devout Hindu throughout his career). His published critiques as well as excerpts from his interviews with me will be referenced here.

Another source referenced here is the philosopher Paul Edwards who authored a thorough and incisive refutation of all varieties of reincarnation titled *Reincarnation: A Critical Examination*.[26] Edwards was a physicalist and denied not just a life after death, but any transphysical reality. But his short chapter in this book on the relation of the brain to consciousness really says nothing relevant to the primary grounds for affirming the survival of the soul: the intellectual and volitional operations of the human person that cannot be described or explained in physical terms. Our concern here is not with Edwards's philosophical views in general, but his analysis of the arguments for reincarnation.

The godfather of modern reincarnation studies was Dr. Ian Stevenson. But, as noted in a *Washington Post* story, Stevenson's prodigious efforts to assemble evidence for reincarnation never won acceptance from the scientific community: "With rare exception, mainstream scientists—the only group Dr. Stevenson really cared to persuade —tended to ignore or dismiss his decades in the field and his many publications. Of those who noticed him at all, some questioned Dr. Stevenson's objectivity; others claimed he was credulous." The article pointed out that "Stevenson himself recognized one glaring flaw in his case for reincarnation: the absence of any evidence of a physical process by which a personality could survive death and transfer to another body."[27]

There are two paradoxes about reincarnation: In one sense it is ultimately no different from physicalism when it comes to the human self. The theory holds that there is no enduring identity of the self and that its ultimate destiny is to be dissolved into the universal Soul. In the long run, *you* cease to be. Secondly, it is also an implicit acknowledgement that the human mind cannot be satisfied with anything less than an embodied soul: as we noted, it is paradoxically an affirmation of resurrection-type views of the after-life.

There are two primary grounds that lead its proponents to affirm reincarnation, although the two are not necessarily related. One is religious belief and the other is the phenomenon of individuals who claim to "remember" their past lives. We consider both.

Religion

The roots of religious belief in reincarnation can be found primarily in the East though there are traces of the belief in some of the Greeks and the Druids. Historically it is a later-stage belief in Hinduism, a belief that is not part of the Vedic vision. The religion of the Vedas, the holiest books of Hinduism, did not teach reincarnation. It was only in some of the later Upanishads and Puranas that reincarnation emerged as a full-blown doctrine.

According to Swami Agehananda Bharati, reincarnation is "not as old as people hope it would be." In fact, "There is the first complete mention, though very brief, in the Brihadaranyaka Upanishad, which is quite old. But the real assumptions having to do with reincarnation come in the Puranic age, at the time that the Puranas were composed, and then of course, through Buddhism. So you might say that it reached a state of common acceptance, I would think, around 300 BC, but not earlier. So it is old, but in its highly articulated form it is not so old—and the way it's talked about now, that's recent; that's 'Theosophical Society.'"[28]

R.C. Zaehner, the great scholar of comparative religion, writes that "there is no trace [of reincarnation] in the Samhitas [the Vedas] or Brahmanas, and it is only when we come to the Upanishads that we first meet with this doctrine, which was to become central to all Hindu thought. In the Rig Veda the soul of the dead is carried aloft by the fire-god, Agni, who consumes the material body at cremation, to the heavenly worlds where it disports itself with the gods in perfect, carefree bliss. There will be eating and drinking of heavenly food and drink, reunion with father, mother, wife, and sons. In the Brihadaranyaka Upanishad (6.2. 15-16), however, a distinction is made.... Here for the first time we meet the doctrine of rebirth."[29]

It should be understood that reincarnation is not portrayed as a desirable state even in those texts that propound it. It is by no means a cheerful view of life after death. Chari points out that "First of all, Hinduism is not committed absolutely to belief in reincarnation. It is not as if Hindu metaphysics condemns every soul to be reborn. In all the systems it is recognized that there are souls that are not reborn at all. Indeed the goal of Hindu metaphysics is not to be reborn. The cycle of rebirth is a fallen state. What the Western reincarnationist does not realize is that the cycle of births and rebirths is a fallen, sinful state. Redemption lies in going beyond the cycle. Even when there is belief in reincarnation in Hinduism it has a secondary place."[30]

The Buddhist Idea of Rebirth

Buddhism, which rejected the teachings and practices of the Vedas, was founded in the sixth century BC. The Buddhist doctrine of rebirth has significant differences from reincarnation in Hinduism. Whereas Hinduism had the idea of unchanging jivatmans that went through numerous rebirths until merging with the Absolute, Buddhism was committed to the idea of anata or no-self. There is no self, only a compound of five skandhas or streams: bodily sensation, feeling, perception, moral dispositions, consciousness. At death the five streams separate and the flow of mental life continues in a cycle of rebirth until release in nirvana.

The historian of philosophy Frederick Copleston points out that there are changing mental states, but no self that has these states. He therefore finds it hard to make sense of the idea of rebirth: "It seems to me difficult to reconcile what is known as the doctrine of 'no-self' with Buddhist acceptance of belief in transmigration. If we suppose that in one terrestrial life x is a human being and in the next terrestrial life a lion, the two bodies are obviously different. What then provides the continuity entitling us to claim that x is the subject of both lives? Further, if x attains liberation from the succession of rebirth and enters Nirvana, and if entry into Nirvana is not interpreted as complete annihilation but as a permanent state, it is natural to ask, a state of what?"[31]

The Case for Reincarnation

But it is not religious belief alone that is responsible for belief in reincarnation. The modern phenomenon of spontaneous and induced "memories" of past lives in the case of certain individuals has spurred widespread acceptance of reincarnation. The allegedly spontaneous cases generally take place in areas where belief in reincarnation is already well entrenched, whereas the "memories" produced by hypnotic regressions are peculiar to the West.

We will consider the case for reincarnation from four standpoints:

1. Its coherence.
2. The evidence in its favor.
3. Possible explanations for it.
4. The background framework it assumes.

The coherence factor concerns the question of how the theory fits in with the hard facts of experience and the established principles of modern science; with regard to evidence, we will consider the nature and reliability of the data that has been adduced in its favor; explanation concerns the possible interpretations of the data; and finally we will consider the kind of framework that has to be assumed for the theory to be true.

To give an example of how these kinds of tests would apply to a theory, let's look at a thesis of timetravel. Is the idea of going back and forth in time coherent? I would submit that the idea turns out to be incoherent once you understand the nature of time. As for evidence, we could look at a case of someone who claims to be from the past or the future. How could such a "traveler" prove the claim of traveling back and forth in time? It is hard to think of any kind of data that would be conclusive (short of our actually "traveling" to another era) and any data that is produced could be interpreted in several different ways. Finally, the background framework requires us to believe that there is some mechanism that enables people to go back and forth in time—a tall order!

Coherence

One question we should ask of any belief is whether it is coherent. Of course the coherence of a belief does not make it true. Neither does its apparent incoherence prove it to be untrue. Nevertheless, the question of coherence is one that should at least be addressed in considering the reincarnation hypothesis. As noted before, the very idea of life after death faces questions of coherence. These questions, I believe, can only be addressed if you take the human person as a unique union of body and soul, and the soul as the animating principle of a body.

When it comes to the coherence of reincarnation, several questions are critical:

- What sense does it make to say that a certain entity, call it soul or subtle body, can become several hundred persons or things and still be thought of as the same being? I do not think there has been an adequate response to this question.

- If a certain person claims to remember events from life as another person, how can we know whether or not these are actually the memories of the person who currently reports them?

- Then there is biology. Reincarnation has to assume a certain view of biological phenomena. According to what we know from biology, the kind of person we become is dictated at least partially by our genetic heritage and our experiences in the world. These are not necessarily the only factors that are relevant, but they are certainly crucial in making us who we are. An Aristotelian model of body and soul would certainly be consistent with these factors, because in that model there is an organic unity of bodily and transphysical processes. But the theory of reincarnation entails the belief that an astral body with certain prior personality traits moves into an embryo over-riding genetic transmission.

- Finally there is the idea that your "soul" after multiple rebirths will "dissolve" into the universal Soul. But souls are not physical entities, and what can possibly be meant by a non-physical entity "dissolving" into another such entity?

Let's take the first issue. What I know from my experience is that I am a unique union of physical and transphysical whose identity springs from one act of being, the soul that individuates the body, and the body that individuates the soul. If we start with this hard fact, then it makes no sense to speak of me as an immaterial being that periodically takes over units of matter (plant, animal, human, extra-terrestrial) with no memory or consciousness of these hundreds of "invasions" and "occupations." Human nature and personhood as we experience it are inextricably linked to our bodies: the unique reality that I am is intrinsically embodied. Granted, after death, I can exist for a time by virtue of a separated soul. But that soul is mine, because it was the soul of my body, and it remains in an unnatural condition until it can animate a body which is truly mine (and by "mine" we mean the "I" that first came to be at the simultaneous inception of body, soul, and person). And the organic unity of body and soul—whereby all my sensory experience comes through the body—results in the emergence of a unique self that is marked forever by what it perceives, conceives, and does from womb to tomb. If the slate is wiped clean by the soul being reborn in a new body (whatever that means), we are talking of the annihilation of the "previous" person whose unique history and identity are simultaneously wiped out. This idea that a soul can be rebooted like a computer is incoherent from the standpoint of our actual experience of what it means to be human. Further, when we speak of reincarnation as a plant or lower animal, it is hard to imagine what is reincarnated: there is no question of a memory or imagination or disposition being passed on.

Braine points out:

- "The capacity for bodily as well as non-bodily activity is integral" to the very nature of the human being. Therefore, "there is no question of a pre-existing soul coming into relation by incarnation or re-incarnation with a separately originating body. Human beings can only come into existence as a unity, "as a unitary psychophysical being." At death, they are deprived of "faculties depending on the body," but it is possible to conceive of them "being resurrected, the body re-constituted."

- Secondly, "the human being has no identity apart from its origin and history."

- Consequently, "although we can make some sense of the notion of resurrection as a restoration of capacities to a being by nature bodily, we can make no sense of a notion of re-incarnation whereby one and the same dualistically conceived soul might live and mature many times through many separate histories associated with different bodies."[32]

H.D. Lewis points out that memories are treacherously unreliable. "While we would normally be inclined to take a sincere memory claim at its face value, we would require exceptionally clear evidence in respect to claims to remember a previous life. Though it is hard for those who have not had such an experience to envisage quite how closely it would have the feel and firmness of a normal memory, it would presumably be cut off from ordinary sequences and be more open to possibilities of delusion.... It follows, in the light of these difficulties, that a claim to remember incidents of a past existence, or a continuous stretch of it, would require, even in one's own case, the support of overwhelming evidence."[33]

Reincarnation vs. Biology

The conflict with what we know from biology is fatal in its implications. Paul Edwards reviews the response of Dr. Ian Stevenson: "Stevenson refers to the critics who think reincarnation cases must, 'accommodate to the current orthodoxy in biology.'" According to Stevenson, "cases of the reincarnation type, if accepted as authentic, challenge orthodox biology." According to B.N. Moore, a Stevenson critic, "If this is so, proof of reincarnation would require disproof of orthodox biology, and thus would require evidence even more vast than that which supports orthodox biology."[34]

Chari goes to the heart of the biological case against reincarnation: "Reincarnation, if it occurs on anything like a major scale, is thinly disguised Lamarckism. The hypothesis demands that the habits, the memories, and even the scars on the bodies, which were acquired by individuals in historically earlier times, are transmitted to later generations by their 'surviving egos' being reborn in large numbers." But modern molecular biology leaves no room for "reincarnating egos to influence genetic information systems directly."[35] If there is an astral body, the problem is, "how does that body carry the memories? How does it invade, at what point does it invade without contradicting biology?"

Prominent reincarnationists have espoused the scientifically discredited ideas of Lamarckism. "Just as Lamarck believed that acquired characteristics can be inherited, so Radhakrishnan would have it that one's acquired character determines the gene pool of the body into which one is reincarnated. On theoretical and empirical grounds the suggestion appears inadmissible because the supposition would involve reversing the normal flow of biological information. We know that the information flows either irreversibly from DNA via RNA to protein, or from the DNA of one generation unchanged (except for chance mutation) to the DNA of the next generation. Reincarnation assumes that genetic information goes from the protein of one generation to the DNA of a later one, which involves formidable theoretical difficulties.... If memories are carried by the 'astral body' even then it would contradict Crick's dogma, the central dogma of molecular biology: the flow of information is in one direction only." If reincarnation is true and there is "some tremendous kind of interaction" with the alleged astral body, then "practically all of biology is at a standstill."[36]

Reincarnation and Pantheism

Another reason for denying the reincarnationist thesis is the absolute and ultimate nature of our personal identity. Reincarnation is closely tied to pantheism, which holds that our sense of being individual persons is an illusion and that we are actually part of the universal mind. H.P. Owen has shown why this theory does not work:

> Pantheism fails to explain our awareness of distinctness and autonomy in things and persons. Our total experience of both personal and sub-personal entities is pervaded by the conviction that each is an independent form of existence. This conviction is immediately and uniquely present in each person's self-consciousness, whereby each is aware of himself as distinct from (and therefore capable of relating himself to) other persons.... It is inconceivable how the Universal Self could include finite selves. A's thought, simply because it is A's, cannot include, though it may coincide with, B's thought." The idea that human selves are appearances or illusory faces two irrefutable challenges. "First, how could such an appearance or illusion of multiplicity be created by a unitary Absolute? Secondly, if our selfhood is illusory, or even if it is only semi-real, none of our individual statements can be true—least of all our statements concerning a supposed Absolute."[37]

For all these reasons, I do not believe that reincarnation as a theory of life after death can pass the coherence test: it does not cohere with what we know from our immediate experience of human nature and it flies in the face of modern biology.

The Evidence

We now consider the evidence offered in favor of reincarnation: it is almost exclusively based on supposed memories of past lives reported by certain individuals. But how good are the data and what viable interpretations are possible from any data that turns out to be reliable?

Hypnotic Regressions: Worthless?

For our purposes, we will focus on claims of spontaneous recall of past lives. Ian Stevenson, for one, regarded induced recall, as in hypnotic regressions, to be worthless. "In my experience, nearly all so-called previous personalities evoked through hypnotism are entirely imaginary and a result of the patient's eagerness to obey the hypnotist's suggestion. It is no secret that we are all highly suggestible under hypnosis. This kind of investigation can actually be dangerous. Some people have been terribly frightened by their supposed memories, and in other cases the previous personality evoked has refused to go away for a long time."[38] One major source of these kinds of "memories" is cryptoamnesia where in an altered state, like hypnosis, the brain releases stored memories of something that was read or discussed.

The relevant data for our purposes are the apparently spontaneous cases of recall of past lives in children. The primary investigator of such data has been Ian Stevenson. Without question, he was a painstaking researcher. But his whole case rests entirely on the quality of his data. According to his critics, these are of dubious value.

"Stevenson's cases," writes Paul Edwards, "read much better in summary than when one examines them in detail. He has admitted that all his cases, even the strongest ones, possess some weaknesses. I think that this is a gross under-statement. They all have big holes, and they do not even begin to add up to a significant counterweight to the initial presumption against reincarnation."[39]

Edwards points to flaws in Stevenson's research methods: "Stevenson's cases then do not amount to even halfway decent evidence. In only 11 of the approximately 1,111 rebirth cases had there been no contact between the two families before investigation was begun. Of those 11, seven were seriously flawed in some respect. What this means is that in the great majority of cases, the two families had met years before a scientific investigation began, and that the likelihood of independent testimony was quite small. The rebirth cases are anecdotal evidence of the weakest sort."[40]

Investigators of these cases have found that "In many cases, there was or easily could have been contact between the parents and persons connected with the 'previous personality' about whose life the child had accurate recollec-tions." Edwards points out that an admirer of Stevenson's research noted "that only in seven of Stevenson's cases were the child's statements about a previous life recorded prior to the attempts at verification. Stevenson has himself admit-ted that where this is not done subsequent developments may lead to embellish-ments of what the child is supposed to have said. Yet, [even!] in all these seven cases, the child lived 'within the geographical or social circumference of the previous personality.' The 'close connection' between the children and the surviving friends and relatives of the previous personality 'raises questions of sensory cues.'"

Moreover, "Stevenson's 'frankly admitted ignorance of Asiatic languages' and the resulting dependence on translators and interpreters must weaken the scientific value of his reports."[41]

Stevenson himself admitted that his research was not conclusive: "Essen-tially I say that the idea of reincarnation permits, but doesn't compel belief. All the cases I've investigated so far have shortcomings. Even taken together, they do not offer anything like proof. But as the body of evidence accumulates, it's more likely that more and more people will see its relevance."[42] In point of fact, Stevenson never disclosed whether or not he personally believed in reincarnation.

Explanation

Different interpretations are possible for the alleged reincarnation data. In the first place, clear cases of fraud and self-deception have been detected, and these can be discarded. Nevertheless some cases seem genuine. But here there are explanations, which are much more plausible if you accept a paranormal dimension (which you have to if you accept the possibility of reincarnation). These explanations—offered by Hindu sages and others—include possession by a spirit and communication from a deceased soul.

As a physicalist, Edwards considers all of the cases to be the result of fraud.

As already noted, before very long, Stevenson's children forget all of their memories of a previous life. 'The children,' he writes, 'nearly always stop talking about their previous lives between the ages of five and eight.' There is surely something very strange about this universal forgetting...the children gradually stop 'remembering' their previous lives because they have become tired of the charade and now have better things to do. The parents, too, for that matter, have by now derived all the publicity and possible financial advantage from the commotion...it should be emphasized that there is no suggestion that the children who forgot their past lives suffered any general amnesia and were also unable to remember events of their current lives. That the child cases are charades is fully confirmed by the experience of Dr. D.R. Barker.[43]

Social Psychology, Not Parapsychology

Barker, an anthropologist, investigated many of the same cases as Stevenson, but "could not find a single case in which there was convincing evidence of the presence of a paranormal process." The most thoroughly investigated case, he said, is "best interpreted as a result of Indian social psychology rather than parapsychology."

"Why is there this disparity in the number and the quality of Eastern and Western cases?" asks Edwards. "I don't believe that the answer is difficult to find, and it has nothing to do with suppression. In the West, we do not have a host of witnesses with an ardent belief in reincarnation who will manufacture the necessary 'proofs'; and if any such proofs were manufactured, we have numerous skeptics right on the spot who would subject them to a much more elaborate and searching scrutiny than any undertaken by Stevenson and his associates."[44]

Chari has several explanations for the phenomenon:

I shall now formulate some theoretical objections to reincarnation regarded as a working hypothesis of survival research. I am not aware that any reincarnationist has stated, in a scientifically testable form, just *what* it is that 'reincarnates' or just how it influences even genetic information transmission which is a kind of biological relay race particularly immune to individual habits, memories, accidents, vicissitudes. The oft-proposed popular reincarnationist hypothesis of 'two streams of heredity,' one 'physical' and the other 'psychical,' dismally fails to account for the curious birthmarks, scars, and the physiological idiosyncrasies of Stevenson's cases, *assuming* that they are 'carried over' from an 'earlier life.'

We have to address 'little-understood influences coming from grandparents and even remote ancestors but also to discarnate possession of indeterminate range, duration and penetrance. My puzzlement as a Hindu parapsychologist arises from the lack of any adequate criterion which would distinguish 'reincarnation' from 'possession.'

My researches have uncovered another trap for the unwary in supposed cases of rebirth. Whether an Asian child's paranormal behavior suggests to the bystanders 'mediumistic possession' or 'reincarnation' depends very much on the kind of imaginative 'reaching out' exercised by the child, which in turn is a function of the cultural setting. There are, in fact, no infallible criteria for 'mediumistic possession' in the Asian area. The late Somasundara Gnanasambandha Desika Paramacharya, the former head of an important Saivite centre in Madurai, Tamilnadu, and the author of a popular book in Tamil on 'spirit communication' was firmly of the opinion that *all* of Stevenson's cases of the 'reincarnation-type' could be explained in terms of 'possession,' keeping well in view the uniformly violent termination of the 'former lives.'"[45]

It should be noted that the possession hypothesis originated from within the Hindu framework where the violent end of a person's life is sometimes seen as the source of mischief caused by the wandering soul. Moreover, in an article titled "Anomalies of Consciousness: Indian perspectives and research," K. Ramakrishna Rao writes, "10 to 20 percent of women sampled in South India belonging to a subset of Brahmins were believed to have been possessed by a spirit at some time in their lives. The event of 'spirit possession,' it is observed, wins attention, prestige, and a deferential treatment that such a woman could not otherwise attain for herself."[46]

Past Life Recall as Cultural and Psychical

Chari believes claims of past life recall spring from two sources: "One is cultural, the other is psychical. [Our] flickering, empirical consciousness is open to invasions. At an empirical level it is very much open to influences: parental influences, social influences. It is open at another level as well, a psychic level: telepathy. It is open to psychic influences coming from the past. Other people's past, not our past. A person dies, but the memories can invade a soul in the present. It is open and the boundaries are not fixed. The empirical consciousness does not have fixed boundaries." Psychic openness to influences from the past, concludes Chari, successfully explains all cases of past-life recall. "Reincarnation is not a scientifically testable hypothesis. The cases of people who claim to 'remember' former lives are explicable by a combination of hidden and disguised normally-acquired memories, extra-sensory tapping of the memories of other people, and a strong empathetic identification with deceased persons. This explanation is not only feasible but actually illustrated by the empirical data of survival research."[47]

NDE-ers and Reincarnation

It should be mentioned at this point that several people involved in NDE research favor the reincarnation hypothesis. But, as Michael Sabom points out, this belief does not originate in the actual NDE event. He cites Raymond Moody who wrote, "Not one of the cases I have looked into is in any way indicative to me that reincarnation occurred." Also Kenneth Ring: "There is no reason why an NDE-ers openness toward reincarnation must stem directly from his NDE. In fact, I am quite convinced that in many cases it is more likely to be a response to an NDE-ers reading and other life experiences *following* an NDE."[48]

Sabom points to a sociological reason why many NDE survivors believe in reincarnation: "Amber Wells interviewed a group of IANDS' near-death experiencers and found that *none* 'claimed to have gained any direct understanding of the nature or process of reincarnation during his or her NDE.' Despite this finding, an incredible 70 percent of these near-death experiencers professed a 'strong belief in reincarnation…which tended to follow the standard view of reincarnation as expressed in much of the New Age literature.' Wells concluded that a belief in reincarnation following a near-death experience is a result of 'reading, discussions with others, and personal reflection,' *not the NDE itself.…* This, it would seem, was the source for the belief in reincarnation, not the NDE."[49]

Framework

The final variable to be analyzed is the background framework assumed by reincarnation. Is it plausible? Edwards, for one, is emphatic that the assumptions made by the theory of reincarnation are simply unacceptable.

Edwards's lays out the implications of astral bodies: "In a simplified form, the question before a rational person can be stated in the following words: which is more likely—that there are astral bodies, that they invade the wombs of prospective mothers, and that the children can remember events from a previous life although the brains of the previous persons have long been dead, or that their very fallible memories and powers of observation have led them to make false statements and bogus identifications."

Edwards cites John Hick's objection that babies are not born with adult egos "as they would be if they were direct continuations of egos which had died at the end of a normal lifespan.' It is little less than scandalous that no reincarnationist has ever attempted to reply to this argument."

What about the billions of years in which there was no life in the Universe? "It is now generally accepted that for many billions of years after the Big Bang the universe contained no life at all. Reincarnation in all forms postulates a series of incarnations stretching back into the past without limit; and this is clearly inconsistent with the facts."[50]

The population argument seems to Edwards to be quite conclusive against reincarnationism. In a 1981 issue of BioScience, Professor Arthur H. Westing of Amherst "estimated that the 1981 population of 4.4 billion amounted to 9 percent of all human beings who ever lived and that it was greater than the number of people who lived through the entire Paleolithic age, a period accounting for 86 percent of the duration of human life." Edwards notes that "these facts are incompatible with the less fanciful version of the reincarnation theory according to which human souls can occupy only human bodies." This is because the reincarnationist holds that "All souls have always existed. Every birth is a *re*birth, the rebirth of a soul that has already existed. All this clearly rules out any population increase.... It is noteworthy that this argument has hardly been explicitly discussed by any of the academically respectable reincarnationists."[51] Of course, this has not stopped some reincarnationists from clutching at bizarre straws. While some have pointed to the possibility of there being other inhabited planets in the universe, others have said that the same soul could occupy more than one soul at the same time!

The Right Fit at the Right Time?

H.D. Lewis asks, "How does it come about that another appropriate life is ready when the time comes for the rebirth? We have to remember that much in our dispositional nature and skills is settled through conception and the transmission of physical characteristics. How, then, can a soul come to an appropriate new birth without suspension of the normal course of natural events? Is there a miraculous modification each time, and how would that square with available evidence? And what, moreover, can we say of changes in the population? On what principle can it be thought that new souls are created?"[52]

The conclusions to be drawn from this long journey into reincarnation are clear:

- ✧ The theory is incoherent as it stands.
- ✧ There is no substantial evidence in its favor.
- ✧ There are various far more plausible counter-explanations for the available data.
- ✧ The general framework that the theory has to assume does not work.
- ✧ For all these reasons, reincarnation is not a viable account of life after death.

Resurrection

The other major account of the survival of the human person is the resurrection of the body. With regard to the evidence in its favor, at best we can say that the soul survives the death of the body, the soul is "formed" by its relation to the body, and the separated soul is oriented to animating a body if it is to subsist in a normal state. This animation of a glorified body called resurrection is entirely different from reincarnation. Here the person and the soul remain the same. All that is different is the matter, but the matter of our bodies keeps changing even in our earthly lives, and yet we remain the same person through all these changes. In reincarnation a new person supposedly comes into being each time the soul passes from body to body.

But whether or not there is a resurrection can only be known through divine revelation. It is also the only coherent account of how the human person can survive death and still retain the fullness of its nature.

A resurrection, if it is possible, is essential for integrity of the person. Peter Geach makes this clear. "The upshot of our whole argument is that unless a man comes to life again by resurrection, he does not live again after death. At best some mental remnant of him would survive death; and I should hold that the possibility even of such survival involves at least a permanent capacity for renewed human life; if reincarnation is excluded, this means: a capacity for resurrection."[53]

The Resurrected Body, Not Necessarily the Pre-Death Body

It should be noted that the resurrection claim does not call for the rising of the pre-death body. "The identity of a body as a whole is safeguarded by the identity of its substantial form," notes Eberle. "Hence, at resurrection, any elementary particles would suffice for the recomposition of a human being's body. No matter from where such particles originate—even if they never had composed that human being's body during his life—they are made to compose his body due to their matter's being informed/configured by his soul."[54]

To reiterate what has been said, the idea of resurrection clearly has to be considered in the context of a claim of divine revelation.

The Separated Soul

We have noted that, at the level of immediate experience, the case for survival flows directly from the nature of the intellectual and volitional acts of the soul. Once we have grasped the non-physical nature of these operations, we realize that their continuance is not necessarily dependent on any physical process (unlike visual consciousness that requires photons, neurons, the optic nerve, and so on). So what happens when a human dies? Clearly the body decomposes—in fact, it ceases to be a body, because there is no soul or principle of life that organizes and animates it. If the soul's operations were entirely limited to physical processes (as is the case in an insect or a cat which also have principles of life), then there is no question of the continued existence of the soul. But in the case of humans, the non-physical nature of some of the soul's operations requires that the soul itself be non-physical and hence capable of independent existence. To be sure, in its essential identity the soul is the principle of life of a body, and so its survival without a body is survival in an unnatural state. The disembodied soul may be capable of intellectual operations, but it would be limited in its ability to perform tasks that require the senses.

Does this mean that the soul cannot "see" or "feel" after death? We have acknowledged that to be separated from the body is to be in an unnatural state. Religious traditions that talk of a resurrection of the body whereby the soul will animate a body—a body that becomes your body because it is the same soul that does the animating—have at least addressed this issue. Moreover, a soul in its separated state could, by an act of God, be infused with new capacities. This is what Aquinas held and what the after-life data including NDEs indicate. But the bottom line is that the soul survives the death of its body. Now we cannot possibly imagine what an existence of this kind is like, but our inability to imagine it does not mean that the soul cannot continue to exist.

At this stage, it would be useful to review the conclusions of thinkers who have specifically considered the nature of disembodied existence. The most important contribution comes from David Braine.

David Braine

Because the act of existing or *esse* of the human person is not of the body but the soul, it will transcend the life of the body. "Since the operations of the human being are, in the case of some operations, not the operations of a bodily organ, the *esse* of the human being does not consist in the *esse* of the ensemble of its bodily organs." For instance, "understanding is not the operation of a bodily organ" but of the person. "If some of the activities, especially ones most nodal to life, transcend the body, then existence and life transcend the body."

After death, it is the person who knows and loves not the soul: "When one has died, one is not a nothing but one has no body. After death it is still the person qua person which primarily knows and loves, not the soul or person supposedly qua soul, just as before death." [55]

Denis Bradley

Bradley points out that "Here and now the human soul acts spiritually because it has a spiritual act of existence which, postmortem, sustains it as a continuing spiritual substance." Its act of being and, consequently, the activity of the intellectual soul "transcends the whole genus of bodies."

Aquinas speculated that there could be a special divine infusion that would enable separated souls to "know" and "communicate" in the manner of the angels: "the human soul's postmortem mode of knowing can be analogized to that of the angelic separate intelligences, who at their creation are connaturally infused with intelligible species. Such infusion, by God via the superior separate intelligences, would also be in accordance with the disembodied human soul's mode of being." [56]

Jason Eberle

Eberle points out that the separated soul will retain its intellective and sensory capabilities, although its ability to actualize these will depend on other factors. "A separated human soul has all the capacities proper to existence as a rational animal, namely intellective, sensitive, and vegetative capacities. Hence, though without his body a human being is unable to actualize many of his capacities, he remains a rational animal by virtue of his soul retaining all the capacities proper to such a nature." Again, "when it subsists apart from the body after a human being's death, each individual human soul retains knowledge, experiential memory, and the blueprint for a particular body." [57]

To Be Continued...

It's time now for a reality check. Let's recap the cumulative case outlined in this book:

- Certain people undergoing the process of dying claim to have left their physical bodies and encountered another state of being.

- If there is a God, it seems likely that he would reveal to us his intentions (if any) for our eternal destiny.

- We know from the primordial-universal testimony of the human race that the overwhelming majority of humanity has seen fit to believe both in God and in a life that follows death. In many cases this belief was built around a claim of direct divine revelation.

- We know of reports throughout history, which persist through the present day, of deceased souls "visiting" the living and of claims of visions of the after-life.

- The claim of the resurrection of Jesus presents a new vision of "life-after-death" that is true to human experience and is integrated with human history.

- We know from our everyday experience that we are a union of physical and transphysical, that we constantly perform intellectual operations that have no basis in matter and that, consequently, there is no reason why this element of our being cannot survive the death of the physical.

- The evidence from encounter complements the evidence from experience.

Based on all of the above, it is eminently reasonable to conclude that there is a life after death. And, if the universal narrative is right, this after-life will be one of union with the divine or separation therefrom.

Has the present book succeeded in building a case for life after death? This is a question that can only be answered by each reader on an individual basis. But whether or not the arguments adduced here are viable, we know this for a fact: the overwhelming majority of human beings took it for granted that there is a life beyond death and that their choices and acts have a definite bearing on their destiny. They knew (without any help from the neuroscientists) that damage to the brain would impair their mental life and that the brain stops functioning at death. And yet they believed that the human person survives death.

At the very least, the dots we have connected indicate that there is a reasonable case to be made for an after-life. No scientific methodologies or technologies are even remotely relevant here (you might as well open a clock to understand the concept of "time"). What we can and do have is a paradigm, a picture that makes sense of the data at hand and all elements of our experience. It is a paradigm that takes seriously our unique identity as psychophysical organisms "organized" by an intellectual soul and oriented to a destiny beyond death. This is a paradigm that appropriates not simply our everyday experience, but also cross-fertilizes the resources available from contemporary NDEs, cross-cultural and inter-religious belief-systems, and even the narratives that emerge from purported visions of the after-life.

Now it must be admitted that some accounts of the after-life sound quite unattractive, even macabre. And this is simply not true of certain ancient texts. We are reminded of the clergyman who, when asked what he thought happened after death, replied, "I suppose we shall enjoy eternal bliss but please let us not discuss such a depressing subject."

Here let me speak personally and candidly. Let us set aside for a moment our philosophical and religious preconceptions. I speak to you as one human person to another, as a fellow traveler on the road to death. We have so little time for niceties and nuances, so little space for abstractions and cliches. We have to get right to the point. There is only one thing that matters to us, to any of us: is death the end or is it the entry-point to some other kind of existence? If an entry-point, how do we prepare ourselves for what is to come?

My personal perspective is one of hope and joy tempered with caution. I believe in a God who loves us unconditionally and infinitely, who seeks union with each one of us. But I am aware that I am a free being and that God respects my freedom. It is here that the exhortations of the sages ring loud and clear: always seek to do God's will: if you turn against him (as we all do), you can always return: above all, never fear and trust totally. As a Christian, I believe that the innermost nature of God is Love, a beginningless, endless act of love of three Centers within the one divine Being, and that we are all called to enter into this Love. Beyond the door of death lies endless ecstasy.

All of us, at every moment of our being, hunger and thirst for love, for acceptance, recognition, security. It is this hunger and this thirst that manifest themselves in nameless longings—"all that men ignored in me," said Browning—which we can hardly comprehend or communicate. In our heart of hearts we know that nothing on earth can ease the pain, the sense of anonymity, the lingering loneliness, which are part and parcel of this seemingly unquenchable quest. And those who have surrendered themselves utterly to him know that, at bottom, this yearning of the inmost self is a call for and from the Source of our being. All who come to him will never hunger and never thirst. All our lives we are searching for him and yet running away from him. Immeasurably more important, He pursues us "down the night and down the days," and his love draws us from darkness to light, from death to life, from lesser goods to the Greatest Good.

Afterword

By Dr. Raymond Moody

Rational inquiry into the mystery of life after death began with the ancient Greek philosophers who founded reason. Despite the intervening 25 centuries of persistent efforts, though, the goal of rational proof still eludes us. Even so, I am confident that breakthroughs will soon bring genuine advances toward rational comprehension of humankind's deepest mystery. Therefore, I am honored to contribute to Roy Varghese's excellent conceptual book on the question of life after death.

The book is conceptual in that Mr. Varghese respects a fundamental limitation that is ignored by many scholars who address the subject. Namely, the question of an after-life is not an easy one. Indeed, great thinkers from Plato to David Hume acknowledged that it may ultimately be unfathomable, and utterly beyond the reach of reason. Nevertheless, human beings naturally desire to know that their conscious personal self-identity will persist after bodily death. So a huge gap is created between what people desire and what is realistic when expecting reason to provide.

Unfortunately, a crowd of enthusiastic believers rushes into that void. These believers are happy to tell people what they want to hear and even to dress it in "scientific" garb. Accordingly, identifying errors introduced by self-deluded pseudo-scientists and "parapsychologists" is essential for restoring reason to this debate. Mr. Varghese has courageously taken on that task at one point in this book. In addition, he presents the works of serious scholars who contend on various grounds that death is a transition into another state of conscious existence.

That frees me to discuss three vital aspects of the question of life after death that generally get short shrift. The first section of what follows discusses the role of the mystery of an afterlife in human psychological development and emotional functioning. The second section then takes up the indispensable role of narratives—specifically, narratives of near-death experiences—in purportedly rational investigations of life after death. Finally, the third section outlines my current research involving a unique new rational method of studying near-death experiences and related phenomena. I predict that ongoing work will soon engender startling new insights into the enduring mystery of the fate of the soul at death.

Life After Death and Human Development

Plato was the first to observe that life after death is partly a developmental question. That is, he observed that the question often first presents itself at certain crucial stages of life development. For example, he pointed out that the aging process itself eventually brings many people around to the question. Aging makes it increasingly difficult for them to deny their own mortality, so they began to worry about the prospects of a life hereafter.

Many others first confront the question of an afterlife when they lose loved ones to death. In fact, grief is one of the most common motivators of rational inquiry into this mystery. People naturally long to know that they will someday be reunited with their lost loved ones.

The trouble is, states of grief and anxiety are not favorable conditions for rational analysis and reflection about a mystery of this magnitude. That makes it easy for pseudo-scientists and true believers to foster their defective reasoning on emotionally vulnerable, anxious, or grief-stricken people.

Nevertheless, it would be exceedingly difficult to eliminate consolation as a motive for rational inquiry into the afterlife. Even Plato acknowledged that he attempted to devise rational arguments for an afterlife partly because he wanted to console himself and others. Afterward, all the schools of ancient philosophers published consolation books for that very purpose. The consolation books marshaled plenty of supposedly rational arguments to reassure readers of an afterlife in the face of the harsh reality of death.

The Stoic philosophers were most famous for the genre of consolation books. But the theme of consolation continues in today's supposedly "scientific" studies of life after death. In recent years, a parapsychologist reportedly told journalists that he undertook his study of mediums in an attempt at consoling his grieving girlfriend.

Now, consoling someone is generally a noble goal. However, in the context of after-life research, it is also a set-up for deceiving oneself or unwittingly helping others deceive themselves. In reality, rational investigations of this mystery require an extraordinary degree of rigor and careful, reflective, logical analysis. Anything short of that borders on scholarly misconduct in this particular field of research. For insofar as consolation is a goal of after-life research, what would happen if the research were subsequently to prove faulty and ill-grounded? People who had taken consolation from the study would be dealt a severe setback. Not only would they suffer a resurgence of their original grief or anxiety, they would have the additional burden of their feelings of disappointment and anger toward the hasty, inept researcher.

Any sound, rational study that moved us forward toward solving the mystery of life after death would naturally console people. Hence, it is not feasible to separate this area of rational inquiry from the emotional dimension of consolation. So we must keep in mind that the best consolation is the truth. In the final analysis, there is no conflict between upholding rigorous procedures of rational inquiry in after-life research and the prospect of consoling people.

Experiences of Almost Dying

I first became acquainted with near-death experiences when reading Plato's *Republic* in 1962, as a first-year philosophy major. I also learned that revenants, or people who had supposedly returned from the dead, played a major role in the origins of ancient Greek philosophy. In 1965, I was walking with a classmate to a shopping area near the University of Virginia. There, my classmate briefly introduced me to a kindly student health psychiatrist who was apparently well-known and respected by students. This man was Dr. George Ritchie. Shortly thereafter, I found out from one of my philosophy professors that Dr. Ritchie had a profound spiritual experience when he nearly died years earlier. Dr. Ritchie often spoke to student groups, so I soon had the opportunity to hear him tell his amazing story. Since then, inspired by Plato and Dr. Ritchie, I have had the great privilege and honor of listening to thousands of people recount such experiences.

Many accounts of near-death experiences are remarkably similar. People say that when they come very close to death they get out of their bodies and see their own physical bodies lying below. They become aware of a tunnel-like passageway and move through the tunnel into a brilliant, comforting, joyous, loving light. They meet deceased loved ones in the light and see their entire lives pass instantly in a holographic life review. They return from this experience transformed, convinced that there is a world beyond death, and that the purpose of this life is to learn to love.

In sum, people recount their near-death experiences in the form of a travel narrative, but with a fascinating twist. Namely, they stipulate that ultimately their experience was ineffable or indescribable in that there are not words that can adequately describe it. And they add that the experience did not take place in the framework of time and space as we know it. So that makes the travel narrative format a paradoxical choice for recounting near-death experiences. For if you think about it, the meaning of a travel narrative presupposes the known, time-space continuum. Without that, we have lost all our ability to interpret the meaning of a travel narrative.

This paradox helps explain the riveting quality of personal accounts of near-death experiences. The intense interest findings about near-death experiences have generated are adequate proof that these stories are inherently fascinating. Or in other words, stories of near-death experiences are powerful inducers of an irresistible mental state psychologists know as narrative transport. For good stories produce in the mind a state of fascinated absorption in the actions narratives supposedly portray.

The patent charm of stories of near-death experiences is a mixed blessing, insofar as rational inquiry into the phenomenon is concerned. Certainly, narrative transport attracted many investigators to the systematic study of near-death experiences. However, that becomes a major disadvantage if narrative transport is also the main factor that holds them in this field of study. For rational study of near-death experiences in relation to the question of an after-life also requires careful logical reasoning and analyzing complex concepts. And for most of us, that is simply not as much fun as hearing these amazing inspirational stories and speculating about what they might mean. And we especially enjoy speculating about whether the stories are possible "evidence of life after death."

I say "stories" to emphasize that personal narratives are the rock bottom origin of all research into near-death experiences. That is, personal narratives are the starting point for rational studies of near-death experiences and their relevance to the question of life after death. But investigators tend to focus on "the experience" and allow the characteristic narrative structure to fade away into the background, unnoticed and unexamined. Yet, this ignored narrative structure is what creates the illusion that near-death experiences could be "evidence" or even "rational proof of an afterlife."

Plato stated precisely what it takes to understand this dilemma for ourselves. He said that it requires patiently following through in one's own mind "a long chain of reasoning touching on many remote points." Plato acknowledged that only a relatively few people would willingly go down that path of careful, logical reasoning.

Compared to the combined thrill of narrative transport and free-form speculation, thinking through a long chain of reasoning initially may seem dull and boring. But it is necessary in order to understand how narratives of near-death experiences are related to the question of life after death.

Plato acknowledged that the narrative element is always needed just to get rational discussion of life after death started. After all, the sentence "There is life after death" is an out-and-out self-contradiction. For "death" just means "the final, irreversible cessation of life." Getting two irreconcilably opposite notions together in the mind as "life after death" requires some sort of story to give the combined notion content. However, reasoning from such stories to the conclusion that they are related in some way to an after-life is a difficult and tricky matter.

The difficulty is compounded by the fact that for an obvious reason most front-line investigators of near-death experiences are medical doctors. Medical doctors have access to patients who have been critically ill and that enables doctors to study near-death experiences. But medical training does not prepare doctors to reason cogently about "evidence of life after death." So even after 40-plus years, it still shocks me to hear fellow medical doctors characterize near-death experiences in those terms.

Furthermore, narrative transport also draws in some for whom near-death experiences eventually become a quasi-religion calling. Even a well-known organization devoted to the study of the phenomenon occasionally displays unmistakably religious aspects including group singing and spiritual rituals. At times, there has even been a tinge of New Age beliefs or an overlapping interest in mediumship! Publications of the organization feature plenty of inspiring stories of personal near-death experiences.

The mesmerizing appeal of narrative transport overpowers the careful logical reasoning needed to connect the narratives to the question of an after-life. In other words, the narrative aspect outweighs the conceptual aspect, and that precludes genuinely rational consideration of near-death experiences and life after death. Acknowledging this difficulty leads to a promising new method of rational inquiry into these experiences in relation to questions about a life hereafter.

A New Logic of the After-life

The Scottish philosopher David Hume (1711-76) contributed to the development of science by challenging fundamental notions of causation and inductive reasoning. He also accurately identified a formidable logical obstacle to the prospect of rational proof of life after death. For he said, "By the mere light of reason, it seems difficult to prove the immortality of the soul. Some new species of logic is required for that purpose; and some new faculties of the mind, that they may enable us to comprehend that logic."

This statement may be another example of Hume's famous irony. He may have thought that this criterion positively ruled out rational proof of life after death. Remember that "There is life after death" is patently self-contradictory. And logic rules out self-contradictions.

Hume's statement is exactly correct, however, and many scholars take that as an insurmountable barrier to rational inquiry into this great mystery. For the classical logic we inherited from Aristotle and other Greek philosophers has served us well for more than 2,000 years. That makes it seem extremely un-likely that someone might discover "some new species of logic." And we know our own minds pretty well, and that makes it seem extremely unlikely that we might discover "some new faculties of the mind."

Some look at Hume's insight as a dead end that necessarily brings a halt to rational investigation into the possibility of an after-life, but we can also look at it as a challenge. Hume's statement entails that rational proof of an after-life would restructure our logical system and expand the capacity of the mind. And that is a far more exciting prospect than what existing methodological approaches offer. For those approaches presuppose the existing logical code and rely on the mind as it is now constituted. In those approaches logic and the mind are static quantities. But if we stick to Hume's renowned requirements, logic and the mind become interactive, dynamic factors. Both logic and the mind would be transformed by the process of rational proof of continued conscious existence after death.

That sounds like an unattainable goal. However, it turns out to be far easier than previously imagined to meet Hume's renowned standard, at least in part. For "proof of the immortality of the soul" is still out of the question. Nonethe-less, we can definitely work out supplementary rational principles and activate untapped capacities of the mind. And that process can definitely result in a genuine advance toward rational understanding of near-death experiences vis a vis life after death. The problem is that this new approach takes a lot of concen-trated effort and reading through a lengthy exposition. And even then, it ap-proaches the question of life after death only as a corollary. The primary goal in this sort of approach must be to enhance our own minds and our capacity for reasoning. For in light of Hume's famous observation, that is the only way we can reshape logic and the mind to handle questions about an afterlife.

My purpose here is only to claim that this can be done and that therefore an alternative rational approach exists. I will publish full details in a forthcoming book, *The Secret World of Nonsense*. In the meantime, I want to challenge colleagues to prove me wrong by uncovering any specific logical flaws in my reasoning. For unless they can do so, the case presented in the forthcoming book represents genuine progress toward rational inquiry concerning life after death. Moreover, this new approach presents grave difficulties for customary parapsychological approaches to the question. The new approach may even entail that parapsychological kinds of reasoning about life after death are intrinsically incoherent.

Again I say this in the present context only to issue a defined challenge to other investigators in an attempt at moving rational debate forward. I am challenging other investigators to a race, in effect. Specifically, conjecture that reshaping the logical mind in advance will affect how they recount their subsequent near-death experiences. I have already made considerable progress in putting this plan into action and perhaps have already achieved some preliminary success.

Time will tell, but I mention this here only to propose a definite test and measure of my claim. That way, this book itself can serve as a vehicle for advancing the rational debate by redirecting and refocusing it. For I remain unconvinced that there is life after death or that reason can prove it. I am convinced, however, that there is another unexplored path of rational inquiry that can enlighten us on the mystery while avoiding pseudo-science.

Roy Varghese, on the other hand, is convinced that there is an after-life and that it can be proven by reason as we know it. He also marshals a lot of interesting information from eminent thinkers to support his positive conclusion. Our shared optimism that this big mystery is amenable to rational inquiry invites readers to consider and reflect for themselves. Mr. Varghese and I do not agree on various specific points, but we do agree on an important specific point. Namely, life after death is the central mystery of human existence and we can use reason in attempts at solving the mystery. So we hope that readers will benefit by considering the whole range of scholarly positions the book presents.

Bibliography

Alper, Matthew. *The God Part of the Brain*. Brooklyn, N.Y.: Rogue Press, 2001.

Ashton, John and Whyte, Tom. *The Quest for Paradise*. New York: Harper San Francisco, 2001.

Baars, Bernard J. "The conscious access hypothesis: Origins and recent evidence," *Trends in Cognitive Science*, January, 2002.

Bartholomew, Anita. "After Life," *Reader's Digest*, August (2003): 122–128.

Beauregard Mario and O'Leary, Denyse. *The Spiritual Brain*. New York: HarperOne, 2007.

Beauregard, Mario. "Mind does really matter: Evidence from neuroimaging studies of emotional self-regulation, psychotherapy, and placebo effect," *Progress in Neurobiology* 81 (2007): 218–236.

Blackmore, Susan. "Serotonin, ergo sum," *New Scientist*, March 2, 2002, *www.newscientist.com/article/mg17323325.900-serotonin-ergo-sum.html*

Blackmore, Susan. Debate with Greg Stone, *www.near-death.com/experiences/articles001.html*

Blakeslee, Sandra. "Flesh Made Soul," *Science and Spirit*, March 1, 2008. *www.science-spirit.org/article_detail.php?article_id=740*.

Bosveld, Jane Bosveld. "Will natural science pin down our supernatural essence?," *Discover,* June 12, 2007.

Boyce, Mary. *Zoroastrianism: It's Antiquity and Constant Vigor.* Costa Mesa, Calif.: Mazda Publishers, 1992.

Bradley, Denis J. M. "To be or not to be?: Pasnau on Aquinas's Immortal Human Soul," *The Thomist*, 2004, 68, 1–39.

Braine, David. *The Human Person—Animal and Spirit.* Cleveland, Ohio: University of Notre Dame Press, 1994.

Braude, Stephen. *Immortal Remains—The Evidence for Life After Death.* Lanham, Md.: Rowman and Littlefield, 2003.

Brown, Peter. *The Cult of the Saints.* Chicago: University of Chicago Press, 1980.

Burkert, Walter. *Homo Necans: The Anthropology of Ancient Greek Sacrificial Ritual and Myth.* Berkeley, Calif.: University of California Press, 1983.

Byassee, Jason "Protestants and Marian Devotion—What about Mary?," *Christian Century*, December 14, 2004.

Cash, William R. "Did atheist philosopher see God when he 'died'?," *National Post*, March 3, 2001.

Chari, C.T.K. "A New Look at Reincarnation," *The Christian Parapsychologist*, Vol.4, 4 (1981): 121–129.

Chari, C.T.K. in B.B. Wolman, ed., *Handbook of Parapsychology.* New York: Van Nostrand Reinhold, 1977.

———. *Handbook of Parapsychology.* New York: Van Nostrand Reinhold, 1977.

———. *The Indian Philosophical Annual.* (1965): 1977–1978.

Churchland, Patricia."How Do Neurons Know?," *Daedalus*, Winter 2004.

Churchland, Paul and Patricia. *On the Contrary.* Cambridge, Mass.: MIT Press, 1998.

Churchland, Paul. *The Engine of Reason, the Seat of the Soul.* Cambridge, Mass.: MIT Press, 1995.

Churchland. "A Neurophilosophical Slant on Consciousness Research," *Progress in Brain Research.* 149, (2005): 285–292.

Clark, Peter. *Zoroastrianism, Introduction to an Ancient Faith.* Brighton: Sussex Library of Religious Beliefs and Practices, 1999.

Connell, Janice T. *Queen of the Cosmos.* Orleans, Mass.: Paraclete Press, 1990.

Coons, John E. "A Grammar of the Self," *First Things*, January 2003, 40.

Copleston, F.C. *Philosophies and Cultures.* Oxford: Oxford University Press, 1980.

Cott, Jonathanand Karen Rester. "Joseph LeDoux's heavy mental," *Salon*, *www.salon.com/mwt/feature/2007/07/25/joseph_ledoux/print.html*

Crick, Francis. *The Astonishing Hypothesis: The Scientific Search for the Soul*. New York: Simon and Schuster, 1994.

Curtain, Cira. "Fact or Fiction?: Living People Outnumber the Dead." *Scientific American* March 2007.

D'Arcy, Martin. *Death and Life*. London: Longmans, Green & Co., 1942.

De Purucker, Gottfried. *The Esoteric Tradition*. San Francisco, Calif.: Theosophical University Press, 1940.

Dean, Cornelia in the *New York Times*, June 26, 2007. *www.nytimes.com/2007/ 06/26/science/26soul.html?_r=1&ref=science*

Dennett, Daniel C. "Facing Backwards on the Problem of Consciousness," *Journal of Consciousness Studies* 3 (1996): 6.

———. *Consciousness Explained*. Boston, Mass.: Little, Brown and Company, 1991.

———. *Kinds of Minds*. New York: Basic Books, 1996.

Dreifus, Claudia. "A Conversation with Joseph LeDoux: Taking a Clinical Look at Human Emotions." *New York Times*, October 8, 2002. *www.nytimes.com/2002/10/08/health/anatomy/08CONV.html*

Eberle, Jason. "Aquinas on the Nature of Human Beings." *The Review of Metaphysics*, 58 (2004): 361.

Eccles, John. "The Creation of the Self," private paper.

———. *Evolution of the Brain: Creation of the Self*. London: Routledge, 1991.

———. *How the Self Controls Its Brain*. Berlin: Springer-Verlag, 1994.

Edelman, Gerald and Giulio Tononi. *A Universe of Consciousness*. New York: Basic Books, 2000.

Edwards, Paul. *Reincarnation: A Critical Examination*. Buffalo, N.Y.: Prometheus Press, 1996.

Emmanuel, Linda. "Reexamining Death: The Asymptotic Model and a Bounded Zone Definition." Hastings Center Report 25 (1995): 27–35.

Ezard, John. "Ayer's Thoughts from the Other Side." *Manchester Guardian Weekly* (1988): 21.

Farrer, Austin. *Finite and Infinite: A Philosophical Essay*. Westminster: Dacre Press, 1943.

Fenwick, Peter and Fenwick, Elizabeth. *The Art of Dying*. London: Continuum, 2008.

Fenwick, Peter. "Dying: a spiritual experience as shown by Near Death Experiences and Deathbed Visions," paper, 2004.

Fox, Douglas. "Light at the end of the tunnel," *New Scientist*, 17 (2006).

Gazzaniga, Michael. "Are Human Brains Unique," April 10, 2007. *www.edge.org/3rd_culture/gazzaniga08/gazzaniga08_index.html*

———. "Prologue,"Human: The Science Behind What Makes Us Unique." San Francisco, Calif.: Ecco, 2008.

Geach, Peter. *God and the Soul*. London: Routledge & Kegan Paul. 1969.

———. *Providence and Evil*. Cambridge, Mass.: Cambridge University Press, 1977.

Gillett, Carl and Barry Loewer, ed. *Physicalism and its Discontents*. Cambridge, Mass.: Cambridge University Press, 2001.

Gilling, Dick and Robin Brightwell, *The Human Brain*. London: Orbis Publishing, 1982.

Gould, Stephen Jay. "Nonoverlapping Magisteria." *Natural History*, 62 (1997): 16–22.

Grossman, Neal. "Four Errors Commonly Made by Professional Debunkers," *Journal of Near-Death Studies*, March 31, 2008.

———. "Who's Afraid of Life After Death?." *IONS Review* 61, (2002).

Haldane, John. *An Intelligent Person's Guide to Religion*. London: Duckworth, 2003.

Hallett, Garth. "The Tedium of Immortality." *Faith and Philosophy*, 288.

Haraldsson, Erlendur. "Survey of Claimed Encounters with the Dead." *Omega* 19(Z) (1988–89): 103–113.

Hartz, Paula. *Zoroastrianism*. New York: Facts on File, 1999.

Hauser, Marc. "The Origin of the Mind." *Scientific American*, September 2009, 44–51.

Iacoboni, Marcoi, et al., "Self-face recognition activates a frontoparietal "mirror" network in the right hemisphere: an event-related fMRI study," *Neuroimage* 25 (2005): 926–935.

Ilibagiza, Immaculee. *Our Lady of Kibeho*. Carlsbad, Calif.: Hay House, 2008.

Kijas, Zdzislaw. "Hell—Myth or Reality?" *Messenger of St. Anthony*, May 2008, 40–43

Kruglinski, Susan. "Evolution in Your Brain," *Discover*, July 3, 2007. *http://discovermagazine.com/2007/brain*.

Lapide, Pinchas. *The Resurrection of Jesus—A Jewish Perspective.* Minneapolis Minn.: Augsburg Publishing House, 1983.

Larson, Edward J. and Larry Witham, "Scientists and Religion in America," *Scientific American,* September 1999, 88–93.

Ledoux, Joseph. *The Synaptic Self: How Our Brains Become Who We Are.* New York: Viking, 2002.

Lemonick, Michael. "Glimpses of the Brain," *Time,* July 17, 1995, 52.

Levenson, Jon. *Resurrection and the Restoration of Israel—the Ultimate Victory of the God of Life.* New Haven, Conn.: Yale University Press, 2006.

Lewis, C.S. *Letters to Malcolm, Chiefly on Prayer.* London: Collins, 1966.

Lewis, H.D. *The Self and Immortality.* London: Macmillan, 1973.

Lund, David. *Death and Consciousness—The Case for Life After Death.* New York: Ballantine Books, 1985.

———. *The Conscious Self.* Buffalo, N.Y.: Prometheus Press, 2005.

Malcolm, Norman. *Wittgenstein: A Religious Point of View.* Ithaca, N.Y.: Cornell University Press, 1994.

Marshall, Catherine. *To Live Again.* London: Collins, 1977.

Mascall, E.L. *The Christian Universe.* New York: Morehouse-Barlow Co., 1966.

Merskey, H. "The manufacture of personalities: The production of multiple personality disorder." *British Journal of Psychiatry,* 160, (1992): 327–340.

Moody, Raymond A. *Life After Life.* Marietta, Ga.: Mockingbird Books, 1975.

Olson, Jay. "Is There Room for Your Soul?" *US News and World Report,* October 23, 2006, 57–63.

Owen, H.P. *Concepts of Deity.* London: Macmillan, 1971.

Papineau, David. *Thinking About Consciousness.* Oxford: Clarendon Press, 2002.

Parnia, Sam. *What Happens When We Die?.* Carlsbad, Calif.: Hay House, 2006.

Parrinder, Geoffrey. *World Religions—From Ancient History to the Present.* New York: Facts on File, 1983.

Penfield, Wilder. "Science, the arts and the spirit," Transactions of the Royal Society of Canada, 7, 1969, 73–83.

Penfield,Wilder. *The Mystery of the Mind*. Princeton, N.J.: Princeton University Press, 1975.

Persinger, Michael A. "Modern Neuroscience and Near-Death Experience: Expectancies and Implications. Comments on 'A Neurobiological Model for Near-Death Experiences," *Journal of Near-Death Studies*, 7/4 (1989): 233–239.

Perszon, Jan ed. *Jan PaweB II a religie wiata. ToruD,* Poland: Wydawnictwo Uniwersytetu MikoBaja Kopernika, 2007.

Phillips, J. B. *Ring of Truth*. London: Macmillan Company, 1967.

Pinker, Steven. *How the Mind Works*. New York: W.W. Norton, 1997.

Popper, Karl R. and Eccles, John C. *The Self and Its Brain*. New York: Springer International, 1977.

Ramachandran, V.S. BBC Reith Lectures, *www.bbc.co.uk/radio4/reith2003. New York Times*, June 26, 2007.

Ring, Kenneth. "Religious Wars in the NDE Movement," *Journal of Near-Death Studies*, Volume 18, Number 4, (2000): 226–7.

Roa, K. Ramakrishna. "Anomalies of consciousness: Indian perspectives and research," *The Journal of Parapsychology*, Vol 58(2), (1994): 149–187

Rodin, Ernst. "Comments on 'A Neurobiological Model for Near-Death Experiences," *Journal of Near-Death Studies*, 7/4 (1989): 255–259.

Rommer, Barbara. *Blessing in Disguise*. St. Paul, Minn.: Llewellyn Publications, 2000.

Rooney, David. "The First Religion of Mankind," *Faith and Reason*, Summer, 1993.

Ross, J. Andrew. "First-Person Consciousness," *Journal of Consciousness Studies*, 9, No. 7 (2002): 260.

Ross, James F. "Immaterial Thought," *The Journal of Philosophy* 89,1992, 136–150.

———. "Review of A. Kenny's Aquinas on the Mind," *The Philosophical Quarterly*, 1993, 537.

Sabom, Michael. *Light and Death*. Grand Rapids, Mich.: Zondervan, 1998.

Sagan, Carl. "In the Valley of the Shadow," *Parade*, March 1996, pp.18–21.

Sapolsky, Robert. "The 2% Difference," *Discover*, April 2006.

Sartre, Jean Paul. *Being and Nothingness*. London: Methuen, 1957.

Saver, Jeffrey and John Rabin, "The Neural Substrates of Religious Experience," *Journal of Neuropsychiatry and Clinical Neurosciences* 9 (1997): 498–510.

Schmidt, Wilhelm. *The Origin and Growth of Religion*. London: Methuen, 1935.

Schroedinger, Erwin. *Collected Papers*. Vienna: Austrian Academy of Sciences.

Schwartz, Jeffrey. "The Mind and the Brain," International Society for Complexity, Information, and Design March 25, 2003.

Schwartz, Jeffrey M. and Sharon Begley. *The Mind and the Brain: Neuroplasticity and the Power of Mental Force*. New York: HarperCollins, 2003.

Searle, John. *The Rediscovery of the Mind*. Cambridge, Mass.: MIT Press, 1992.

Secrest, Meryle. Interview with Ian Stevenson, *Omni Magazine* 10(4) (1988), 76.

Sheed, F.J. *Where Will You Spend Eternity?*. London: Sheed and Ward, 1977.

Shermer, Michael. A New Phrenology?, *Scientific American,* May 2008, 48.

Sherrington, Charles Scott. *Man on His Nature*. Edinburgh: MacMillan 1978.

Shroder, Tom. "Ian Stevenson, Sought To Document Memories of Past Lives in Children," *Washington Post*, February 11, 2007.

Sister Emmanuel. *The Amazing Secret of the Souls in Purgatory – An Interview with Mary Simma*. Goleta, Calif.: Queenship Publishing, 1997.

Smart, Ninian. *The World's Religions*. Cambridge: Cambridge University Press, 1998.

Sperry, Roger W. "A Mentalist View of Consciousness," *Social Neuroscience Bulletin*, Vol 6, No.2 (1993): 17–18.

———. "Turnabout on Consciousness: A Mentalist View," paper delivered at the First International Conference on the Study of Consciousness Within Science, February, 1990, UC San Francisco.

Stanley, Charles, *Eternal Security—Can You Be Sure?*, Nashville, Tenn.: Oliver Nelson, 1990

Stix, Gary. "Jacking into the Brain," *Scientific American* November 2008, 59.

Thomas, Lewis. "On Science and Uncertainty," *Discover* magazine, October 1980, 58–59.

Thong, Chan Kei. *Faith of Our Fathers—God in Ancient China*. Shanghai: Orient Publishing Center, 2006.

Van Biema, David. "Hail Mary," *Time*, Volume 165, 12, March 21, 2005.

Van Lommel, Pim. "Near-death experience in survivors of cardiac arrest: a prospective study in the Netherlands," *Lancet* 2001, 358: 2039–45.

Wilkes, Kathleen V. *Real People: Personal Identity Without Thought Experiments*. Oxford: Clarendon, 1988.

Williams, Daniel. "At the Hour Of Our Death," *Time*, Friday, Aug. 31, 2007, *www.time.com/time/magazine/article/0,9171,1657919-2,00.html*

Wittgenstein, Ludwig. *Culture and Value*, transl. Peter Winch. Oxford: Blackwell, 1984.

Zaehner, R.C. *Hinduism*. London: Oxford University Press, 1962.

Zaleski, Carol. *OtherWorld Journeys*. New York: Oxford University Press, 1987.

Zimmerman, Anthony. "The Afterlife Among Hunter-Gatherers," *Faith and Culture*, 1992.

Notes

Chapter 1

1. Jean Paul Sartre, *Being and Nothingness* (London: Methuen, 1957), p.539-540.

2. Carl Sagan, "In the Valley of the Shadow," *Parade*, March 1996.

3. Stephen Jay Gould, "Nonoverlapping Magisteria," *Natural History*, 106:62, March 1997, 16–22.

4. Cira Curtin, "Fact or Fiction?: Living People Outnumber the Dead", *Scientific American*, March 2007, *www.scientificamerican.com/article.cfm?id=fact-or-fiction-living-outnumber-dead.*

5. Lewis Thomas, "On Science and Uncertainty," *Discover*, October 1980, 58–59.

6. Edward J. Larson and Larry Witham, "Scientists and Religion in America," *Scientific American*, September 1999, 88–93.

7. Erlendur Haraldsson, "Survey of Claimed Encounters with the Dead," *Omega*, Vol. 19(Z), 1988–89.

Chapter 2

1. Daniel Williams, "At the Hour Of Our Death," *Time*, Friday, Aug. 31, 2007, *www.time.com/time/magazine/article/0,9171,1657919-2,00.html*

2. "Reexamining Death: The Asymptotic Model and a Bounded Zone Definition," *Hastings Center Report* 25 (July-August 1995): 27–35.

3. Michael Sabom, *Light and Death* (Grand Rapids, Michigan: Zondervan, 1998), 51.

4. "Near-Death Experiences: What Really Happens?," *LiveScience*, Sept. 12, 2008. *www.livescience.com/health/080912-near-death.html*

5. Raymond A. Moody, *Life After Life* (Marietta, Georgia: Mockingbird Books, 1975).

6. *http://www.pimvanlommel.nl/?near_death_experiences*

7.   Carol Zaleski, *OtherWorld Journeys* (New York: Oxford University Press, 1987).

8.   Plato, *The Republic,* Book X, 614b.

9.   Zaleski, op. cit., 5–7.

10.   K. Ramakrishna Rao, "Anomalies of consciousness: Indian perspectives and research," *The Journal of Parapsychology*, Vol 58(2), June 1994, 149-187

11.   *Time*, op. cit., Friday, Aug. 31, 2007

12.   *http://www.iands.org/nde_index.php*

13.   "Near-Death Experiences and Survival of Bodily Death, An Esalen Invitational Conference," December 6-11, 1998. *www.esalenctr.org/display/confpage.cfm?confid=3&pageid=22&pgtype=1*

14.   Barbara Rommer, *Blessing in Disguise* (St. Paul, Minnesota: Llewellyn Publications, 2000).

15.   *Time*, op. cit., Friday, Aug. 31, 2007.

16.   Dr. Van Lommel. "Near-death experience in survivors of cardiac arrest: a prospective study in the Netherlands," *Lancet* 2001, 358: 2039–45.

17.   *Time*, op. cit., Friday, Aug. 31, 2007

18.   "Dying: a spiritual experience as shown by Near Death Experiences and Deathbed Visions," paper, 2004.

19.   Van Lommel, op. cit., Friday, Aug. 31, 2007

20.   Susan Blackmore, Debate with Greg Stone, *www.near-death.com/experiences/articles001.html*

21.   Jeffery Saver and John Ravin. "The Neural Substrates of Religious Experience," *Journal of Neuropsychiatry and Clinical Neurosciences* 9 (1997), 498–510.

22.   Sabom, op. cit., 177–8.

23.   Michael A. Persinger, "Modern Neuroscience and Near-Death Experience: Expectancies and Implications. Comments on 'A Neurobiological Model for Near-Death Experiences," *Journal of Near-Death Studies*, 7/4 (Summer 1989):233-239.

24.   Ernest Rodin, "Comments on 'A Neurobiological Model for Near-Death Experiences," *Journal of Near-Death Studies*, 7/4 (Summer 1989):255–259.

25.   Sabom, op. cit.,178-181

26.   *www.iands.org/nde_index/ndes/key_facts_about_near-death_experiences_4.html*

27.   *Time*, op. cit., Friday, Aug. 31, 2007

28.   *www.iands.org/nde_index/ndes/key_facts_about_near-death_experiences_4.html*

29.   Douglas Fox, "Light at the end of the tunnel," *New Scientist*, 17 October 2006. *www.newscientist.com/article/mg19225731.300-light-at-the-end-of-the-tunnel.html*

30.   *Time*, op. cit., Friday, Aug. 31, 2007

31.   Douglas Fox. "Light at the end of the tunnel," *New Scientist*, 17 October 2006.

32.   *http://www.near-death.com/experiences/evidence01.html.*

33.   Spetzler quoted in *www.anitabartholomew.com/Tunnel%20Visions.htm*

34.   Anita Bartholomew, "After Life," *Reader's Digest*, August, 2003, 122–128.

35.   *www.ianlawton.com/nde2.htm*

36.   *www.near-death.com/experiences/articles009.html*

37.   Sabom, op. cit., 49.

38.   *Time*, op. cit., Friday, Aug. 31, 2007

39.   Mario Beauregard and Denyse O'Leary, *The Spiritual Brain* (New York: HarperOne, 2007), 292.

40.   Sam Parnia, *What Happens When We Die?* (Carlsbad, CA: Hay House, 2006).

41.   Neal Grossman. "Who's Afraid of Life After Death?," *IONS Review* #61, Sept.–Nov. 2002 *www.noetic.org/publications/review/issue61/r61_Grossman.html.*

42.   Jane Bosveld, "Will natural science pin down our supernatural essence?," *Discover* June 12, 2007. *http://discovermagazine.com/2007/jun/soul-search*

43.   "Power of the Paranormal," *New Scientist*, March 13, 2004.

44.   Kenneth Ring, "Religious Wars in the NDE Movement," *Journal of Near-Death Studies*, Volume 18, Number 4, Summer 2000, 226–7.

CHAPTER 3

1.   Ninian Smart, *The World's Religions* (Cambridge: Cambridge University Press, 1998), 37.

2.   Walter Burkett. *Homo Necans: The Anthropology of Ancient Greek Sacrificial Ritual and Myth*, Transl Peter Bing, (Berkeley, California: University of California Press, 1983), 17.

3.   David Rooney. *Faith and Reason*, Summer, 1993.

4.   Wilhelm Schmidt, *The Origin and Growth of Religion*, (London: Methuen, 1935), 275–6.

5.   Anthony Zimmerman. "The Afterlife Among Hunter-Gatherers," *Faith and Culture*, 1992. Online article no longer available in its original from. Modified version found at *www.lifeissues.net/writers/zim/ae/ae_03religionadameve6.html.*

6.   David Rooney, "The First Religion of Mankind," *Faith and Reason*, Summer, 1993. *www.ewtn.com/library/HUMANITY/FR93206.TXT*

7.   *Epic of Gilgamesh* VII, 34-42, cited in Geoffrey Parrinder, *World Reli-gions—From Ancient History to the Present* (New York: Facts on File, 1983), 124.

8.   *www.sacred-texts.com/cla/homer/ody/ody10.htm, Book Eleven.*

9.   John Ashton and Tom Whyte, *The Quest for Paradise* (New York: Harper SanFrancisco, 2001), 41.

10.   Chan Kei Thong, *Faith of Our Fathers—God in Ancient China*, (Shang-hai: Orient Publishing Center, 2006), 89-90.

11.   Geoffrey Parrinder, *World Religions—From Ancient History to the Present* (New York: Facts on File, 1983), 314.

12.   *Encylopedia of Death and Dying, www.deathreference.com/Ce-Da/Chinese-Beliefs.html)*

13.   Parrinder, op. cit., 339.

14.   Parrinder, op. cit., 66.

15.   Henryk Zimo, "African spiritual and religious values as the basis for interreligious dialogue" in *Jan PaweB II a religie [wiata* ed. by Jan Perszon (ToruD, Poland: Wydawnictwo Uniwersytetu MikoBaja Kopernika, 2007).

16.   *www.wsu.edu/~dee/ANCINDIA/VEDICAGE.HTM*

17.   *www.religionfacts.com/hinduism/texts/vedas.htm*

18.   *Rig Veda*, Mandala 7, Verse 89.

19.   Excerpts from a version edited and translated by Maurice Bloomfield, *Sacred Books of the East*, volume 42.

20.   Atharva Veda 6.120.3. *www.newworldencyclopedia.org/entry/Afterlife*

21.   Parrinder, op. cit., 195,197

22.   Mary Boyce, *Zoroastrianism: It's Antiquity and Constant Vigor*, (Costa Mesa, California: Mazda Publishers, 1992).

23.   Farhang Mehr, *www.deathreference.com/Vi-Z/Zoroastrianism.html).*

24.   Paula Hartz, "Zoroastrianism" (New York: Facts on File, 1999), 105-6.

25.   Peter Clark, *Zoroastrianism, Introduction to an Ancient Faith* (Brighton: Sussex Library of Religious Beliefs and Practices), 1999, 15.

26.   Parrinder, 178.

27.   Jon Levenson. *Resurrection and the Restoration of Israel—the Ultimate Victory of the God of Life* (New Haven, CT: Yale University Press, 2006).

28.   Ibid., 39, 20-2, 46, 53, 83, 105.

29.   Ibid.,106, 112, 106.

30.   Ibid., 132, 162, 180, 187, 189, 213, 215.

31.   Ibid., 215, 218.

32.   Ibid., 225.

33. Pinchas Lapide, *The Resurrection of Jesus—A Jewish Perspective* (Minneapolis: Augsburg Publishing House, 1983), 125–6, 130.

34. Karl R. Popper and John C. Eccles, *The Self and Its Brain*, (New York: Springer International, 1977), 556, 557.

35. John Haldane, *An Intelligent Person's Guide to Religion* (London: Duckworth, 2003), 204.

36. Garth Hallett, "The Tedium of Immortality," *Faith and Philosophy*, 288.

37. Martin D'Arcy, *Death and Life* (London: Longmans, Green & Co., 1942), 153–4, 156–160, 96,

38. Ibid., 177.

39. Zdzislaw Kijas, "Hell—Myth or Reality?," *Messenger of St. Anthony*, May 2008, 42.

40. Norman Malcolm,*Wittgenstein: A Religious Point of View?* (Ithaca: Cornell University Press, 1994), 10.

41. *Messenger of St. Anthony*, op. cit., 41.

42. Peter Geach, *Providence and Evil* (Cambridge: Cambridge University Press, 1977), 144

43. Ibid., 145.

44. E.L. Mascall, *The Christian Universe* (New York: Morehouse-Barlow Co., 1966), 146-148.

45. Catherine Marshall, *To Live Again* (London: Collins, 1977), 218–9, 221.

46. Charles Stanley, *Eternal Security—Can You Be Sure?* (Nashville: Oliver Nelson, 1990), 127.

47. *Letters to Malcolm, Chiefly on Prayer* London: Collins, 1966, 109–111

48. F.J. Sheed, *Where Will You Spend Eternity?* (London: Sheed and Ward, 1977), 57–8.

49. Peter Brown, *The Cult of the Saints* (Chicago: University of Chicago Press, 1980).

50. "Hail Mary," *Time*, March 21, 2005.

51. Jason Byassee, "Protestants and Marian Devotion—What about Mary?," *Christian Century*, December 14, 2004.

52. John Haldane, *An Intelligent Person's Guide to Religion* (London: Duckworth, 2003), 198.

CHAPTER 4

1. *The Secret of Fatima*, by Sr. Lucia dos Santos

2. Janice Connell, *Queen of the Cosmos*, (Orleans, MA: Paraclete Press, 1990).

3. Ibid., 60-7, 94, 26-8, 38-9, 28, 87, 119-121.

4.   Immaculee Ilibagiza, *Our Lady of Kibeho* by (Carlsbad, CA: Hay House, 2008), 135, 137-8.

5.   *Diary: Divine Mercy in My Soul,* 1146

6.   *Treatise on Purgatory*, Chapter I

7.   Sister Emmanuel, *The Amazing Secret of the Souls in Purgatory – An Interview with Mary Simma* (Goleta, CA: Queenship Publishing, 1997), 7-8, 10, 12, 13, 26, 27, 29, 36.

CHAPTER 5

1.   John Ezard, "Ayer's Thoughts from the Other Side," Manchester Guadian Weekly, September 11, 1988, 21

2.   William R. Cash, "Did atheist philosopher see God when he 'died'?," *National Post*, March 3, 2001.

3.   J. B. Phillips, *Ring of Truth* (Macmillan Company, 1967), 118–119.

4.   http://www.loymershimer.blogspot.com/2005/09/theology-of-ghosts.html

5.   Personal Interview

6.   *www.GloriaPolo.com*

CHAPTER 6

1.   Michael Lemonick, "Glimpses of the Brain," *Time*, July 17, 1995, 52.

2.   Cornelia Dean in the *New York Times*, June 26, 2007, *www.nytimes.com/ 2007/06/26/science/26soul.html?_r=1&ref=science*

3.   Francis Crick, *The Astonishing Hypothesis: The Scientific Search for the Soul* (New York: Simon and Schuster, 1994), 1.

4.   Ian Sample, "We are the final frontier," *Guardian*, Thursday February 10, 2005.

5.   BBC Reith Lectures, *ww.bbc.co.uk/radio4/reith2003. New York Times*, June   26,   2007.   *www.nytimes.com/2007/06/26/science/ 26soul.html?_r=1&ref=science*

6.   Joseph LeDoux, *The Synaptic Self: How Our Brains Become Who We Are* (New York: Viking, 2002), 2.

7.   Gerald Edelman and Giulio Tononi, *A Universe of Consciousness* (New York: Basic Books, 2000), 72.

8.   Jay Olson, "Is There Room for Your Soul?," *US News and World Report*, October 23, 2006, 57–63

9.   *A Universe of Consciousness*, xi

10.   Susan Kruglinski, "Evolution in Your Brain," *Discover*, July 3, 2007. *http:/ /discovermagazine.com/2007/brain.*

11.   *The Synaptic Self*, op. cit., 2.

12.   Jonathan Cott and Karen Rester, "Joseph LeDoux's heavy mental," *Salon*, (*www.salon.com/mwt/feature/2007/07/25/joseph_ledoux/ print.html*

13.   Claudia Dreifus, "A Conversation with Joseph LeDoux: Taking a Clinical Look at Human Emotions," *New York Times*, October 8, 2002). *www.nytimes.com/2002/10/08/health/anatomy/08CONV.html*

14.   Susan Blackmore, "Serotonin, ergo sum," *New Scientist*, March 2 2002, *www.newscientist.com/article/mg17323325.900-serotonin-ergo-sum.html*

15.   *V.S. Ramachandran,* "The Neurology of Self-Awareness," January 8, 2007, The Edge 10th Anniversary Essay*, www.edge.org/3rd_culture/ ramachandran07/ramachandran07_index.html).*

16.   Gary Stix, "Jacking into the Brain," *Scientific American* November 2008, 59.

17.   Ibid., 60.

18.   Bernard J. Baars, "The conscious access hypothesis: Origins and recent evidence,"_*Trends in Cognitive Science*, January, 2002. *www.nsi.edu/ users/baars/BaarsTICS2002.pdf.*

19.   Ian Tattersall, *Monkey in the Mirror: Essays on the Science of What Makes Us Human.* Oxford: Oxford University Press, 2002.

20.   Sandra Blakeslee, "Flesh Made Soul," *Science and Spirit*, March 1, 2008. *www.science-spirit.org/article_detail.php?article_id=740.*

21.   "Self-face recognition activates a frontoparietal "mirror" network in the right hemisphere: an event-related fMRI study", *Neuroimage*

22.   "Politics and the Brain," *New York Times*, November 14, 2007. *http://query.nytimes.com/gst fullpage.html?res=9907E1D91E3CF937A25752C1A9619C8B63*

23.   Michael Shermer, A New Phrenology?, *Scientific American,* May 2008, 48).

24.   Robert Sapolsky, "The 2% Difference," *Discover*, April 2006. *http:// discovermagazine.com/2006/apr/chimp-genome.*

25.   Patricia Churchland, "How Do Neurons Know?," *Daedalus*, Winter 2004, 44).

26.   Daniel Dennett, *Kinds of Minds*, New York, Basic Books, 1996, 55.

27.   Daniel Dennett, *Consciousness Explained* (Boston, MA: Little, Brown and Company, 1991), 218.

28.   Daniel C. Dennett, "Facing Backwards on the Problem of Consciousness", *Journal of Consciousness Studies*, 3 (1), 1996, 6.

29.   Daniel Dennett, *Consciousness Explained*, 37.

30. Paul Churchland, *The Engine of Reason, the Seat of the Soul* (Cambridge, MA: MIT Press, 1995), 322.

31. Paul and Patricia Churchland, *On the Contrary* (Cambridge, MA: MIT Press, 1998), 305-6.

32. Patricia Churchland, "A Neurophilosophical Slant on Consciousness Research," *Progress in Brain Research*, Volume 149, Elsevier, 2005, 285, 290, 292.

33. Gary Stix. "Jacking into the Brain," *Scientific American* November 2008, p.58.

34. Marc Hauser, "The Origin of the Mind," *Scientific American* September 2009, 44–51.

35. "The Transcript: Tom Wolfe + Michael Gazzaniga," *Seed Magazine*, July 1, 2008, *h t t p : / / s e e d m a g a z i n e . c o m / c o n t e n t / a r t i c l e / the_transcript_tom_wolfe_michael_gazzaniga/*

36. *Journal of Near-Death Studies*, March 31, 2008, 238.

37. Michael Gazzaniga, "Are Human Brains Unique," April 10, 2007. *www.edge.org/3rd_culture/gazzaniga08/gazzaniga08_index.html*. Also appears in "Prologue," Human: The Science Behind What Makes Us Unique (San Francisco: Ecco, 2008).

38. Roger W. Sperry, "A Mentalist View of Consciousness," *Social Neuroscience Bulletin*, Vol 6, No.2, Spring 1993, 17–18.

39. David Papineau, "The Rise of Physicalism"in Carl Gillett and Barry Loewer ed. *Physicalism and its Discontents* (Cambridge University Press, 2001).

40. David Papineau, *Thinking About Consciousness*, (Oxford: Clarendon Press, 2002), 94, 4.

41. John Searle, *The Rediscovery of the Mind* (Cambridge, MA: MIT Press, 1992), 9.

42. The Transcript: Tom Wolfe + Michael Gazzaniga," op.cit.

43. Kathleen V. Wilkes, *Real People: Personal Identity Without Thought Experiments* (Oxford: Clarendon, 1988), 39, 46

44. "Jacking into the Brain." Gary Stix, Scientific American November 2008, p.58.

45. Andrew Ross, "First-Person Consciousness," *Journal of Consciousness Studies*, 9, No. 7, 2002, 260.

46. David Lund, *The Conscious Self* (Buffalo New York: Prometheus Press, 2005), 13, 14, 20, 385, 386.

47. Austin Farrer, *Finite and Infinite* (Westminster: Dacre Press, 1943), 229, 221.

48. Steven Pinker, *How the Mind Works* (New York: W.W. Norton, 1997).

49. Mario Beauregard and Denyse O'Leary, *The Spiritual Brain* (New York: Harper One, 2007), 114.

50. David Lund, 144.

51. Merskey, H. (1992a). "The manufacture of personalities: The production of multiple personality disorder." *British Journal of Psychiatry,* 160, 327-340.

52. Jeffrey Schwartz, "The Mind and the Brain," *International Society for Complexity, Information, and Design* March 25, 2003 (90).

53. Jeffrey M. Schwartz and Sharon Begley, *The Mind and the Brain: Neuroplasticity and the Power of Mental Force* (New York: HarperCollins, 2003), 54-5.

54. Mario Beauregard, "Mind does really matter: Evidence from neuroimaging studies of emotional self-regulation, psychotherapy, and placebo effect", *Progress in Neurobiology* 81 (2007), 218–236.

55. Planck, as cited in de Purucker 1940, ch. 13; de Purucker, Gottfried. 1940. *The Esoteric Tradition*. California: Theosophical University Press.

56. Erwin Schroedinger, "General Scientific and Popular Papers," in *Collected Papers,* Vol. 4. Vienna: Austrian Academy of Sciences. Friedr. Vieweg & Sohn, Braunschweig/Wiesbaden, 334. (Excerpted from 50 Nobel Laureates and Other Great Scientists Who Believe in God," by Tihomir Dimitrov *http://nobelists.net).*

57. Charles Scott Sherrington *Man on His Nature*, Edinburgh: New York: MacMillan 1978), page 229.

58. Sir John Eccles. *How the Self Controls Its Brain* (Berlin: Springer-Verlag, 1994)

59. Sir John Eccles. *Evolution of the Brain: Creation of the Self* (London: Routledge, 1991)

60. Ibid., 241.

61. Roger W. Sperry, Turnabout on Consciousness: A Mentalist View, First International Conference on the Study of Consciousness Within Science, February, 1990, UC San Francisco.

62. Wilder Penfield. *The Mystery of the Mind*, (Princeton, NJ: Princeton University Press, 1975), p. 80.

63. Edward J. Larson and Larry Witham, "Scientists and Religion in America," *Scientific American*, September 1999, 88–93.

64. Wilder Penfield. "Science, the arts and the spirit," Transactions of the Royal Society of Canada, 7, 1969, 73-83.

65. Gilling, Dick and Robin Brightwell, *The Human Brain* (London: Orbis Publishing, 1982), 180.

66. Interview with Sir John Eccles

CHAPTER 7

1. David Braine, *The Human Person—Animal and Spirit*, (Notre Dame: University of Notre Dame Press, 1994), 338.

2. Jason Eberle, "Aquinas on the Nature of Human Beings," *The Review of Metaphysics*, 58, December 2004, 361.

3.   Boethius De Persona et Duabus Naturis, c. ii.

4.   *Summa Theologica* III, Q. xvi, a. 12, ad 2um

5.   *The Disputed Questions on the Soul*, Article 14.

6.   Peter Geach, *God and the Soul* (London: Routledge & Kegan Paul. 1969), 37.

7.   James Ross. "Immaterial Thought", *The Journal of Philosophy* 89,1992,, 136, 143.

8.   David Braine, op. cit., 537. "The Human Person—Animal and Spirit," 219.

9.   Ibid., 449, 450, 459, 451, 461, 451.

10.   Ibid.,474.

11.   John E. Coons, "A Grammar of the Self," *First Things*, January 2003, 40.

12.   Ibid., 40-41

13.   Ibid., 43.

14.   Austin Farrer, *Finite and Infinite: A Philosophical Essay.* Westminster: Dacre Press, 1943. 220.

15.   Denis J. M. Bradley, "To be or not to be?": Pasnau on Aquinas's Immortal Human Soul", *The Thomist*, 2004, Volume 68, 11.

16.   James F. Ross, "Review of A. Kenny's Aquinas on the Mind," *The Philosophical Quarterly*, 1993, 537.

17.   David Braine, op. cit., 538,

18.   Jason Eberle, op. cit., 341,

19.   John Eccles, "The Creation of the Self"

20.   Stephen Braude, *Immortal Remains – The Evidence for Life After Death* (Lanham, MD: Rowman and Littlefield, 2003).

21.   Ibid., 302-303.

22.   Neal Grossman. "Four Errors Commonly Made by Professional Debunkers," *Journal of Near-Death Studies*, March 31, 2008.

23.   *Death and Consciousness—The Case for Life After Death* (New York: Ballantine Books, 1985, 233.

24.   David Lund. *The Conscious Self,* (Buffalo New York: Prometheus Press, 2005), 10, 11.

25.   Peter Fenwick and Elizabeth Fenwick, *The Art of Dying* (London: Continuum, 2008), 241–2.

26.   Paul Edwards, *Reincarnation: A Critical Examination* (Buffalo, New York: Prometheus Press, 1996)

27.   Tom Shroder, "Ian Stevenson, Sought To Document Memories Of Past Lives in Children," *Washington Post*, February 11, 2007

28.   Interview with Mark Albrecht and Johannes Aagaard, 15 December 1981 *www.dci.dkindex.php?option=com_content&view=article&id=360:interview-agehananda-bharati&catid=146&Itemid=36*

29.   R.C. Zaehner, *Hinduism* (London: Oxford University Press, 1962), pp. 75, 77.

30.   Personal interview.

31. Frederick Copleston. *Philosophies and Cultures* (Oxford: Oxford University Press, 1980), 80.

32. David Braine, op. cit., 542.

33. Lewis *The Self and Immortality*, (London: Macmillan, 1973), 101.

34. Paul Edwards, 259

35. C.T.K. Chari in B.B. Wolman, ed., *Handbook of Parapsychology* (New York: Van Nostrand Reinhold, 1977), 818.

36. Chari, Personal Interview

37. H.P. Owen, *Concepts of Deity* (London: Macmillan, 1971), 123,71–2.

38. *Omni* magazine interview with Ian Stevenson, Meryle Secrest, *Omni Magazine* 10(4) (1988), 76.

39. Paul Edwards, op. cit., 256.

40. Ibid., 276-7.

41. Ibid., 260, 261.

42. *Omni* op. cit.

43. Paul Edwards, op. cit., 262-3.

44. Ibid., 268.

45. C.T.K. Chari, "A New Look at Reincarnation," *The Christian Parapsychologist*, Vol.4, No. 4 (1981), 121–129, and *Handbook of Parapsychology*, op. cit.

46. K. Ramakrishna Rao, *"Anomalies of consciousness: Indian perspectives and research,"* *The Journal of Parapsychology*, Vol 58(2), June 1994, 149–187

47. Private interview.

48. Michael Sabom, *Light and Death* (Grand Rapids, Michigan: Zondervan, 1998), 138–139.

49. Ibid., 138.

50. Paul Edwards, op. cit., 255, 256, 223, 225.

51. Ibid., 226-7.

52. *The Self and Immortality*, op. cit., 93.

53. *God and the Soul*, op. cit., 28.

54. Jason Eberle, op. cit., 359.

55. David Braine, op. cit., 538, 539, 540, 541.

56. Denis J. M. Bradley, op. cit., 68, 22, 17.

57. Jason Eberle, op. cit., 340–1, 345.

Index

About the Author

Roy Abraham Varghese is the author/editor of nine books on science, religion and theology. *Cosmos, Bios, Theos*, a book he edited, included contributions from 24 Nobel Prize-winning scientists and was widely reviewed in technical and popular publications including *Chronicle of Higher Education*, *The Science Teacher* and *Foundations of Physics*. *Time* magazine called *Cosmos* "the year's most intriguing book about God." *Cosmic Beginnings and Human Ends*, a subsequent work, won a Templeton Book Prize for *Outstanding Books in Science and Natural Theology*. His book *The Wonder of the World* was an exploration of the relationship between modern science and the existence of God. It was endorsed by two Nobel Prize winners, the inventor of the laser and the scientist who established the Big Bang theory, as well as by leading Jewish, Hindu, Moslem and Christian thinkers. In 2007, he co-authored (with Antony Flew) the internationally publicized *There is a God: How the World's Most Notorious Atheist Changed His Mind*. He was a panelist at the science and religion forum in the Parliament of World Religions held in Chicago in 1993 and an invitee and participant in the Millennium World Peace Summit of Religious and Spiritual Leaders held at the United Nations in August 2000. He has also organized several international conferences of theists and atheists on such topics as the existence of God and the soul. Participants in one such conference, *Artificial Intelligence and the Human Mind*, held at Yale University, included four Nobel Prize winners and prominent AI scientists. He helped produce the documentary "Has Science Discovered God" featuring Antony Flew, Gerald Schroeder, John Haldane and Paul Vitz. He has been interviewed on TV and radio (including the popular show "Coast to Coast").